Promoting Health and Well-being through Schools

The contribution schools can make to improving students' health and well-being is increasingly recognised. Schools that have embraced this role and adapted policies and practices to create an environment in which young people feel safe and happy have reported broad and significant gains.

Through expert contributions from active researchers and experienced practitioners, *Promoting Health and Well-being through Schools* combines recent research with knowledge of the current climate in which schools are operating. Offering authoritative advice on effective intervention, this book provides an overview of the key issues that need to be addressed, including:

- alcohol use
- sexual health
- drug use
- obesity
- mental health.

This accessible text is innovative in its focus on how schools can build partnerships with young people, parents and health professionals to promote their commitment to health and well-being. It highlights successful approaches for promoting health and educational goals, and provides useful advice on planning and evaluation.

Promoting Health and Well-being through Schools is invaluable reading for professionals working in and with schools to implement healthy schools programmes and to bring about improvement in health and well-being, including teachers, nurses, and health and education managers. It is also of interest to students, researchers and policy makers.

Peter Aggleton is Professor of Education, Health and Social Care, and Head of the School of Education and Social Work, at the University of Sussex, UK. He is a Visiting Professor in the Faculty of Arts and Social Sciences at the University of New South Wales, Australia, and in the Section for International Community Health at the University of Oslo, Norway.

Catherine Dennison is Research Manager for the Children and Young People's Public Health Programme at the Department of Health, UK.

Ian Warwick is Senior Research Officer at the Thomas Coram Research Unit at the Institute of Education, University of London, UK.

Promoting Health and Well-being through Schools

Edited by Peter Aggleton,
Catherine Dennison and
Ian Warwick

Routledge
Taylor & Francis Group

LONDON AND NEW YORK

First published 2010
by Routledge
2 Park Square, Milton Park, Abingdon, Oxon OX14 4RN

Simultaneously published in the USA and Canada
by Routledge
270 Madison Avenue, New York, NY 10016

Routledge is an imprint of the Taylor & Francis Group, an informa business

Typeset in Garamond by
GreenGate Publishing Services, Tonbridge, Kent
Printed and bound in Great Britain by
TJ International Ltd, Padstow, Cornwall

British Library Cataloguing in Publication Data
A catalogue record for this book is available from the British Library

Library of Congress Cataloging-in-Publication Data
Promoting health and wellbeing through schools /
edited by Peter Aggleton, Catherine Dennison and Ian Warwick.
  p. cm.
  Includes bibliographical references.
  1. School health services–Great Britain.   I. Aggleton, Peter.
  II. Dennison, Catherine.   III. Warwick, Ian.   IV. Title: Promoting health
  and wellbeing through schools.
  LB3409.G7P76 2010
  371.7'10941–dc22   2009031317

ISBN10: 0-415-49341-2 (hbk)
ISBN10: 0-415-49342-0 (pbk)
ISBN10: 0-203-86009-8 (ebk)

ISBN13: 978-0-415-49341-3 (hbk)
ISBN13: 978-0-415-49342-0 (pbk)
ISBN13: 978-0-203-86009-0 (ebk)

Contents

Contributors   vii
Acknowledgements   xi

1 Introduction   1
PETER AGGLETON, CATHERINE DENNISON AND IAN WARWICK

2 The health of children and young people   8
FIONA BROOKS

3 Promoting mental health through schools   24
KATHERINE WEARE

4 Reducing disaffection and increasing school engagement   42
COLIN NOBLE AND MARILYN TOFT

5 Tackling obesity: promoting physical activity and
  healthy eating in schools   56
WENDY WILLS

6 The role of schools in reducing alcohol-related
  harm among young people   69
WILLM MISTRAL AND LORNA TEMPLETON

7 The role of schools in drug education and wider
  substance misuse prevention   84
MARTINE STEAD AND ROBERT STRADLING

8 Promoting sexual health   99
ROGER INGHAM AND JULIA HIRST

9 Children and young people as partners in health and
well-being 119
JO BUTCHER

10 The contribution of parents 134
CLAIRE JAMES

11 The role of the school nurse 147
VIV CROUCH AND HELEN CHALMERS

12 Evaluating health and well-being in schools:
issues and principles 162
CATHERINE DENNISON, IAN WARWICK AND PETER AGGLETON

Index 172

Contributors

Peter Aggleton has worked in the young people, schools and health field for over twenty years. He is Professor of Education, Health and Social Care and Head of the School of Education and Social Work at the University of Sussex, and holds visiting professorships in Norway and Australia. He has published widely and is the editor of the Routledge journal *Culture, Health and Sexuality*.

Fiona Brooks is Professor of Health Services Research and Head of Adolescent and Child Health Research at the University of Hertfordshire. A medical sociologist, she is leading a number of projects addressing young people's and children's voices in health encounters. She is a co-principal investigator for England on the WHO International Health Behaviour in School-aged Children study.

Jo Butcher has worked with and for children and young people for sixteen years in face-to-face and local and national strategic development, coordination and policy roles, mainly in the third sector, but also in the statutory sector and within government, in England. She is Assistant Director of Health, Well-being and Environment at the National Children's Bureau in London, where she leads a national unit on improving children and young people's health and well-being.

Helen Chalmers is a retired nurse and nurse teacher and now a part-time research associate at the Thomas Coram Research Unit at the Institute of Education, University of London. Her professional interests include promoting health for all age groups and enabling health care professionals to offer care, support and advice of a high quality. Helen also has an interest in specialist palliative care.

Viv Crouch is employed by NHS Bath and North East Somerset as a school nurse, a young people's sexual health worker and the lead nurse for the Teenage Pregnancy Strategy Board. Viv is particularly interested in teaching sex and relationships education and training other professionals who are working with young people to help develop friendly and confidential services.

Catherine Dennison is Research Manager for the Children and Young People's Public Health Programme within the Department of Health (DH), UK, as part of which she has responsibility for projects evaluating and informing the National Healthy Schools Programme. Prior to this she worked with the DH's Sexual Health and Substance Misuse Team and the Government's Teenage Pregnancy Unit. Her background is in research with young people, especially in relation to their physical, emotional and sexual health.

Julia Hirst has worked with young people and teachers throughout her professional life. She is a former secondary teacher of sex and relationships education in schools and a local authority adviser for school-based sexual health and HIV/AIDS education. Currently, Julia is a senior lecturer in sociology, research lead on sexualities, health and youth, and faculty lead on public health at Sheffield Hallam University.

Roger Ingham is Professor of Health and Community Psychology at the University of Southampton, where he is also director of the multidisciplinary Centre for Sexual Health Research. He has carried out research on many aspects of sexual health for many years. Roger is a member of the Independent Advisory Group on Teenage Pregnancy and was a member of the 2008 ministerial review on sex and relationships education in schools.

Claire James is a policy officer at the Family and Parenting Institute, which carries out research and policy development to improve the services families use and the environment in which children grow up, including a focus on parental involvement in schools. Her interests span a broad range of family policy areas.

Willm Mistral manages the Mental Health R&D Unit, a joint enterprise of the University of Bath and the Avon & Wiltshire Mental Health Trust. He has over fifteen years' experience of research into alcohol and drug-related issues, and has published widely in peer-reviewed journals.

Colin Noble began his career as a secondary teacher, drugs awareness coordinator and local authority adviser for Personal, Social and Health Education (PSHE). Having previously been the national coordinator of the National Healthy Schools Programme, he is now a senior adviser with the National Strategies' Behaviour and Attendance Programme. Colin has written a number of articles and books about PSHE, raising boys' achievement and pupil responsibility.

Martine Stead is Deputy Director of the Institute for Social Marketing (ISM) at the University of Stirling and the Open University. ISM applies marketing concepts and research methodologies to the understanding of health behaviour and to the evaluation of behaviour change interventions and policies. Martine has particular research expertise in young people's health behaviour, drug education, and programme evaluation in real-world settings.

Robert Stradling is Senior Research Fellow in the School of Education at the University of Edinburgh. He is currently seconded to the Scottish Executive to evaluate the integration of children's services in Scotland. Prior to this he was evaluating the provision of drug education and sex education in Scotland and was a member of the team which evaluated the Blueprint Drug Use Prevention Programme in England.

Lorna Templeton is Deputy Manager of the Mental Health R&D Unit in Bath, a joint enterprise of the University of Bath and the Avon & Wiltshire Mental Health Trust. Lorna has specific responsibility for the alcohol, drugs and family research programme. She publishes and presents widely, sits on the Board of Trustees for Adfam and is a founder member of ENCARE – a European Network for Children Living in Risky Family Environments.

Marilyn Toft has worked as a secondary school teacher in London and Bristol for over fourteen years. In 1988 she became a training and development officer at the former Bristol Polytechnic, evaluating a government video for schools and leading training for local authorities and voluntary organisations. She was appointed as an advisory teacher for health education in the early 1990s, later becoming the director of the National Healthy Schools Programme. More recently, Marilyn has led the National Strategies' programme on behaviour, attendance and SEAL.

Ian Warwick is Senior Researcher at the Thomas Coram Research Unit and a senior lecturer in the Department of Education and International Development at the Institute of Education, University of London. He has been involved in evaluations of healthy school initiatives as well as studies of how health and well-being might best be promoted in early years settings and in further education.

Katherine Weare is Emeritus Professor of Education at the University of Southampton. She works in the field of the mental, emotional and social well-being learning of children. She has advised government departments on policy in the area of social and emotional learning and was a key contributor to the writing and development of the secondary Social and Emotional Aspects of Learning (SEAL) programme. She is currently helping various agencies to develop their education and mental health services, and working with the EU to develop an international database of effective mental health programmes.

Wendy Wills is Senior Research Fellow in adolescent and child health at the University of Hertfordshire's Centre for Research in Primary and Community Care. She is a sociologist and also a public health nutritionist. She works with children, young people and families, and the practitioners and professionals with whom they come into contact, to undertake research on the factors which drive everyday food and eating practices and lay perceptions of diet, health, weight and obesity. Wendy is a co-convenor of the British Sociological Association's specialist food study group.

Acknowledgements

We dedicate this book to the late Kim Rivers, who served as an inspiration to us all and who played a key role in leading early evaluations of the National Healthy Schools Standard in England and the National Healthy Schools Programme.

We would also like to thank all those who have contributed to our thinking about health in schools in recent years and, in particular, Marilyn Toft, National Strategies' Programme Director for behaviour, attendance and SEAL, and Karen Turner, Deputy Director for Delivery Programmes, Children Families and Maternity, Department of Health.

We are grateful to all the contributors for their flexibility, timeliness and responsiveness to feedback on their chapters. Sincere thanks to Daisy Ellis, who with diligence and attention to detail liaised with contributors and prepared the manuscript for publication.

Finally, we are grateful to our partners, Preecha, Darren and Terry, for their support and understanding of the time needed to work on this book.

Chapter 1

Introduction

*Peter Aggleton, Catherine Dennison and
Ian Warwick*

The last two decades have seen a growing focus within the UK on the ways in which schools might promote physical and mental health. From an initial concern with the physical and mental well-being of pupils, this has broadened to engage the wider school community, including teachers, classroom assistants, school meals providers, health workers and others working in and with schools. Yet more recently, through notions of the extended school, the National Healthy Schools Programme and in other ways, schools have been promoted as beacons for the engagement of entire communities in health-related work and activities (DCSF, 2008).

Concurrent with the above changes, there has been a broadening of definition as to what might count as school-based health promotion, with work being extended to include colleges of further education and early years settings. Perhaps it is better now to talk of 'health promotion through educational settings' rather than health-promoting schools, healthy schools or one of the other narrower definitions used earlier. In parallel with this broadening of scope, there has been growing recognition of the close synergy between health- and education-related goals. Health promoting activities in schools tend to be associated with better education outcomes (Powney *et al.*, 2000; Stewart-Brown, 2006; Murray *et al.*, 2007; Fuller, 2009), and schools which perform well academically often have healthier members and are part of a healthy community (Lister-Sharp *et al.*, 1999; St Leger and Nutbeam, 2000; Mukoma and Flisher, 2004; St Leger *et al.*, 2007).

But we should never forget that there are exceptions to this general rule. Some high-performing schools achieve success at the expense of the emotional health and well-being of at least some of their pupils. And pupils in some schools with more modest academic results can show high levels of physical and mental health and well-being. Nevertheless, as chapters in this book make clear, the reciprocal relationship between education and health and between health and education is clear; it is one in which both school staff and health professionals should be interested.

The idea of using schools and colleges as settings in which to improve health is not new and models of how to work towards becoming a health-promoting school have existed internationally since the 1970s. However, within the UK this agenda is gaining increasing impetus. Developments in government policy mean that, as part of the *Every Child Matters* agenda, schools are assessed on their contribution to health-related outcomes. Several initiatives, most notably the National Healthy Schools Programme (NHSP) in England and the Health Promoting Schools initiative in Scotland, have been put in place or transformed to support this. The NHSP provides a framework for schools to enhance pupils' emotional and physical health. Its popularity is almost unparalleled in the history of UK education, with 99 per cent of all English schools voluntarily participating in the programme, and 76 per cent having gained National Healthy School Status. Most recently, new legislation has conferred on schools statutory responsibility for the well-being of pupils and, as we write, indicators of a school's efforts to promote well-being are being issued which confirm the requirement that schools must now support the needs of children and young people beyond attainment and achievement and will be judged on this (Ofsted, 2009). A similar emphasis is being placed on integrating health into a broad range of education settings across the UK.

Within this context, headteachers, governors, curriculum leaders and others are looking for support as to how to meet their new responsibilities, and a growing number of other professionals are partnering with schools to make their contribution. Health professionals including teenage pregnancy co-ordinators, school and community nurses, drug action teams, child and adolescent mental health services, and voluntary sector agencies need support in identifying the contribution they might make and the best way to make it. Too often the evidence base is elusive and inaccessible to those working in and with schools. There is an urgent need to share what is known about the key issues children and young people are facing, and to disseminate research evidence concerning effective programmes and examples of promising practice. This book aims to satisfy this need. Prepared for a broad but critical readership, it aims to increase readers' awareness of the health needs of young people, to share with them current evidence in relation to 'what works' – or rather, what we know has worked in the past (Biesta, 2007) – and to draw out implications for practice. Rather than taking a single topic focus, it covers a wide range of health issues, highlighting their inter-relatedness together with links to broader educational goals. It aims to help educators and health professionals think, sort fact from fiction, and identify practical ways forward across a range of school and college settings.

In twelve chapters, the book brings together contributions from a range of prominent writers including researchers, policy leads and advocates, and practitioners. It offers an up-to-date summary of what is known about particular health topics and issues, together with guidance on how schools might engage with these. The experience and guidance it provides are firmly rooted in the current policy context with its emphasis on raising education standards, minimising social exclusion and health inequality, and maximising health gain. While it focuses predominantly on the UK, international research and experiences are drawn upon where appropriate. Our focus throughout is on children and young people in mainstream education. However, chapter authors have been encouraged to consider the diverse range of individuals this represents, including girls and boys, young women and young men, young people from differing ethnic backgrounds, and children and young people growing up in challenging circumstances or with special needs. Throughout the text, authors stress the importance of working with the wider community and parents, and the value of participation as a means of enhancing engagement; for unless schools and all those within them feel they 'own' a health issue or problem, little headway can be made in promoting health and well-being.

Chapter 2, by Fiona Brooks, provides a comprehensive overview of the health and well-being of young people. While focusing on the UK, it also examines international and historical trends. It describes findings from a variety of health surveys, pointing to key issues and topics which are taken up in detail later in the book. These include mental health and well-being, sexual health, alcohol and substance use, and physical activity, healthy diet and healthy weight. The chapter examines individual and social differences in health and stresses the importance of considering young people's own perspectives on health and well-being. Rather than seeing health risk behaviours as 'bad' choices made due to lack of understanding and immaturity, we need to appreciate how environmental and socio-economic inequalities shape the options available to young people, constraining the 'choices' they can make.

In Chapter 3, Katherine Weare offers a detailed account of mental health issues and problems arising in schools together with the steps that schools can take to promote the mental and emotional health and well-being of their members. The chapter describes the recent growth of interest in schools as settings for the promotion of mental health and well-being, and details findings from recent evaluations of programmes and interventions in school and college settings. These include those focusing on the social and emotional aspects of learning as well as anti-bullying initiatives, particularly those involving a whole school approach.

Chapter 4 has as its theme reducing disaffection and increasing school engagement, which links closely with health and well-being outcomes. Its authors, Colin Noble and Marilyn Toft, examine how teachers and other professionals working in schools can go about reducing disaffection and increasing engagement, particularly for those children and young people who may be especially vulnerable or who are at risk of exclusion. Disengagement from school can occur for a number of reasons: problems at home, care responsibilities, poor mental and emotional health, substance misuse and physical health problems. Whatever the cause, schools are required to ensure that they reach and engage all pupils, irrespective of ability and background. The chapter offers a number of ways forward, stressing in each case the importance of belonging and participation.

Since the 1970s, rates of obesity among school-aged children have doubled or tripled in countries such as the UK, USA, Canada and Australia, with major short- and long-term consequences for individuals and society. Chapter 5, written by Wendy Wills, addresses this problem, explaining carefully what childhood obesity is and why both healthy eating and physical activity matter. A range of positive frameworks for reducing obesity are outlined, including socio-cultural and assets-focused approaches to promoting physical activity and healthy eating in schools. The importance of schools engaging with parents and the wider community is stressed in order to address structural barriers and influence pupils' choices.

In Chapter 6, Willm Mistral and Lorna Templeton look at another topic of ongoing public concern – levels of alcohol use and alcohol-related harm among young people. Media panics over binge drinking and drunkenness make it difficult for those working with young people in school settings to take a balanced approach. This chapter examines the evidence along with young people's own perspectives on the role of alcohol in their lives. Stressing the importance of using methods known to be effective, the chapter describes traditional and more innovative ways of educating children and young people about alcohol use. It highlights the potential contribution that schools can make as part of a comprehensive and multi-component approach.

Chapter 7, by Martine Stead and Robert Stradling, focuses on the no less contentious issue of drug education. Throughout the UK, young people have access to a growing range of illegal substances at an increasingly accessible cost. Drug misuse continues to be a difficult issue for schools to address. With a focus on illicit drug use, this chapter examines the evidence base for effective curricular and whole school approaches, looks at some of the conflicting expectations surrounding school drug education, and argues for a more realistic assessment of schools' role within broader substance use prevention efforts. While drug education's long-term impact on drug use behaviour is unclear, there is evidence to suggest that well-developed programmes implemented in schools can have important short-term effects in terms of reducing and delaying the uptake of substances.

Chapter 8 looks at sexual health. Against the background of national priorities to prevent teenage pregnancy and sexually transmitted infections, Roger Ingham and Julia Hirst explore the role that schools can have in delivering high-quality sex and relationships education as well as health services with a sexual health component. The chapter reviews the current policy context before identifying key components of what has been shown internationally to be an effective response. So as to engage with young people's needs and real-life circumstances, the chapter stresses the need for schools to take a broader view of sexual health; not solely focusing on a 'prevention' agenda, but ensuring that young people are equipped to make healthy choices in relation to sex and relationships.

Chapters 9, 10 and 11 stress in complementary ways the importance of partners and partnership in efforts to promote health and well-being. In Chapter 9, by Jo Butcher, the focus is on children and young people themselves. The need to engage with children and young people in efforts to improve health and well-being is increasingly recognised. However, knowledge about effective ways of doing so is not widespread. The chapter describes a number of innovative and successful approaches, the benefits to be gained, and the skill and resource requirements needed effectively to involve children and young people. Examples of promising practice along the spectrum from tokenism to authentic participation are provided.

In Chapter 10, Claire James looks at the contribution that parents (and carers) can make to promoting health and well-being in schools. The chapter identifies a number of general principles on how best to work with and involve parents, illustrating these with suggestions as to how schools might better involve parents in health-related programmes and activities. Building upon issues explored earlier in the book, the chapter looks at three key areas in which parental involvement might be strengthened: healthy eating and the introduction of healthier school meals; improving young people's sex and relationships education; and promoting children's emotional well-being and mental health through family support. While including parents as partners in promoting health is not necessarily straightforward, an open and respectful approach can minimise conflict, and an understanding of parents' perspectives is likely to increase any programme's chance of success.

In Chapter 11, Viv Crouch and Helen Chalmers examine the role of the nurse in supporting health-related work in schools. There is a long history of nurses being engaged with schools. Nurses' early responsibilities were often restricted to checking for health problems and preventing childhood infectious diseases such as diphtheria and measles through immunisation. In recent years, however, there has been an extension of their role to include organising activities on healthy eating, smoking cessation and alcohol and drug use, running school health services, and supporting wider initiatives such as the delivery of PSHE. Such actions and interventions are often welcomed by young people, who may experience difficulties in accessing traditional health services. This chapter describes the different partnerships nurses have forged with teachers and other school members, the relationships they have built, and the value of an integrated approach in which the contributions of the health and education sectors are brought closer together.

Throughout this book, we have tried to stress approaches to undertaking health-related activities in school that 'work' in the sense that they engender worthwhile relationships and bring about desirable outcomes. Yet how do we know that a particular approach or style of work 'works', and how can we improve upon the methods that are being used in schools? These and related questions are addressed by Catherine Dennison, Ian Warwick and Peter Aggleton in the final chapter of this book. In addition to detailing different styles of evaluation, they describe experiences of evaluating healthy school activities. In so doing, they aim to provide teachers and health professionals with a realistic appreciation of what might be expected from evaluation, and what evaluation can and cannot do.

For many years, teachers have been interested in promoting the health and well-being of students and pupils. Yet they have often sought to do this through 'educational' means, hoping that what is taught will lay the foundations for a healthy physical and mental life in adulthood. In recent times, the narrowness of a perspective which stresses educational inputs alone has been questioned – education can do a lot to promote health, but it can achieve much in synergy with others, including parents, health professionals and the wider community. Recent interest in healthy and health-promoting schools recognises and responds to this concern. We hope you enjoy reading this book and that it provides you with some useful ideas to try out in your own work. We hope too that it contributes to a broader understanding of the ways in which schools may or may not produce the health benefits that children and young people deserve.

References

Biesta, G. (2007) 'Why "what works" won't work: Evidence-based practice and the democratic deficit in educational research', *Educational Theory*, 57(1): 1–22.

DCSF (Department for Children, Schools and Families) (2008) *Extended Schools: Building on Experience*. London: DCSF.

Fuller, E. (2009) *The Relationship between National Healthy School Status and Selected School Outcomes*. London: NatCen.

Lister-Sharp, D., Chapman, S., Stewart-Brown, S. and Sowden, A. (1999) 'Health promoting schools and health promotion in schools: Two systematic reviews', *Health Technology Assessment*, 3(22): 1–207.

Mukoma, W. and Flisher, A. J. (2004) 'Evaluations of health promoting schools: A review of nine studies', *Health Promotion International*, 19(3): 357–368.

Murray, N. G., Low, B. J., Hollis, C., Cross, A. W. and Davis, S. M. (2007) 'Coordinated school health programs and academic achievement: A systematic review of the literature', *Journal of School Health*, 77(9): 589–600.

Ofsted (2009) *Indicators of a School's Contribution to Well-Being*. London: Ofsted.

Powney, J., Malcolm, H. and Lowden, K. (2000) *Health and Attainment: A Brief Review of Recent Literature*. Glasgow: SCRE Centre, University of Glasgow.

St Leger, L. and Nutbeam, D. (2000) 'Research into health promoting schools', *Journal of School Health*, 70(6): 257–259.

St Leger, L., Kolbe, L., Lee, A., Douglas, S., McCall, D. and Young, I. M. (2007) 'School health promotion: Achievements, challenges and priorities', in D. V. McQueen and C. M. Jones (eds) *Global Perspectives on Health Promotion Effectiveness*. New York: Springer.

Stewart-Brown, S. (2006) *What is the Evidence on School Health Promotion in Improving Health or Preventing Disease and, Specifically, What is the Effectiveness of the Health Promoting Schools Approach?* Copenhagen: WHO Regional Office for Europe (Health Evidence Network Report).

Chapter 2

The health of children and young people

Fiona Brooks

This chapter looks at the health and well-being of children and young people in Britain. The focus is primarily on the health of the school-aged population. Where the existing evidence base allows, data are presented that provide comparisons across time, and among different demographic groups. International comparative studies and data sources have also been drawn upon to provide contextual insight.

The chapter also describes inequalities in children's and young people's health, according to gender, age, geography and socio-economic status. Age and gender distinctions are particularly significant categories for understanding the health and well-being of the school-aged population. The relationship between gender and health in childhood and adolescence is marked in terms of both protective and risk behaviours, as well as health outcomes.

One of the key difficulties in offering a comprehensive and detailed depiction of the health and well-being of the school-aged population is the paucity of the data, with gaps relating to, for example, the health of Black and minority ethnic (BME) young people and young people with disabilities. However, there are a number of studies that provide invaluable insights into the health and well-being of children and young people, the most notable being the *Health Behaviour in School-Aged Children* study (Currie *et al.*, 2008), the *European School Survey Project on Alcohol and Other Drugs* (ESPAD) (Hibell and Guttormsson, 2009) and the *Exeter Schools Health Study* (Balding, 2007).

As other chapters stress (e.g. Chapters 4 and 9), and as work within the new social studies of childhood (Wills *et al.*, 2008) has asserted, young people are active social agents who have their own strategies for navigating the surrounding world and for negotiating in relation to their health. These may differ from adult perspectives and health maintenance strategies. As a result, understanding and taking seriously the experience and perspective of young people themselves is necessary if health promotion policies and health services are to address children and young people's needs. Consequently, this chapter will also show how important an understanding of the perspectives of young people is for interpreting their health behaviour and for responding to their health and well-being needs.

Children and young people in the UK

Children and young people constitute a major part of the population, both globally and closer to home. In 2007, there were 7.8 million young people aged 10–19 and 7 million children under 10 years of age in the UK – an increase of more than 11 per cent from a decade earlier (Coleman and Brooks, 2009).

Life circumstances have a profound impact on how far children and young people are able to establish and sustain their health and well-being. Socio-economic status, gender, race and ethnicity, geographical location and environmental conditions, as well as young people's relative access to a range of resources within households, combine cumulatively to affect young people's health. It has been estimated that upwards of 3.6 million children in Britain live in poverty (House of Commons, 2004). A family's socio-economic status is likely to be one of the most important determinants of the health of children within the household; the lower the socio-economic status of a household, the higher risk of childhood mortality and long-term and acute illness (Spencer, 2003).

Socio-economic disadvantage is also strongly associated with poorer emotional health and development (Graham and Power, 2004). In addition, the relative impact of lower socio-economic status may be increasing as over the past thirty years the 'socialisation gap' (Margo and Dixon, 2006), whereby relatively affluent parents can purchase access to a range of resources, activities and institutions that enhance children's social and academic development, has become an increasingly significant determinant of young people's life chances and their ability to maintain health and well-being.

Family and household structures have also dramatically changed, with one-quarter living in a household headed by a lone parent (Coleman and Brooks, 2009). While lone parenthood often correlates with socio-economic disadvantage within the household, research suggests that for children and young people the quality of the communication within the home may be as integral to young people's well-being as family structure (Pedersen et al., 2004). Adult health status also affects the well-being of children and young people: poor adult health has long been associated with reductions in socio-economic status for the whole family; moreover, over 50 per cent of children with an emotional disorder have been found to have a parent who also scored very low for psychological health (Meltzer et al., 2000).

Significant numbers of children and young people take on long-term informal caring responsibilities for family members, often parents (Dearden and Becker, 2004). The 2001 census identified that over 114,000 children aged between 5 and 15 act as carers for family members, with 27,000 providing twenty or more hours a week (Doran et al., 2003). Children with ill or disabled parents do not inevitably provide informal care as, again, wider social determinants play a role in structuring the responsibilities of young people. Young carers, for example, are more likely to be found in single-parent families and those living in poverty (Dearden and Becker, 1998, 2004). Moreover, girls are more likely than boys to have considerable caring responsibilities, and around 15 per cent of all young carers come from BME communities (Dearden and Becker, 1998). A worrying finding in relation to the lives of young carers is that many report their own health to be poor (Doran et al., 2003).

Outside of the home and family context, school is the environment where children and young people spend most of their time. The school setting represents a significant potential resource for health among children; enjoying school is associated with positive self-esteem, lower levels of risk-taking behaviour and higher levels of self-rated health, while a dislike of school is associated with the reverse (Nutbeam et al., 1993; Samdal et al., 1998). From middle childhood onwards, young people may spend up to one-third of their waking time with peers and friends, with the school being an important arena for the development of peer relationships (Brown and Klute, 2003). Peers and friendship groups can be a major determinant of risk-taking behaviour among young people. Pressure to conform can create norms that lead to an acceptability of risk-taking behaviour within a group, especially substance use (Settertobulte and Gaspar de Matos, 2004). Moreover, persistent relational or physical bullying can isolate and marginalise children and young people, with detrimental effects on their health.

However, having a close circle of supportive friends can be a protective health asset and young people gain considerable support and pleasure from spending time with friends. Peers can enable young people to develop social competence and successfully manage stressful situations (Settertobulte and Gaspar de Matos, 2004). Even some youth sub-cultures that may appear challenging to adult definitions of appropriate behaviour can provide a protective sense of community for otherwise marginalised young people (Hodkinson, 2002).

Physical health, mortality and morbidity

The school years, especially in economically rich countries, are generally assumed to be a time of good health. However, ill health and disability during childhood and adolescence can have a marked effect on the attainment of life and educational goals, as well as restricting social and emotional development (Currie et al., 2008).

Mortality in childhood in the UK is rare and fell continually during the latter half of the twentieth century. Apart from mortality in children under the age of 1, death rates among children and young people are highest between 15 and 19 years. For example, in the UK in 2006 there were 430 deaths of young people aged 10–14, but 1,654 among those aged 15–19 (ONS, 2008). This increase with age is due primarily to preventable deaths, caused by injury, self-poisoning and road traffic accidents. In the UK, just over 1,000 young people aged 15–24 years die each year as a result of accidents, and the majority are road traffic related (Donaldson, 2008).

Media reports abound with concerns relating to young people as a risk to others. However, in reality young people are as likely to be victims of violence as the perpetrators of harm to others. The 2006–7 British Crime Survey identified that just over 20 per cent of all young people aged 16–24 years, and 14 per cent of young men, had been a victim of violent crime compared to around 4 per cent of those aged 45–64 (Home Office, 2007). Recent data from London indicate that one-third of all victims of rape and sexual offences are children and young people, predominantly girls aged under 17 years (Greater London Authority, 2007). While violence against young people is often perpetrated by peers, in many cases individuals they may know from their community are responsible for the crime (Home Office Statistical Bulletin, 2008). In 2007, nearly 28,000 UK children were identified as being at risk of serious abuse from their parents or other carers and placed on Children and Young People Child Protection Registers. Overall, violence, abuse and injury (either accidental or intentional) represent a significant health risk for young people.

In relation to morbidity, the vast majority of health issues among the pre-school and school-aged population are managed at home under the care of parents or guardians, with only 20 per cent of all disease and illness among young people resulting in a consultation with a general practitioner (Bruijnzeels *et al.*, 1998). Consultation rates with a general practitioner among the school-aged population have remained relatively stable over the last decade at about two consultations per young person a year. Among young men, the consultation rate remains constant through to early adulthood; however, for young women late adolescence (15–19 years) marks a doubling of general practice consultations to four per year (Hippisley-Cox *et al.*, 2007). In relation to young people's experience of general practice, a recent questionnaire study reported that 23 per cent of girls surveyed from school years 8 to 10 (aged 12–15 years) felt either 'quite' or 'very uneasy' with their doctor during their most recent consultation, with highest rates of unease being found among younger girls (Balding, 2007).

In terms of acute health service usage, and in contrast to the adult population, emergency hospital admissions are more common than planned admissions among children and young people under the age of 15. Moreover, across the 5–19 age group in England, the number of emergency admissions to hospital has steadily increased over the last decade from 352,841 in 1996–7 to 419,414 in 2006–7, an increase that has been most dramatic among the 16–19 age group (Cochrane, 2008; Coleman and Brooks, 2009). In the main, emergency admission rates reflect the higher rates of accidents and violent injury among young people; however, children and young people are also at risk from being admitted to hospital due to a long-term or chronic condition.

Over the last ten years, the prevalence of longstanding illnesses (e.g. diabetes or asthma) among children aged 2–15 has fluctuated between 20 per cent and 29 per cent for boys and between 16 per cent and 25 per cent for girls (Nessa, 2004). The most common longstanding illness or disability among the school-aged population (5–19 years) is asthma, followed by autism and behavioural disorders (Nessa, 2004). Nessa's analysis of both the General Household Survey 2000 (GHS) and the Family Fund Trust's register of applicants showed that mild disability prevalence (any longstanding condition or illness that limits activities) is about 20 per cent among the school-aged population, is more prevalent in the 5–19 population than the pre-school age group (under 4), and is slightly lower for girls than boys. In terms of understanding the prevalence and character of severe disability among young people, there is a dearth of recent reliable data. Data from 2000 does, however, indicate that the prevalence of severe disability among BME young people is disproportionate to the general UK population (Nessa, 2004).

The overall trend appears to indicate a decrease in the prevalence rates of both longstanding and limiting conditions among children (Health and Social Care Information Centre, 2008). In contrast, there has been a rise in hospital admission rates for the three key chronic and long-term conditions that affect young people the most (Coleman and Brooks, 2009). The most dramatic increase has been for asthma admissions, which among 10–19 years increased by 19 per cent to 11,291 in the five years between 2002–3 and 2006–7 (Donaldson, 2008). A number of sources indicate that policies relating to the management of long-term conditions within school settings may play an important role in the health of young people. For example, a recent study of asthma in school-aged children in two UK cities found strong evidence that peaks in hospital admissions coincide with the end of the summer school holidays and the return to school (Julious et al., 2007).

In order to gain an understanding of the quality of children and young people's health, it is important to look at how they perceive their own health. Self-rated health is a good indicator of subsequent long-term health outcomes and, importantly, measures health in an in-depth way that cannot be covered by traditional morbidity and mortality measures, thereby adding significant insight into our understanding of children and young people's health. Young people's self-rated health as a subjective measure of general health shows strong associations with mental health, family structure and parental communication, as well as school experience and attainment. During the primary school years and up to the first year of secondary school, between 80 and 95 per cent of young people surveyed in the UK report their health to be 'good' (Currie et al., 2008; Health and Social Care Information Centre, 2008). However, the proportions of young people reporting to have good health declines with age, and significantly so for young women. The HBSC study also highlights a continued inverse relationship between social class and the proportions of young people who rate their health as 'good' or 'excellent' (Brooks et al., 2009).

Emotional well-being and mental health

The absence of disease is an important aspect of health, but equally the absence of distress and the presence of a sense of well-being are also central components of the best possible health (Seligman and Csikszentmihalyi, 2000). Self-reported life satisfaction among school-aged children has been associated with a range of health-related outcomes such as healthy weight, physical activity levels, substance use and attainment of goals (Thorne and Espelage, 2004; Zullig et al., 2001). The HBSC study asked young people to rate their life satisfaction on a score of 0–10 on a Cantril ladder; a score of 0 is the 'worst possible life' and 10 is the 'best possible life' (Cantril, 1965). Findings suggest that the majority of young people in England, Scotland and Wales report that they are happy with their lives; for example, 85 per cent of all young people included in the study from England rated their life satisfaction to be 6 or above (Brooks et al., 2009). Levels of life satisfaction found in Britain are also not too dissimilar to levels found in the rest of Europe; for example, in the Netherlands, the highest-scoring country, 94 per cent of 15-year-old boys reported high life satisfaction compared to 89 per cent in England (Currie et al., 2008). However, life satisfaction decreases from the age of 11 years and significantly more boys than girls are reporting higher life satisfaction by the mid to late teens (Currie et al., 2008).

Although the majority of children and young people report being happy and satisfied with their lives, the prevalence of conduct disorders and poor mental health among some young people has been an issue of public and policy concern (Coleman and Brooks, 2009). The prevalence of any emotional, conduct or hyperkinetic disorder among young people has remained relatively unchanged over the past five years at about 12–13 per cent for boys and 9–10 per cent for girls aged 11–15 (Green et al., 2005; Meltzer et al., 2000). Among the 5–11 age group, the prevalence of any disorder is much higher for boys than for girls, especially in relation to conduct of hyperkinetic (hyperactivity) disorders; among girls emotional disorders are more common. The disparity between boys and girls, in relation to emotional disorders increases with age (Brooks et al., 2009). Girls also report being worried by schoolwork issues, including exams and friendship and family problems, more frequently than boys of the same age (Balding, 2007).

Although girls and young women are more likely to report feeling low and experience low self-esteem, it is young men who are at greatest risk from extreme feelings of hopelessness and suicide, with older young men being most at risk (Bradford and Urquhart, 1998). Suicide among the younger school-aged population is rare, but among the 15–24 age group this figure for 2006 jumps to 543, the overwhelming majority of whom were male (431) (Samaritans, 2008). However, the suicide rates in the UK for young men do appear to be gradually reducing, so that in 2006 the rate for young men aged 15–24 was the lowest for a decade and comparable with rates in other European countries such as Germany and France (EUROSTAT, 2008).

Psychological distress and diagnosed psychiatric disorders are also significantly more common among children aged 11–16 from the Black and Black African/Caribbean communities (14 per cent) than among White (12 per cent) or Pakistani and Bangladeshi (7.8 per cent) communities, highlighting the need for better understanding of the relative experiences of living in the UK for children from different BME and minority communities (Samaritans, 2008).

Life circumstances and the experience of abuse and neglect play a role in the emotional well-being of children. Poor psychological health is common among the UK's most vulnerable children; a recent study identified that just over 45 per cent of young people aged 5–17 who were looked after by local authorities had a diagnosed psychiatric disorder (Ford *et al.*, 2007). In addition, 'looked after children' with a psychiatric disorder are much more likely to be in residential care than in a foster or kinship placement (Ford *et al.*, 2007).

In terms of the sources of support for emotional well-being, there is evidence that relatively fewer young people look to general practitioners as a means of support. Churchill *et al.* (2000) found that over a twelve-month period, consultations among young people for psychological conditions accounted for only a tiny minority of consultations. Instead, young people appear more likely to turn to family and friends as a means to address negative and distressing feelings (Balding, 2007).

Health risk and protective behaviours

In the media, and to a certain extent in the academic literature, the health of young people is often considered to be determined by health risk behaviours, especially within a deficit model that portrays young people's behaviour as intrinsically and recklessly damaging to their future health. As we have seen, however, young people's health is as much influenced by social determinants and constraints as it is by risk behaviours. The remainder of the chapter will therefore attempt to offer this more balanced perspective, looking at some of the health issues that are examined in more detail later in this book.

Sexual health

Sexual health is an essential component of well-being and encompasses the concept of a positive, pleasurable and safe sexual relationship (World Health Organization, 2006). During the teenage years, sexual health is often seen as a cause for adult anxiety, due to the potential for a clash with dominant societal norms, as well as possible exposure to unplanned pregnancy and sexually transmitted infections (STIs).

Early sexual intercourse is one element of a set of health risk behaviours, each of which may reinforce other risk-taking behaviour and put the individual at increased risk of negative outcomes, including pregnancy, STIs and negative self-rated life satisfaction (Godeau *et al.*, 2008). Sexual initiation during the early years of adolescence is associated with other risk behaviours such as substance use, most notably alcohol use (Robertson and Plant, 1988). Moreover, sexual initiation earlier than age 14 is linked with lower self-rated quality of life in girls and higher levels of psychosomatic health complaints such as regular headaches, stomach aches and feeling low (Currie *et al.*, 2008).

In terms of the prevalence of both early sexual initiation and sexual experience, young people in England, Scotland and Wales are comparable in their behaviours with those in other Northern European countries, with a number of studies concluding that around 20–30 per cent of 15-year-olds report ever having had sex (Brooks *et al.*, 2009; Testa and Coleman, 2006). Experience of first sexual intercourse under 16 years has been found to be higher in some groups such as Black African Caribbean boys (43 per cent) and lower among Asian boys (12 per cent) and girls (4 per cent) (Testa and Coleman, 2006).

Prevention of unintended pregnancy and STIs has been a central component of public health strategy within the UK. A recent study looking at sexual activity among young people in London found that the majority of sexually active young people do appear to use contraception, with non-use during first-ever sexual intercourse reported to be in the region of 17 per cent (Testa and Coleman, 2006). However, there appear to be important variations by socio-economic status, with those from more affluent backgrounds being more likely to use contraception than other economic groups (Brooks *et al.*, 2009). Variations have also been found between ethnic groups; non-use of contraception during first-ever sexual experience is more likely among Black African teenage men than White British young men. Although fewer Asian young people report ever having sex, among those who do use contraception much higher proportions of males and females reported not using any method of contraception than White British young people (Testa and Coleman, 2006).

The use of the contraceptive pill is highest in Western European countries, such as the Netherlands, where 61 per cent of sexually active 15-year-old girls reported using the contraceptive pill the last time they had sexual intercourse compared to 23 per cent of sexually active girls in England (Currie *et al.*, 2008). Condom use is more frequently reported by boys and is highest in Southern European countries such as Spain, Portugal and Greece, with between 85 and 95 per cent of young people reporting using a condom the last time they had sexual intercourse (Currie *et al.*, 2008). Condom use is also high among sexually active teenagers in England (82 per cent, both genders), Scotland (78 per cent) and Wales (75 per cent) (Brooks *et al.*, 2009).

Over the last decade, there has been considerable policy attention given in England to a reduction in the teenage pregnancy rates. In the UK, statistical data over the decade (since 1998) suggests a general downward trend in the teenage conception rate and a respective rise in terminations (TPU, 2008). However, among the most vulnerable teenagers conception rates remain high. For example, looked after young women are twice as likely to become pregnant under 18 as other teenagers, and it is estimated that one in four girls leaving care are already mothers or pregnant (SCIE, 2005).

Turning to STIs and HIV, globally millions of children are at increasing risk of HIV infection, in the majority of cases contracted from their mother during pregnancy or breast-feeding (UNAIDS, 2003). This contrasts with under 2,000 UK diagnoses of HIV in children under 14 years of age (ONS, 2008). New diagnoses of infectious syphilis are somewhat low in the UK, amounting to about 100 cases a year in under 16s and 16–19-year-olds combined (HPA, 2008). Gonorrhoea rates are higher, with over 30,000 new cases among young people each year, although recent data since 2002–3 indicate a downward trend in new infection rates (HPA, 2008). Time trend analysis does, however, reveal that some STIs represent an increasing risk to young people's health; for example, between 1998 and 2007, chlamydia-diagnosed infection rates for 16–19-year-olds increased by over 100 per cent, and in 2007 there were 32,038 newly diagnosed cases of chlamydia in the 16–19 age group (HPA, 2008).

In terms of supporting the development of sexual health among young people, greater levels of understanding and knowledge need to be developed to fully understand how young people can develop positive value frameworks that lead to mature, pleasurable sexual relationships (Ingham, 2007).

Alcohol and substance use

The UK has consistently been identified as having higher numbers of young people drinking alcohol regularly and to the point of drunkenness than many other countries in Europe and North America (Currie et al., 2004, 2008; Hibell and Guttormsson, 2009). Although the proportion of young people who report having drunk alcohol in the previous seven days appears to have fallen slightly since 2001 (Fuller et al., 2007), recent findings also indicate that in the UK over 88 per cent of 16-year-olds surveyed have consumed alcohol in the previous twelve months, 57 per cent have been drunk at least once over the previous year (Hibell and Guttormsson, 2009) and between 12 and 14 per cent of young people aged 11–15 in England, Wales and Scotland reported more than four occasions of lifetime drunkenness (Brooks et al., 2009).

Children and adolescents are especially vulnerable to alcohol poisoning due to a lower body mass and metabolic processing of alcohol, and over the last decade excessive alcohol consumption has resulted in an increasing number of under 18-year-olds being admitted to hospital for an alcohol-related condition, and in particular alcohol poisoning (Miller *et al.*, 2001). For both males and females, rates of admission across England were highest in the North West and North East and lowest in London and the East of England (NWPHO, 2007).

Potentially, reflecting a shift in risk-taking behaviour among young women, girls in the UK, unlike in the majority of other European countries, have either achieved parity with boys in terms of frequency of drunkenness or are slightly more likely to report at age 15 having been drunk than boys of the same age (Currie *et al.*, 2008; Hibell and Guttormsson, 2009). Significantly, there were more female alcohol-related hospital admissions than male in 2004–5 (57 per cent of admissions were female), a pattern that occurred consistently across all regions of the UK (NWPHO, 2007).

Apart from alcohol consumption, levels of substance misuse and smoking among young people in the UK appear to be on a downward trend (Hibell and Guttormsson, 2009; The Information Centre, 2008a). Smoking in particular is less prevalent among children and young people in the UK than in other European countries, with 22 per cent reporting having smoked a cigarette in the previous 30 days compared to a 29 per cent European average (Hibell and Guttormsson, 2009). In 2007, 19 per cent of girls and 12 per cent of boys in England were regularly smoking at least once a week; however, this represents a significant reduction from the rates two years previously of 25 per cent for 15-year-old girls and 16 per cent for boys (Fuller, 2007; The Information Centre, 2008a).

Use of cannabis can also be seen to be relatively common among the UK school-aged population, with about one-third of young people reporting that they have tried the drug (Currie *et al.*, 2008; Hibell and Guttormsson, 2009). Aside from cannabis, the proportion of school-aged pupils who use any form of drug, including class A drugs and other drugs such as solvents, is relatively low in the UK, accounting for 6.5 per cent of 11–15-year-olds (The Information Centre, 2008a) and 9 per cent of 16-year-olds (Hibell *et al.*, 2009).

In considering young people's substance use and alcohol consumption it is important to note that early onset is a key indicator of future and long-term usage, as drug-related risk-taking behaviours operate in tandem with other health risk behaviours, especially those relating to sexual health. Consequently, it is important that rates of smoking are reducing among young people in the UK, but also especially concerning to note is the high level of alcohol consumption, especially the increase among girls. Overall, levels of substance misuse among girls in the UK now mirror those of boys and we are seeing the serious consequences of this pattern, with high levels of alcohol hospital admissions among young women. The increase in girls' and young women's substance use highlights the need for a renewed attention to gender issues and how societal and environmental vulnerability operate as determinants of young people's health.

Physical activity, healthy diet and healthy weight

Active lifestyles have been demonstrated to have an array of positive impacts on the health and emotional well-being of children and young people (Brooks and Magnusson, 2006). Despite the benefits of an active lifestyle, worldwide many children's lives are becoming increasingly sedentary (World Health Organization, 2002). In the UK, identifying and promoting ways to sustain an active lifestyle among children has become a policy priority.

During the primary school years, levels of physical activity are high, with over 70 per cent of both sexes regularly participating in sport, exercise or active play such as 'running about' or riding a bike. By age 15, however, a marked gender differentiation has become apparent as girls' participation in physical activity reduces. Studies have found that around 15 per cent of 15-year-old boys but 30 per cent of girls are undertaking significantly less than the recommended one hour of any moderate physical activity a day (Craig and Mindell, 2008). Moreover, participation in any sport or exercise, while dropping by about 10 per cent for boys, declines for girls from 75 per cent participation at age 10 years to 45 per cent at age 15 (Craig and Mindell, 2008). Although the causes of such gender differences are complex, findings suggest that the character of physical activity provision for girls warrants detailed consideration.

Linked to the concern over young people's sedentary lifestyles has been a growing concern over levels of obesity and being overweight among young people. Quality of nutrition is key to the health and development of young people. In 1995, 11 per cent of children aged 2–15 in England were classified as clinically obese. One decade later, in 2006, this figure had risen to 16 per cent, with more boys (17 per cent) than girls (15 per cent) being likely to be obese. Social determinants appear to play a significant role in the construction of childhood obesity; in 2006 among the lowest income group 20 per cent of both genders were obese, while among the highest income group 15 per cent of boys and 9 per cent of girls could be classified as obese. Overweight and obesity prevalence among children is also associated with parental Body Mass Index. For example, in 2006 22 per cent of girls aged 2–15 living in households where the parents were overweight or obese were also classed as obese; this contrasts with just 8 per cent of girls in normal-weight households (The Information Centre, 2008b).

In terms of the diet of children and young people in the UK, recent evidence suggests that the consumption of fruit and vegetables has increased; young people aged 11–15 in England in particular are more likely to report eating fruit daily than in the overwhelming majority of countries in Europe and North America (Currie et al., 2008). School-aged young people consuming significant portions of fruit and vegetables still remain in a minority, however. Among those aged 5–15 years, in 2006 only 19 per cent of boys and 22 per cent of girls consumed five or more portions of fruit and vegetables a day, although this does represent an increase from 2004 levels (The Information Centre, 2008b).

Young people's body image and self-esteem have been linked in a number of studies (Bergman and Scott, 2001; Ter Bogt *et al.*, 2006; Williams and Currie, 2000). Studies consistently report that throughout adolescence girls are more likely to report being unhappy about their body size than boys. For example, only 28 per cent of UK school year 10 boys wanted to lose weight compared to 57 per cent of girls in school year 10 (aged 14–15 years) (Balding, 2007). In this same survey, however, the majority of girls who wanted to lose weight were actually of healthy weight or even underweight (Balding, 2007). Consequently, it is not surprising that girls in the secondary school population are most at risk of eating disorders (Currin *et al.*, 2005).

Sedentary behaviours, such as two or more hours of computer gaming or television watching a day, have been associated with increased consumption of high-calorie food and lower consumption of fruit and vegetables (Vereecken *et al.*, 2006). Boys may participate in physical activity more than girls, but higher proportions of boys spend considerable amounts of time gaming on computer consoles (Brooks *et al.*, 2009). However, boys may also gain social status from playing computer games that may serve to strengthen peer relationships in school, and for both sexes it may also be very important emotionally to be able to participate in peer discussions relating to popular television programmes. It is important therefore to understand how participation in some sedentary activities may offer both benefits and risks to the health of young people.

Conclusion

The majority of the UK school-aged population appear to enjoy good health and high life satisfaction. However, the data presented in this chapter have demonstrated that the health of young people is differentially mediated by socio-economic inequalities, age, ethnicity and gender. Although boys and young men have historically been more likely to engage in risk behaviours, girls and young women have been closing this gap. Girls are more likely to smoke and be vulnerable to the serious effects of excessive alcohol consumption. Internationally, there are marked differences in the health status of the school-aged population, and the UK compares well for life satisfaction, but poorly for some health risk behaviours, such as alcohol misuse.

The psychological development of children and adolescents is highly dependent upon their social environment, with family, peers and school having a critical role. Education and school can function both as a determinant of health status and as a means to promote health and well-being among young people. A positive experience of school, family life and supportive peer relationships can be protective, supporting the development of high life satisfaction and lower levels of reported stress; conversely, negative school experiences, such as bullying, can generate a predisposition towards depression (Rutter *et al.*, 1979; Torsheim and Wold, 2001).

The data presented in this chapter have illuminated how health risk behaviours are not simply risky or 'bad' choices made due to poor judgement and immaturity; rather, the apparent choices made by children and young people are constructed through the lens of social determinants. While young people should not be seen as passively being moulded by the surrounding adult world, environmental conditions and socio-economic inequalities shape the character of the choices that are available to young people. Overall, in order to improve the health and well-being of the school-aged population, it is essential to acknowledge how young people are socially and economically positioned by forces outside their immediate control and, as a result, come to feel about their lives.

References

Balding, J. (2007) *Young People into 2007*. Exeter: Schools Health Education Unit.

Bergman, M. and Scott, J. (2001) 'Young adolescents' wellbeing and health-risk behaviours: Gender and socio-economic differences', *Journal of Adolescence*, 24: 183–197.

Bradford, S. and Urquhart, C. (1998) 'The making and breaking of young men: Suicide and the adolescent male', *Youth and Policy*, 61: 28–41.

Brooks, F. and Magnusson, J. (2006) 'Taking part counts: Adolescents' experiences of the transition from inactivity to active participation in school based physical education', *Health Education Research*, 21: 872–883.

Brooks, F., Klemera, E., Morgan, A., Magnusson, J., Nic Gabhainn, S., Roberts, C., Smith, R. and Van Der Sluijis, W. (2009) *Young People's Health in Great Britain and Ireland: Findings from the Health Behaviour in School-Aged Children Study*. Hatfield: University of Hertfordshire.

Brown, B. B. and Klute, C. (2003) 'Friendships, cliques and crowds', in G. R. Adams and C. Klute (eds) *Handbook of Adolescence*. Oxford: Blackwell.

Bruijnzeels, M., Foets, M., Van Der Wouden, J., Van Den Heuvel, W. and Prins, A. (1998) 'Everyday symptoms in childhood: Occurrence and general practitioner consultation rates', *British Journal of General Practice*, 48: 880–884.

Cantril, H. (1965) *The Pattern of Human Concern*. New Brunswick, NJ: Rutgers University Press.

Churchill, R., Allen, J., Denman, S., Williams, D., Fielding, K. and Von Fragstein, M. (2000) 'Do the attitudes and beliefs of young teenagers towards general practice influence actual consultation behaviour?' *British Journal of General Practice*, 50: 953–957.

Cochrane, H. (2008) *Trends in Young People's Care: Emergency Admission Statistics 1996/7–2006/07, England*. London: Chief Nursing Officers' Directorate, Department of Health.

Coleman, J. and Brooks, F. (2009) *Key Data on Adolescence 2009*. Brighton: Association for Young People's Health and Trust for the Study of Adolescence.

Craig, R. and Mindell, J. (eds) (2008) *Health Survey for England 2006*. Vol. 2: *Obesity and Other Risk Factors in Children*. London: The Information Centre, Lifestyle Statistics.

Currie, C., Roberts, C., Morgan, A., Smith, R., Settertobulte, W., Samdal, O. and Barnekow-Rasmussen, V. (2004) *Young People's Health in Context: Health Behaviour in School-aged Children (HBSC) Study. International Report from the 2001/2002 Survey*. Copenhagen: World Health Organization.

Currie, C., Nic Gabhainn, S., Godeau, E., Roberts, C., Smith, R., Currie, D., Picket, W., Richter, M., Morgan, A. and Barnekow, V. (eds) (2008) *Inequalities in Young People's Health: HBSC International Report from the 2005/2006 Survey.* Copenhagen: WHO Regional Office for Europe.

Currin, L., Schmidt, U., Treasure, J. and Hershel, J. (2005) 'Time trends in eating disorder incidence', *British Journal of Psychiatry*, 186: 132–135.

Dearden, C. and Becker, S. (1998) *Young Carers in the United Kingdom: A Profile.* London: Carers National Association.

Dearden, C. and Becker, S. (2004) *Young Carers in the UK: The 2004 Report.* London: Carers UK.

Donaldson, L. (2008) *On the State of Public Health: Annual Report of the Chief Medical Officer.* London: Office for National Statistics (ONS).

Doran, T., Drever, F. and Whitehead, M. (2003) 'Health of young and elderly informal carers: Analysis of UK census data', *British Medical Journal*, 327: 1388.

EUROSTAT (2008) *Europe in Figures: Eurostat Yearbook 2008.* Luxembourg: European Communities.

Ford, T., Vastanis, P., Meltzer, H., Goodman, R. and Vostanis, P. (2007) 'Psychiatric disorder among British children looked after by local authorities: Comparison with children living in private households', *British Journal of Psychiatry*, 190: 319–325.

Fuller, E. (ed.) (2007) *Smoking, Drinking and Drug Use among Young People in England in 2006.* London: The Information Centre, NHS.

Godeau, E., Vignes, C., Duclos, M., Navarro, F., Cayla, F. and Grandjean, H. (2008) 'Factors associated with early sexual initiation in girls: French data from the international survey Health Behaviour in School-aged Children (HBSC)/WHO', *Gynécologie, obstétrique & fertilité*, 36: 176–182.

Graham, H. and Power, C. (2004) 'Childhood disadvantage and health inequalities: A framework for policy based on lifecourse research', *Child Care, Health and Development*, 30: 671–678.

Greater London Authority (2007) *The State of London's Children Report.* London: Greater London Authority.

Green, H., McGinnity, A., Meltzer, H., Ford, T. and Goodman, R. (2005) *The Mental Health of Children and Young People in Great Britain.* London: Palgrave Macmillian.

Health and Social Care Information Centre (2008) 'Health Survey for England 2007: Latest trends', in R. Craig and J. Mindell (eds) *Health Survey for England.* London: Health and Social Care Information Centre.

Hibell, B. and Guttormsson, U. (2009) *The European School Survey Project on Alcohol and Other Drugs: The 2007 ESPAD Report.* Stockholm: Swedish Council for Information on Alcohol and Other Drugs (CAN).

Hippisley-Cox, J., Fenty, J. and Heaps, M. (2007) *Trends in Consultation Rates in General Practice 1995 to 2006: Analysis of the QRESEARCH database. QRESEARCH Research Highlights.* Leeds: The Information Centre.

Hodkinson, P. (2002) *Goth: Identity, Style and Sub-culture.* Oxford: Berg.

Home Office (2007) *Crime in England and Wales 2006/7: Home Office Statistical Bulletin.* London: Home Office.

Home Office Statistical Bulletin (2008) *Young People and Crime: Findings from the 2006 Offending and Crime Justice Survey.* London: Home Office.

House of Commons (2004) *Child Poverty in the UK: Second Report of Session 2003–04.* London: The Stationery Office.

HPA (2008) *Diagnosis of Selected STIs by Sex and Age Group 2003–2007*. London: Health Protection Agency UK (HPA).

Information Centre, The (2008a) *Drug Use, Smoking and Drinking among Young People in England 2007*. London: The Information Centre, NHS.

Information Centre, The (2008b) *Statistics on Obesity, Physical Activty and Diet: England*. London: The Centre, NHS.

Ingham, R. (2007) 'Some reflections on encouraging abstinence and delay as possible approaches to reducing sexual ill health among young people', in P. Baker, K. Guthrie, C. Hutchinson, R. Kane and K. Wellings (eds) *Teenage Pregnancy and Reproductive Health*. Dorchester: Royal College of Obstetricians and Gynaecologists.

Julious, S., Osman, L. and Jiwa, M. (2007) 'Increases in asthma hospital admissions associated with the end of summer vacation for school age children with asthma in two cities from England and Scotland', *Public Health*, 121: 482–484.

Margo, J. and Dixon, M. (2006) *Freedom's Orphans: Raising Youth in a Changing World*. London: Institute for Public Policy Research (IPPR).

Meltzer, H., Gatwood, R., Goodman, R. and Ford, T. (2000) *Mental Health of Children and Adolescents in Great Britain*. London: The Stationery Office.

Miller, E., Kilmer, J., Kim, E., Weingardt, K. and Marlatt, G. (2001) 'Alcohol skills training for college students', in P. Monti, S. Colby and T. O'Leary (eds) *Adolescents, Alcohol and Substance Abuse*. New York: Guilford Press.

Nessa, N. (2004) 'Disability', in Office for National Statistics (ed.) *The Health of Children and Young People*. London: The Stationery Office.

Nutbeam, D., Smith, C., Moore, L. and Bauman, A. (1993) 'Warning! Schools can damage your health: Alienation from school and its impact on health behaviour', *Promotion and Education*, 2: 4–7.

NWPHO (2007) *Alcohol Specific Admission for Those Aged 16 and Under: NWPHO Monthly (North West Public Health Observatory)*. Liverpool: John Moores University, Centre for Public Health. Available at www.nwpho.org.uk/monthly/mar07/ (last accessed 15 October 2009).

ONS (2008) *Population Trends 132*. London: Office for National Statistics (ONS).

Pedersen, M., Carmen Granado Alcon, M. and Moreno Rodriguez, C. (2004) 'Family and health', in C. Currie, C. Roberts, A. Morgan, R. Smith, W. Settertobulte, O. Samdal and V. Barnekow-Rasmussen (eds) *Young People's Health in Context: Health Behaviour in School-aged Children (HBSC) Study. International Report from the 2001/2002 Survey*. Copenhagen: World Health Organization.

Robertson, J. and Plant, M. (1988) 'Alcohol, sex and risks of HIV infection', *Drug and Alcohol Dependence*, 22: 75–78.

Rutter, M., Maugham, B. and Mortimore, P. (1979) *Fifteen Thousand Hours: Secondary Schools and Their Effects on Children*. London: Open Books.

Samaritans (2008) *Samaritans Information Resource Pack*. London: The Samaritans.

Samdal, O., Nutbeam, D., Wold, B. and Kannas, L. (1998) 'Achieving health and educational goals through schools: A study of the importance of school climate and students' satisfaction with school', *Health Education Research*, 13: 383–397.

SCIE (2005) *SCIE Research Briefing 9: Preventing Teenage Pregancy in Looked After Children*. London: SCIE. Available at www.scie.org.uk/publications/briefings/briefing09/index.asp (last accessed 7 July 2009).

Seligman, M. and Csikszentmihalyi, M. (2000) 'Positive psychology: An introduction', *American Psychologist*, 55: 5–14.

Settertobulte, W. and Gaspar de Matos, M. (2004) 'Peers and health', in C. Currie, C. Roberts, A. Morgan, R. Smith, W. Settertobulte, O. Samdal and V. Barnekow-Rasmussen (eds) *Young People's Health in Context: Health Behaviour in School-aged Children (HBSC) Study. International Report from the 2001/2002 Survey*. Copenhagen: World Health Organization.

Spencer, N. (2003) 'Social, economic and political determinants of child health', *Pediatrics*, 112: 704–706.

Ter Bogt, T., Van Dorsselaer, S., Monshouwer, K., Verdurmen, J., Engels, R. and Vollebergh, W. (2006) 'Body mass index and body weight perception as risk factors for internalizing and externalizing problem behavior among adolescents', *Journal of Adolescent Health*, 39: 27–34.

Testa, A. and Coleman, L. (2006) *Sexual Health Knowledge, Attitudes and Behaviours among Black and Minority Youth in London*. Brighton: Trust for the Study of Adolescence (TSA) and the NAZ Project. Available at www.tsa.uk.com (last accessed 7 July 2009).

Thome, J. and Espelage, D. (2004) 'Relations among exercise, coping, disordered eating and psychological health among college students', *Eating Behaviours*, 5: 337–351.

Torsheim, T. and Wold, B. (2001) 'School-related stress, school support and somatic complaints: A general population study', *Journal of Adolescent Research*, 24: 293–303.

TPU (Teenage Pregnancy Unit) (2008) *Under 18 Conception Data for Top Tier Local Authorities LAD1 1998–2006*. London: Office for National Statistics and Teenage Pregnancy Unit.

UNAIDS (2003) *AIDS Epidemic Update. UNAIDS: The Report on the Global HIV/AIDS Epidemic. Focus: AIDS and Orphans*, July 2002. Available at www.unaids.org (last accessed 7 July 2009).

Vereecken, C. A., Todd, J., Roberts, C., Mulvihill, C. and Maes, L. (2006) 'Television viewing behaviour and associations with food habits in different countries', *Public Health Nutrition*, 9: 244–250.

Williams, J. M. and Currie, C. (2000) 'Self-esteem and physical development in early adolescence: Pubertal timing and body image', *Journal of Early Adolescence*, 20: 129–149.

Wills, W., Appleton, J., Magnusson, J. and Brooks, F. (2008) 'Exploring the limitations of an adult-led agenda for understanding the health behaviours of young people', *Health and Social Care in the Community*, 16: 244–252.

World Health Organization (2002) *World Health Report 2002*. Geneva: World Health Organization.

World Health Organization (2006) *Defining Sexual Health: Report of a Technical Consultation on Sexual Health 28–31 January 2002*. Geneva: World Health Organization.

Zullig, K., Valois, R., Huebner, S., Oeltmann, J. and Drane, J. (2001) 'Relationship between perceived life satisfaction and adolescents' substance abuse', *Journal of Adolescent Health*, 29: 279–288.

Chapter 3

Promoting mental health through schools

Katherine Weare

Children and young people spend a large amount of time in schools and the school represents an easy-access environment with direct day-to-day contact with children, young people and, often, their families. Schools not only establish the competencies for learning, but are an important setting for mental health promotion, through their role in helping to establish identity, interpersonal relationships and other transferable skills (Greenberg *et al.*, 2003). This wider role is gradually being clearly recognised in mainstream education in the UK, where recent reviews of both primary education commissioned by the Government from independent experts (DCSF, 2008; University of Cambridge, 2009) and a new National Curriculum for secondary schools (QCA, 2008) strongly emphasise the need to help young people develop generic skills for learning and for life.

Schools are also workplaces for school staff, who, as some of the most dedicated but overstretched public workers, also deserve to have their own mental health needs met, not least because otherwise they are unlikely to be able to promote the mental health of those of whom they have charge. The school has for some time now been seen as a unique community resource to promote and foster mental, emotional and social well-being, and calls for it to be more active in this respect are growing (Mental Health Foundation, 1999; Hosman *et al.*, 2004; WHO/HBSC Forum 2007 Task Force, 2007; Fundación Marcelino Botín, 2008).

This chapter will explore what is meant by mental health promotion in schools, examining approaches which attempt to promote the positive mental health of all, and those which attempt to address mental health problems of various levels of intensity. It will provide a brief overview of work across the world, and examine what is happening in the UK in a little more detail. It will look at the evidence that mental health promotion in schools 'works', outline the various issues it has been shown to address, and suggest the key principles that lie behind effective approaches.

Mental health and mental health problems

Positive mental health

The concept of health as a positive state, not just the absence of illness, is now well accepted within health promotion. Applying this 'salutogenic' or health-focused approach is moving approaches to mental health in schools from a focus on mental health problems to a focus on actions to promote well-being, to recognise strengths, capacities and the characteristics of mentally healthy people, a move strongly assisted by the recent growth of interest in positive psychology (Snyder and Lopez, 2005).

In recent years, there have been several attempts to create positively focused taxonomies of mental health skills. A categorisation which underpins several of the best-known social and emotional programmes found in schools across the world is one popularised by Goleman (1996):

- self-understanding: having a positive and accurate sense of yourself, acknowledging strengths and limitations, having a sense of coherence about your life;
- understanding and managing feelings: relating skilfully to difficult feelings and impulses such as anger, sadness, anxiety and frustration, and promoting positive states such as happiness, elation, joy and calm;
- motivation: showing optimism, persistence and resilience, planning and setting goals;
- social skills: communication, assertion, relationships, solving social problems; and
- empathy: seeing another's point of view, celebrating diversity and difference, listening.

Mental health skills are critical throughout life, but are especially important during the school years (Harden et al., 2001). They can help in negotiating the challenges of growing up and making transitions (Newman and Blackburn, 2002) and may act as protective factors by preventing the development of risky behaviour. They lead to increased school attainment and completion, less involvement in the criminal justice system, lower costs to public services, higher earning potential, and resilience for life (Catalano et al., 2002; Zins et al., 2004).

It is gratifying, then, that most young people report at least reasonable levels of mental health. A recent overview (Graham, 2004) concluded that, contrary to stereotypes, most young people enjoy and work hard at school, get along with their parents and do not engage in high levels of risky behaviour. So, there is much positive mental health capacity on which to build.

Mental health problems

Alongside a positive approach to mental health promotion, it is important to recognise that a substantial minority of young people do experience mental health problems. A recent report by UNICEF (2007) compared various aspects of well-being of children in twenty-one of the world's richest countries, including relationships with family and friends, behaviours and risks and what young people themselves said about how they feel, and found that the UK ranked bottom of the league. Some 25 per cent of children and young people have an identifiable mental health problem (Harden *et al.*, 2001), of whom 10 per cent fulfil criteria for a mental health disorder which justifies specialist assessment and treatment (Green *et al.*, 2005). A review of mental health and young people (Harden *et al.*, 2001) found anti-social behaviour (here defined as conduct disorder, oppositional defiant disorder) to be the most common mental health problem presenting to psychiatrists, affecting over 5 per cent of children, particularly boys. Anxiety and depression affect 4 per cent. Suicide is thankfully relatively rare, but is still one of the three most common causes of death in youth, while self-harm and eating disorders are a growing problem, particularly in girls (Harden *et al.*, 2001).

Poor mental health impacts severely on life chances, and can increase the risk of delinquency, trouble with the police, smoking, substance use disorders and teenage pregnancy (Graham and Power, 2003). It also depresses educational attainment (Edwards, 2003): in a recent survey of child mental health in Great Britain (Green *et al.*, 2005), 44 per cent of children with emotional disorders were behind in their overall educational attainment, 43 per cent missed at least five school days in the previous term, one in three children had officially recognised special educational needs, and 12 per cent were excluded. These rates are even higher for children with recognised behavioural (conduct) problems. Mental health problems in childhood are also major predictors of mental health problems in adulthood: half of all lifetime mental disorders are reported as beginning before the age of 14 years (WHO/HBSC Forum 2007 Task Force, 2007).

Mental health promotion in schools: a global snapshot

Some terminology

The past two decades have seen a significant growth of research and good practice on mental health prevention and promotion in schools (WHO/HBSC Forum 2007 Task Force, 2007; Fundación Marcelino Botín, 2008). Across the world, an increasing number of schools are engaging in a wide range of mental health-related initiatives and policies, which in many places are showing promising results. Activities operate under a variety of headings, such as 'social and emotional learning', 'emotional literacy', 'emotional intelligence', 'resilience', 'lifeskills' or 'character education' (Weare, 2004).

Mental health promotion can refer to interventions at a range of levels, from the promotion of positive mental health, through the prevention of problems, to tackling mental health problems once they have occurred. It is often helpful to move beyond the catch-all phrase of 'mental health promotion' to terminologies that make more subtle distinctions clear. The Department for Children, Schools and Families in England suggests a 'three-wave' model, which is proving generally helpful and acceptable in creating a clear vocabulary to distinguish both a variety of levels of mental health need and an escalating intensity of appropriate response:

- 'wave one': universal approaches aimed at all in the school, including students without particular problems, e.g. whole class, whole school approaches;
- 'wave two': more targeted approaches for those who appear to school staff to show clear but relatively mild mental health difficulties and/or showing early signs and/or in a high-risk group;
- 'wave three': highly targeted therapeutic interventions for those identified by professionals as having severe mental health problems.

(DCSF 2009a)

Throughout this chapter, the terminology of these three different 'waves' will be utilised.

Mental health promotion in schools across the globe

The world leader in the field, in terms of both sheer numbers of programmes and also the amount of resources put into attempts to evaluate them rigorously, is undoubtedly the USA, where literally thousands of what are effectively mental health programmes are operating for all three waves, with various levels of demonstrable success. Twenty or so major programmes, such as *Promoting Alternative Thinking Strategies (PATHS)* (2009) and the *Metropolitan Area Child Study* (2009), are consistently identified as successful by rigorous systematic reviews (Zins *et al.*, 2004). There are several major US research and practitioner networks, most notably CASEL (the Collaborative for Academic, Social and Emotional Learning; CASEL, 2009a), which have produced some influential collations of programmes and their characteristics, reviews of the evidence for effectiveness and meta-analyses of studies to determine the key principles for the characteristics of effective interventions.

Australia is also the scene of thriving work for all three waves of need, and some of its programmes are starting to produce robust and positive evaluations (Adi *et al.*, 2007; Shucksmith *et al.*, 2007). Australia has long taken a whole school, whole community approach, developing strong networks of healthy and resilient schools (Stewart *et al.*, 2004). Specific programmes aimed clearly at mental health have emerged over the last ten years, including *Roots of Empathy* (2009), *MindMatters* (2009) and most recently the overarching national strategy of *Kidsmatter* (2009), which includes specific programmes such as *Friends*. Robust evaluations suggest that these programmes are effective (Adi *et al.*, 2007; Shucksmith *et al.*, 2007).

Programmes and approaches are also to be found across Europe, often under titles such as mental health, social and emotional competency, violence prevention, anti-bullying and cognitive and coping skills, with programmes aimed at all three waves of need (WHO/HBSC Forum 2007 Task Force, 2007; Fundación Marcelino Botín, 2008). They include adapted US programmes such as *PATHS* (see above) and *Second Step* (Committee for Children, 2009). The European Union has long been very active in formulating policy and collating the evidence for effectiveness, and is now moving to create a database of effective programmes which will be in place by 2010 (European Union, 2009).

In the UK

In the UK, an increasing number of schools are engaged in what is effectively mental health work, again under a range of titles. Many voluntary sector agencies have been actively working for some time to promote the mental health of young people in the school context, working on a wide range of initiatives, most of them targeted at students with wave two and three levels of need, i.e. with mental health problems. Two particular examples are *Place 2 Be* (2009), which supports counsellors in schools, and *Pyramid Clubs* (Continyou, 2009), localised initiatives in schools to identify children with mental health problems, providing multi-agency help and quiet places for troubled children to gain a sense of safety.

Some UK approaches have focused mainly on the creation of whole school environments to support and promote mental health, aimed mostly at students at wave-one level of need and providing a universal backdrop against which more intensive work at levels two and three can more effectively take place and find support. In mainstream schools, starting in the 1980s a major government-led focus has been on creating healthy schools/health-promoting schools networks in all four countries of the UK, each of which have had a strong emphasis on emotional well-being, and anti-bullying strategies (e.g. DCSF/NHS, 2009). Within this overall approach, curriculum time is given to discussion of such mental health issues as emotional well-being, assertive communication and building relationships, in contexts such as tutorial time, circle time and Personal, Social, Health and Citizenship Education (PSHCE). Meanwhile, a well-known and highly active independent organisation, Antidote, the campaign for emotional literacy, has focused particularly on creating emotionally literate whole school environments which focus particularly on pupil engagement and dialogue (Antidote, 2009).

More recently, building on this environmentally focused work, approaches in some parts of the UK have focused more specifically on explicit learning and teaching of social and emotional skills, most of it aimed at pupils with wave-one level of need, and some of it including more targeted approaches. Starting in the 1980s, some UK schools and local authorities have taken up successful US skills-based programmes and approaches such as *PATHS* (see above), *Second Step* (see above) and *Incredible Years* (2009), all of which have convincing evidence behind them (Adi *et al.*, 2007; Shucksmith *et al.*, 2007). Some schools and local authorities are using programmes developed by UK-based organisations such the *School of Emotional Literacy* (2009) and the *Developing Emotional Awareness and Learning* (DEAL) project to develop skills in 14–19-year-olds developed by the Samaritans (Samaritans, 2009). Some have taken on European projects such as *Zippy's Friends* (Partnership for Children, 2009).

Some localities devised their own programmes, such as Cumbria with its behaviour curriculum and Southampton and Edinburgh with a focus on emotional literacy, although most such initiatives have now been subsumed into national approaches such as SEAL (see below). This localised approach to mental health predominates in Scotland, where detailed decision making is devolved to local level (rather than the more centralised approaches now favoured by the English DCSF in the form of national programmes such as SEAL and TaMHS, which will be discussed below). The Scottish approach has been to use existing structures, organisations and individuals to work with a variety of specific initiatives and projects as they choose. Scottish projects include *Being Cool in School* (Better Behaviour Scotland, 2009) and *Creating Confident Kids* (2009) and, until recently, the national framework *Heads Up Scotland* (2008). The role of central government in Scotland is seen as providing vision, energy, leadership and coordination rather than detailed programme development. The new Scottish *Curriculum for Excellence* (Learning and Teaching Scotland, 2009) intends to support universal approaches to mental health by putting emotional and social well-being at the heart of the educational process, alongside, and equal to, more traditional educational concerns.

SEAL

In an attempt to consolidate and develop appropriate work on social and emotional skills and provide clear and free entitlement for all pupils to high-quality, evidence-based work, over the last decade the DCSF in England has committed considerable resources to developing its own *Social and Emotional Aspects of Learning* (SEAL) programmes in primary and secondary schools (DCSF, 2009b). Primary SEAL (ages 4–11) is now well established and can be found, delivered with various levels of intensity and success, in two-thirds of all primary schools in England, with a developing presence in Wales. It is based on a set of curriculum materials which cover seven main themes, and provide material aimed at wave-one level of need for one lesson a week across the primary school years, plus materials for assemblies, whole school guidance, as well as wave-two work for small groups of students with special needs and outreach work with parents. Evaluations are showing some encouraging results, including a clear impact on behaviour and learning across the whole school (Hallam *et al.*, 2006), and some positive impact on students with special needs through the small group work (Humphrey *et al.*, 2008).

Following the success of Primary SEAL, Secondary SEAL was created. Secondary SEAL started more definitively with a whole school approach rather than the strong curriculum focus of Primary SEAL. The web-based guidance materials explore how social and emotional skills can be supported by the whole school context, including management and leadership, teaching and learning, policy development, staff development and relations with parents and the community. Learning materials have been developed for years 7–9 (11–14 years), including both generic SEAL lessons to be taught within a PSHE or tutorial group context, and work to explore SEAL in mainstream school subjects. Secondary SEAL was piloted in over 60 schools, with successful process evaluations by NFER and by Ofsted (Smith *et al.*, 2006), and is now being extended to 10 per cent of secondary schools, with the aim of being offered in all by 2010.

Targeted approaches

Looking nationally, to complement the whole school approach of SEAL, starting in 2007 the UK Government has put £60 million into development of the *Targeted Mental Health in Schools* (TaMHS) project in England, aimed at children 5–13 with wave two and three levels of need (DCSF, 2009a). Resources have been given to a growing number of 'pathfinders', each of which is funded to develop and deliver an innovative model of mental health support for children with mental health problems. Pathfinders are expected to work at two levels of approach. At the first level of 'strategic integration', all the agencies involved in the delivery of child and adolescent mental health services (schools, local authority services, primary care trusts, other health trusts and the voluntary sector) are expected to work together strategically and operationally to deliver flexible, responsive and effective early-intervention mental health services for children and young people. Second, and more specifically, each pathfinder follows a named intervention or 'evidence-informed practice', aimed at children and families at risk of and experiencing mental health problems. Pathfinders are expected to base this interventionist work on the universal approach provided by SEAL and integrate new work into that context.

The evidence base

The evidence that mental health promotion in schools works

Alongside this international outpouring of school-based programmes, the last twenty years or so have seen a growing evidence base for the effectiveness of this work. Systematic reviews of programmes, using the most rigorous and exacting criteria, are repeatedly demonstrating definitively that the best of them are effective, a fact which the recent NICE reviews of work in primary schools (Adi et al., 2007; Shucksmith et al., 2007), and a forthcoming review of work in secondary schools, support. Taken together, the reviews provide growing evidence that well-designed programmes to promote mental health and social and emotional well-being and learning can have a very wide range of positive impacts, and at all three waves of need.

For example, a review of whole school approaches which looked at how effective they appeared to be in 'promoting mental health' found seventeen programmes which stood up to the rigorous methodological criteria customarily employed in systematic reviews, such as allocating participants to control or intervention groups on a randomised basis, and having large numbers in the study (Wells et al., 2003). These programmes reduced specific mental health problems, such as aggression and depression, reduced commonly accepted risk factors, such as impulsiveness and anti-social behaviour, and developed the competences that promote mental health, such as cooperation, resilience, a sense of optimism, empathy and a positive and realistic self-concept. Programmes have also been shown to help prevent and reduce early sexual experience, alcohol and drug use, and violence and bullying in and outside schools (Greenberg et al., 2003), promote pro-social behaviour (Durlak and Wells, 1997) and in some cases reduce juvenile crime (Caplan et al., 1992). A recent major US meta-analysis across the whole field (CASEL, 2009b) summarised research on 207 social and emotional programmes and suggested that schools with effective programmes showed an 11 per cent improvement in achievement tests, a 25 per cent improvement in social and emotional skills, and a 10 per cent decrease in classroom misbehaviour, anxiety and depression.

Links between mental health and learning

One reason why schools are becoming more enthusiastic about mental health promotion is the growing body of research which demonstrates the centrality of mental, emotional and social well-being and learning to academic success (Weare, 2004; Zins et al., 2004; CASEL, 2009b). Children who receive effective and well-designed mental health and social and emotional learning programmes are more likely to do well academically, in some cases achieving higher marks in subjects such as mathematics and reading, to make more effort in their school work, and to have improved attitudes to school, with fewer exclusions and absences.

Implementing mental health promotion in schools

The evidence for the efficacy of programmes is becoming so well established that the main focus of enquiry has now moved on to implementation (Devaney et al., 2006). Meta-analyses of successful programmes have identified the characteristics of the most effective programmes (Catalano et al., 2002; Weare and Gray, 2002; Zins et al., 2004); these evidence-based characteristics will be explored next.

Holistic approach

The healthy/health-promoting schools approach has long emphasised the need to look at the setting in which the promotion of health takes place, and ensure that the total environment is congruent with the promotion of health. Although evaluating whole school approaches is a methodological challenge, there is sound empirical evidence from systematic reviews that approaches to mental health in schools which cover more than one base are more effective than single-focused approaches (Lister-Sharpe et al., 2000; Adi et al., 2007).

It is increasingly common for effective school mental health programmes to be implemented within several aspects of school life at once. Most successful programmes include work in the curriculum and staff development to promote social and emotional skills, but the consensus is clear that a range of further steps are necessary in implementing a whole school approach successfully (Weare and Gray, 2002; Devaney et al., 2006; CASEL, 2009b). Programmes need to run over a prolonged period of time. They require a clear and systematic action planning process, which starts small and strategic but with a clear view of the end result, and which ensures that developments are coherent, consistent and coordinated. Surrounding school policies need to be consistent with mental health aims and ethos, audited at the outset for their compatibility, adapted as necessary, and kept under review. Committed and skilled leadership and management is vital, creating leaders who 'walk the talk' of social and emotional learning, who understand that mental health programmes have an effect on all aspects of school life, who are prepared to lead, inspire and organise the process, have a clear vision, set an overall framework for action, delegate responsibility appropriately and ensure that progress is monitored and evaluated.

Sound mental health delivery requires strong teamwork and joined-up working at the local level. This is true for all children and young people, but is absolutely vital for those with identifiable mental health problems, mild or severe. Children and young people live their lives within a wide range of settings, including their homes, schools, youth organisations, local community and, sometimes, in health care settings. To promote mental health and tackle mental health problems, links must be built between these different contexts to encourage agencies to work in and with schools, and enhance the social inclusion of vulnerable young people. Specialist interventions should be part of a multi-agency approach to support the child and their family (Shucksmith *et al.*, 2007; DCSF, 2009a).

Supportive contexts and environments

There is considerable consensus on the kind of contexts, cultures and ethos that can be created in schools and classrooms by staff and students working together, and which can support mental health, help tackle mental health problems, and encourage the development of appropriate mental health skills. Several overviews have attempted to draw these environmental features together (Weare, 2000; Antidote, 2003; Devaney *et al.*, 2006). The broad consensus is outlined below.

At the heart of any mentally healthy context, whether it be school, classroom or one-to-one relationship, is a central focus on warm relationships, which place respectful and empathic compassionate concern for the individual and their emotional well-being at the centre of the process. Such a climate of warmth and caring helps to give everyone a sense of significance and belonging, a feeling of being accepted, valued, listened to and respected, which are all essential prerequisites for motivation to learn and good behaviour as well as good mental health. Behaviour management is positive, focusing mainly on what students do well and on the effort they make, supported by staff attention, encouragement and appropriate and realistic levels of praise, motivating children through incentives such as 'golden time' to spend as they wish, rather than relying only on punishments for undesirable behaviour. This warm, positive climate helps everyone, but is particularly important for children who have mental health difficulties due to problems with family relationships and a lack of attachment to a caring figure in their lives.

Linked with this sense of warmth is a drive for genuine participation and inclusion, and a feeling of engagement and ownership by everyone involved. Student voice is encouraged, helping students, and especially those with problems, to be active participants in the process rather than negative, withdrawn and depressed victims. Peer learning is seen as a tool for building a sense of engagement, including more formal approaches such as mentoring, mediation, conflict resolution and buddying, which can help more vulnerable children in particular to feel safe and befriended. The school encourages genuine partnerships between all stakeholders, including students, staff, the community, and education and mental health agencies.

Parental involvement is seen as particularly essential, both with the education of individual children, to ensure consistency between home and school, and in the life of the school more generally, so parents feel they have a real influence. Where children have mental health difficulties, some schools are organising parenting education to support parents in relating to their children more skilfully, such as showing more warmth and empathy and managing behaviour in positive ways.

Mental health is not about conformity and rule following; it involves encouraging students and staff to make free and informed choices, develop a sense of autonomy or capability, and exhibit appropriate levels of independence, self-determination, reflection, critical thinking and self-control. Pupils and staff are empowered to make real choices, and have appropriate levels of genuine decision making and responsibility. Building autonomy is particularly important for children with mental health difficulties, who can feel disempowered by their difficult circumstances and be prone to fatalism and blame, and who especially need to build an inner sense of control and empowerment.

For people to achieve appropriate levels of warmth, participation and autonomy requires them to feel secure and safe enough to engage with the process. Safety is based on clarity about, for example, aims, discipline, expectations, rules and boundaries. Behaviour and actions need to have real-life, logical and known rewards and consequences, both positive and negative. Anti-bullying actions are essential if all are to feel free of the threat of intimidation and violence.

Getting the right mix of all these features is not a simple matter: it involves finding the optimum balance of key elements, the ratio of which will change for different students with different needs and at different ages. Children with low self-esteem and high anxiety may well need a greater sense of warmth and belonging, while others with higher self-esteem but who are prone to conduct disorders and bullying may need stronger clarity and boundaries.

Skills development

Developing the key features of effective environments depends to a large extent on the skills of all who learn and work in schools, whose behaviour and attitudes shape those environments. The evidence is clear that more effective programmes include explicit work on the development of the relevant mental health skills in students and staff (Catalano *et al.*, 2002; Adi *et al.*, 2007; Shucksmith *et al.*, 2007).

Children with mental health problems particularly need to develop skills they may not have learned at home, and need to develop resilience to tackle their difficulties. Schools that provide the opportunities for students to learn and use their social and emotional skills, and positively reinforce emotionally and socially literate behaviour, encourage motivation for learning, more positive beliefs and a greater sense of attachment to the school, which leads in turn to better mental health, improved behaviour and greater academic achievement (Hawkins and Catalano, 1992).

There is considerable consensus among those who have developed and reviewed successful programmes on how skills-based work can best be developed (Antidote, 2003; Weare, 2004; Devaney et al., 2006). Skills-based programmes need to start early and take a long-term developmental approach through a spiral curriculum in which key learning is constantly revisited. Teaching and learning methods need to be diverse, participative and experiential rather than didactic, appeal to a range of learning styles, engage learners' attention and ensure that skills are practised. Effective teaching requires all the active and engaging methods of teaching and learning at a school's disposal – whole class, groups, one to one, circle time, peer work, games, simulations and projects. Learning mental health skills involves more than talking about what is desirable: it involves behavioural strategies such as identification, practice, re-run, coaching and feedback. Students can be provided with clear frameworks to scaffold and support specific issues such as problem solving, resolving conflict, or calming down. Skills learned in designated lessons can be generalised throughout the school day, in and out of the classroom, and outside the school context. Skills can be integrated into the normal process of pupil assessment, feedback and reward. Parents and carers can be involved in the learning process, for example through 'take home' ideas to promote family and community involvement.

If it is to support young people to be autonomous, the teaching of emotional and social skills must avoid being reductionist, behaviourist or normative. The process of skills development needs to be explored with pupils, so they are enabled to select the skills they see as relevant and useful for their own lives and contexts, make their own sense of them and use them flexibly to give themselves greater choice to do what they want to do.

In terms of where in the school day this might fit, most effective programmes include specific and designated work on mental, emotional and social skills in the curriculum. Mental health skills can be developed specifically in discrete lessons, located, for example, in tutorial time, circle time, PSHE and Citizenship, and in whole school assemblies. Programmes such as SEAL are attempting to extend this work into whole school/out-of-class activities such as school councils, peer mentoring, clubs and societies, breaks and lunchtimes, school visits, work experience and volunteering. School staff can support students' skills development outside the classroom structure by, for example, setting them structured tasks for homework, encouraging personal reflection and diary writing, and using 'golden moments' outside the classroom to help pupils consolidate and practise skills. Students who are needing support at waves two and three may spend a good deal of their time developing key skills and attitudes they may lack and which may be holding them back, such as impulse control, self-belief, self-discipline and the ability to relate to others, in small groups, including nurture groups (DCSF, 2009a).

teachers' impact on students.

Staff development

teachers empowerment

A lack of staff engagement is one of the key reasons why programmes fail, while modelling is possibly the most powerful determinant of whether or not pupils acquire the skills. Unsurprisingly, then, the evidence from reviews of effective programmes supports the need for strong professional development opportunities for staff (Adi *et al.*, 2007; Shucksmith *et al.*, 2007).

Staff are not likely to take an interest in promoting the mental health of students if they feel their own mental health needs are not met. Staff will need to spend some time exploring their own emotions, consider ways to promote their own well-being and feel supported and understood before they see this work as part of their role with students (Weare and Gray, 2002; Morris and Casey, 2006). Staff development can enable staff to improve their own flexibility and capability to relate to pupils in emotionally sound ways, by managing their own reactions and impulses, strengthening their positive behaviour strategies and their ability to solve problems, teaching in more engaging ways, applying effective classroom management skills, promoting emotionally literate behaviour and reducing problem behaviour such as aggression in their students.

Sound staff development is best linked with existing systems of professional networking and development opportunities, such as training, peer support, coaching and mentoring, so that staff do not feel overburdened with new initiatives. It needs also to be supported by the rest of the school and conducted in a safe, cooperative and supportive atmosphere, with plenty of fun, laughter and enjoyment, as mental health is for some staff a somewhat alien, threatening and uncomfortable issue.

Supporting those with special needs

Everything said so far about the development of strategies to promote mental health in schools applies to children at all three waves of mental health need. Evidence is clear that there need be no conflict between the three waves, and that the mental health both of those with problems and of those who fall into the normal range is best promoted by a joined-up approach in which work at the three waves is systematically coordinated. Having a backdrop of entitlement for all makes it easier to provide extra support. It helps avoid the stigma that so often attaches to specialist mental health interventions, and provides a 'critical mass' of emotionally literate people in the school to assist those with problems using strategies known to all, for example strategies to calm down, manage anger, resolve conflicts and solve problems. Students with mental health difficulties generally need 'more' (intensive, explicit, long-term) rather than 'different' forms of provision (Rutter *et al.*, 1998). Any additional therapeutic help that is indicated for those with severe difficulties needs therefore to be delivered within the backdrop of a broad, universal approach.

Universal measures are necessary but not sufficient, and students with a greater degree of difficulty will need their problems addressing earlier, more energetically and forcefully, and with some more specific inputs than are needed by the majority. Students who are likely to need more targeted help include those who are clearly exhibiting signs of disturbance and stress, and who may or may not have a definable mental health problem. They include 'troubled' children with so-called internalising disorders such as anxiety and depression, suicide and eating disorders, and 'troubling' children with so-called externalising disorders, which include conduct, hyperkinetic disorders such as attention deficit hyperactivity disorder and oppositional defiant disorders (Harden et al., 2001).

Students who need special help may also be part of a social group with known high-risk factors for mental health problems (DCSF, 2008). Children currently targeted in European initiatives include refugee/asylum-seeking children, children whose parents have a mental illness, looked after children, families experiencing separation, bereaved children and young carers – all of whom are likely to need some extra help and support (WHO/HBSC Forum 2007 Task Force, 2007). For children with such difficulties, schools need to provide a range of specific interventions that have been proven to be effective, according to the child's needs and at the level appropriate to their severity.

For children with wave-two level of need – that is, those whose problems are clear but fairly mild – it is imperative to start early and give energetic help before problems grow (Shucksmith et al., 2007). Small group sessions to develop cognitive problem-solving and social skills, such as those used successfully by the small group work of Primary SEAL (Humphrey et al., 2008) and the Penn Prevention Programme (Jaycox et al., 1995), have been shown to be helpful. Other approaches with good evidence behind them include nurture groups, the use of play-based approaches, close liaison with parents, work to develop parenting skills, and follow-up booster sessions for children (Shucksmith et al., 2007; DCSF, 2009a). Energetic and early intervention of this kind may be sufficient to help these children and their families through their difficulty.

Children and young people with wave-three level of need – that is, with more complex or critical needs and whose problems are intense and disabling – require all of the above to be present, but will need more specific help than this. They are in urgent need of early identification and a sensitive appraisal of their problems by appropriate professionals, problems which may be multi-faceted. Approaches need to be clearly therapeutic, with cognitive behaviour therapy and play-based therapies having been shown to be particularly effective (Shucksmith et al., 2007). The children and young people may well need to take appropriate medication. Such children and young people will need small group or one-to-one sessions to be delivered by appropriately trained specialists receiving clinical supervision, and tailored to their particular problem. Interventions will almost invariably need to look at the child or young person in the context of their family structure and work with all family members. Intensive sessions for the parents or carers of these children, run in parallel with the children's sessions, can be useful.

Conclusion

There is increasing recognition of the wider role of the school in promoting mental health, helping to create concerned citizens who are able to understand themselves, relate effectively to others, care about their community and their environment, and make their own, informed choices in a rapidly changing world. The next few years will probably see a continuation of the rapid growth of interest and practical initiatives, with a greater integration of work to develop mental health and emotional and social well-being into the mainstream of school life, including into academic school subjects and teaching and learning. There is likely to be a great deal more activity created in secondary schools to match the fairly well-developed work in primary schools, and there may be some developments in further and higher education. It is to be hoped that targeted work for children with special needs will be successful in reducing the high levels of mental health problems; to achieve this, targeted initiatives will need to be dovetailed with whole school initiatives and be supported by a joined-up approach from services.

Perhaps then the child and young person will, after many decades of pendulum swinging, finally start to be placed firmly at the centre of the educational and mental health processes.

References

Adi, Y., Killoran, A., Janmohamed, K. and Stewart-Brown, S. (2007) *Systematic Review of the Effectiveness of Interventions to Promote Mental Wellbeing in Primary Schools: Universal Approaches Which do not Focus on Violence or Bullying.* London: National Institute for Clinical Excellence.

Antidote (2003) *The Emotional Literacy Handbook: Promoting Whole School Strategies.* London: David Fulton Publishers.

Antidote (2009) Online. Available at www.antidote.org.uk (accessed 20 April 2009).

Better Behaviour Scotland (2009) *Being Cool in School.* Online. Available at www.betterbehaviour scotland.gov.uk/initiatives/cool.aspx (accessed 20 April 2009).

Caplan, M., Weissberg, R. P., Grober, J. S., Sivo, P. J., Grady, K. and Jacoby, C. (1992) 'Social competence promotion with inner-city and suburban young adolescents: Effects on social adjustment and alcohol use', *Journal of Consulting and Clinical Psychology*, 60: 56–63.

CASEL (2009a) Online. Available at www.casel.org (accessed 20 April 2009).

CASEL (2009b) *Social and Emotional Learning and Student Benefits.* Online. Available at www.casel.org/downloads/EDC_CASELSELResearchBrief.pdf (accessed 6 March 2009).

Catalano, R. F., Berglund, L., Ryan, A. M., Lonczak, H. S. and Hawkins, J. (2002) 'Positive youth development in the United States: Research findings on evaluations of positive youth development programs', *Prevention and Treatment*, 5(15). Online. Available at http://aspe.hhs.gov/hsp/PositiveYouthDev99 (accessed 22 April 2009).

Committee for Children (2009) *Second Step for Violence Prevention*. Online. Available at http://www.cfchildren.org/ (accessed 20 April 2009).

Continyou (2009) 'Pyramid clubs', *About Pyramid*. Online. Available at www.continyou.org.uk/ what_we_do/children_and_young_people/pyramid/about_pyramid (accessed 22 April 2009).

Creating Confident Kids (2009) Online. Available at www.edinburgh.gov.uk/internet/ Learning/Learning_publications/CEC_creating_confident_kids (accessed 20 April 2009).

DCSF (2008) *Independent Review of the Primary Curriculum*. Online. Available at www.dcsf.gov.uk/primarycurriculumreview (accessed 20 April 2009).

DCSF (2009a) *Targeted Mental Health in Schools Project: Using the Evidence to Inform Your Approach. A Practical Guide for Headteachers and Commissioners*. Nottingham: DCSF Publications.

DCSF (2009b) *Social and Emotional Aspects of Learning*. Online. Available at http:// nationalstrategies.standards.dcsf.gov.uk/inclusion/behaviourattendanceandseal (accessed 22 April 2009).

DCSF/NHS (2009) *Healthy Schools*. Online. Available at www.healthyschools.gov.uk (accessed 6 March 2009).

Devaney, E., Utne O'Brien, M., Resnik, H., Keister, S. and Weissberg, R. (2006) *Sustainable School-Wide Social and Emotional Learning: Implementation Guide*. CASEL. Chicago: College of Liberal Arts and Sciences, University of Illinois.

Durlak, J. and Wells, A. (1997) 'Primary prevention mental health programs for children and adolescents: A meta-analytic review', *American Journal of Community Psychology*, 25(2): 115–152.

Edwards, L. (2003) *Promoting Young People's Wellbeing: A Review of Research on Emotional Health*. Glasgow: University of Glasgow.

European Union (2009) *Scientific Support to Policies: DataPrev*. Online. Available at http://ec.europa.eu/research/fp6/ssp/dataprev_en.htm (accessed 6 March 2009).

Fundación Marcelino Botín (2008) *Social and Emotional Education: An International Analysis*. Santander: Fundación Marcelino Botín.

Goleman, D. (1996) *Emotional Intelligence*. London: Bloomsbury.

Graham, H. and Power, C. (2003) *Childhood Disadvantage and Adult Health: A Lifecourse Framework*. London: Health Development Agency.

Graham, P. (2004) *The End of Adolescence*. Oxford: Oxford University Press.

Green, H., McGinnity, A., Meltzer, H., Ford, T. and Goodman, R. (2005) *Mental Health of Children and Young People in Great Britain, 2004*. Basingstoke: Palgrave.

Greenberg, M. T., Weissberg, R. P., O'Brien, M. U., Zins, J. E., Fredericks, L., Resnik, H. and Elias, M. J. (2003) 'School-based prevention: Promoting positive social development through social and emotional learning', *American Psychologist*, 58(6/7): 466–474.

Hallam, S., Rhamie, J. and Shaw, J. (2006) *Evaluation of the Primary Behaviour and Attendance Pilot*. London: Department for Children, Schools and Families.

Harden, A., Rees, R., Shepherd, J., Ginny, B., Oliver, S. and Oakley, A. (2001) *Young People and Mental Health: A Systematic Review of Research on Barriers and Facilitators*. London: Institute of Education, University of London EPPI-Centre.

Hawkins, J. D. and Catalano, R. (1992) *Communities That Care: Action for Drug Abuse Prevention*. San Francisco: Jossey-Bass.

Heads Up Scotland (2008) Online. Available at www.headsupscotland.co.uk (accessed 20 April 2009).

Hosman, C., Jané-Llopis, E. and Saxena, S. (2004) *Prevention of Mental Disorders: Effective Interventions and Policy Options. Summary Report.* Geneva: World Health Organization.

Humphrey, H., Kalambouka, A., Bolton, J., Lendrum, A., Wigelsworth, M., Lennie, C. and Farrell, P. (2008) *Primary Social and Emotional Aspects of Learning (SEAL) Evaluation of Small Group Work*, DCSF Report No. RR064. London: Department for Children, Schools and Families.

Incredible Years (2009) Online. Available at www.incredibleyears.com (accessed 20 April 2009).

Jaycox, L., Gillham, J., Reivich, K. and Seligman, M. (1995) 'Prevention of depressive symptoms in school children: Two-year follow-up', *Psychological Science*, 6: 343–351.

Kidsmatter (2009) Online. Available at www.kidsmatter.edu.au (accessed 20 April 2009).

Learning and Teaching Scotland (2009) *Curriculum for Excellence.* Online. Available at www.ltscotland.org.uk/curriculumforexcellence (accessed 20 April 2009).

Lister-Sharp, D., Chapman, S., Stewart-Brown, S. L. and Sowden, A. (2000) 'Health promoting schools and health promotion in schools: Two systematic reviews', *Health Technology Assessment*, 3(22). Online. Available at www.ncchta.org/fullmono/mon322.pdf (accessed 22 April 2009).

Mental Health Foundation (1999) *Bright Futures: Promoting Children and Young People's Mental Health.* London: Mental Health Foundation.

Metropolitan Area Child Study (2009) Online. Available at www.psych.uic.edu/fcrg/macs.html (accessed 20 April 2009).

MindMatters (2009) Online. Available at www.mindmatters.edu.au (accessed 20 April 2009).

Morris, E. and Casey, J. (2006) *Developing Emotionally Literate Staff.* London: Paul Chapman.

Newman, T. and Blackburn, S. (2002) *Transitions in the Lives of Young People: Resilience Factors.* Edinburgh: Scottish Executive.

Partnership for Children (2009) *Zippy's Friends.* Online. Available at www.partnershipforchildren. org.uk/zippy-s-friends (accessed 20 April 2009).

Place 2 Be (2009) Online. Available at www.theplace2be.org.uk (accessed 20 April 2009).

Promoting Alternative Thinking Strategies (2009) Online. Available at www.channing-bete.com/ prevention-programs/paths (accessed 20 April 2009).

QCA (2008) *National Curriculum, Key Stages 3 and 4, Skills.* Online. Available at http:// curriculum.qca.org.uk/key-stages-3-and-4/skills/index.aspx (accessed 20 April 2009).

Roots of Empathy (2009) Online. Available at www.rootsofempathy.org (accessed 20 April 2009).

Rutter, M., Hagel, A. and Giller, H. (1998) *Anti-social Behaviour and Young People.* Cambridge: Cambridge University Press.

Samaritans (2009) *Welcome to DEAL.* Online. Available at www.samaritans.org/our_services/ work_in_schools/work_in_schools.aspx (accessed 20 April 2009).

School of Emotional Literacy (2009) Online. Available at www.schoolofemotional-literacy.com (accessed 20 April 2009).

Shucksmith, J., Summerbell, C., Jones, S. and Whittaker, V. (2007) *Mental Wellbeing of Children in Primary Education (Targeted/Indicated Activities).* London: National Institute of Clinical Excellence.

Smith, P., O'Donnell, L., Easton, C. and Rudd, P. (2006) *Secondary Social, Emotional and Behavioural Skills (SEBS) Pilot Evaluation.* London: National Foundation for Educational Research.

Snyder, C. R. and Lopez, S. J. (2005) *Handbook of Positive Psychology.* Oxford: Oxford University Press.

Stewart, D., Sun, J., Patterson, C., Lemerle, K. and Hardie, M. (2004) 'Promoting and building resilience in primary school communities: Evidence from a comprehensive "health promoting school" approach', *International Journal of Mental Health Promotion*, 6(3): 26–33.

UNICEF (2007) *Child Poverty in Perspective: An Overview of Child Wellbeing in Rich Countries. Innocenti Report Card 7*. Florence: UNICEF Innocenti Research Centre.

University of Cambridge (2009) *The Cambridge Primary Review: Special Report on the Curriculum*. Online. Available at www.primaryreview.org.uk (accessed 20 April 2009).

Weare, K. (2000) *Promoting Mental, Emotional and Social Health: A Whole School Approach*. London: Routledge.

Weare, K. (2004) *Developing the Emotionally Literate School*. London: Sage.

Weare, K. and Gray, G. (2002) *What Works in Promoting Children's Emotional and Social Competence?* London: Department of Education and Skills.

Wells, J., Barlow, J. and Stewart-Brown, S. (2003) 'A systematic review of universal approaches to mental health promotion in schools', *Health Education*, 103(4): 197–220.

WHO/HBSC Forum 2007 Task Force (2007) *Social Cohesion for Mental Well-being among Adolescents*. Copenhagen: World Health Organization Regional Office for Europe.

Zins, J. E., Weissberg, R. P., Wang, M. C. and Walberg, H. (2004) *Building Academic Success on Social and Emotional Learning*. New York: Columbia Teachers College.

Chapter 4

Reducing disaffection and increasing school engagement

Colin Noble and Marilyn Toft

In this chapter, we explore how teachers and other professionals working in schools can reduce disaffection and increase school engagement among children and young people. It has been suggested that engagement with school has a protective role to play in relation to children and young people's health, particularly with regard to promoting emotional well-being and reducing smoking and drug use (West, 2006; Carter *et al.*, 2007; Fletcher *et al.*, 2009). For the purposes of this chapter, we focus particularly on the ways that schools in England have been moving towards supporting the engagement of pupils. Our perspective derives from being involved with and taking a lead in the National Strategies in England. These are professional development programmes for school improvement which include embedding good practice and building local capacity to achieve a sustainable basis for continued improvement in local authorities, schools and settings.

In this chapter, we interpret engagement as implying a sense of belonging and a willingness to participate meaningfully in school by taking advantage of the opportunities offered. If children and young people have a range of skills to contribute confidently to school life, their engagement can be strengthened further. Engagement in itself can be seen to contribute to promoting pupil health and well-being. The symbiotic relationship between education and health is clear when considering the engagement of young people, and it appears repeatedly to underpin nearly all the strategies needed to improve schools and pupil achievement. The inclusion of teachers and other staff is a very necessary, but obviously insufficient, part of a school's drive to increase engagement. A major part of both the diagnosis and the prescription offered in this chapter is that schools have to re-emphasise their role of building learning communities, and that the process of increasing school engagement involves teachers reflecting upon their own role as learners as much as pupils.

The Welsh word *dysgu*, implying both 'teaching' and 'learning', lies at the heart of our approach. Optimum school engagement cannot be reached until everybody in school views themselves primarily as learners. The mindset, and consequent expectations and behaviour, of a teacher or teaching assistant who arrives at school with the self-definition of 'learner' is very different from that of a person who sees her- or himself as simply a 'teacher', a classroom manager or a support worker. Similarly, pupils who regard themselves predominantly as learners are already engaged with what the school might be offering them. School engagement – belonging and participation – will in itself encourage a commitment to learning, increase motivation, enhance a sense of responsibility, and support pupils in maximising their achievements (CASEL, 2008). Thus, increasing school engagement is a two-way process that can result in a virtuous circle: the greater the engagement of staff in the school, the greater the impact of this on pupil attitudes and behaviour. This in turn helps to increase pupil engagement and thus enhance staff effectiveness and commitment.

Although a school will often mirror – and even perpetuate or amplify – some of the disadvantages apparent in society, it is also able to play a leadership role by promoting key values, beliefs and principles. Schools experience variable success in leading the way, and we need to understand why. Some of the most successful schools make effective use of universal and targeted action – promoting pupil entitlement and pupils as partners in learning – but, at the same time, pinpointing interventions based on data analysis (i.e. constantly *learning* about their pupils) that reveals barriers to learning and specific challenges faced by pupils (Ofsted, 2008a).

Data analysis can enable the school to develop intelligent, informed responses and ensure that its structures and systems reflect a positive ethos. For pupils who lead complex lives, the school environment can offer safety and security and a relatively 'problem-free' zone, in which, through a personalised approach, learning can be supported. Schools, by increasing the accuracy and appropriateness of their actions, have the chance to narrow the gap that exists between different groups of pupils, and individuals, when they enter school. This personalisation of the school offer to pupils can only be established by significant staff engagement – and of course will result in greater pupil engagement (West-Burnham and Coates, 2005). This practice supports part of the general thrust of current government policy in England, exemplified in the one-to-one tuition programmes recently introduced in Key Stages 2 and 3 (DCSF, 2008a, 2008b).

Every Child Matters: building on children and young people's strengths

The *Every Child Matters* White Paper and subsequent legislation in 2003–4 are gradually having an impact in English local authorities and schools, and are informing subsequent guidance and policy directives. The *Children's Plan* published in late 2007 (DCSF, 2007) and the subsequent vision of *21st Century Schools* in December 2008 (DCSF, 2008c) provide further opportunities to develop the *Every Child Matters* agenda at a local level. The following quotation from the *Children's Plan*, later reiterated in the Steer Report (Steer, 2009a), is worth considering: 'Too often we focus on the problems of a few young people rather than the successes of the many – we want a society where young people feel valued and in which their achievements are recognised and celebrated' (DCSF, 2007: 12).

The relevance of these ideas to this chapter lies in the implied challenge that schools need to face when placing greater emphasis on engaging pupils by celebration and recognition, and less on problem behaviour. The goal is one of getting schools 'on the front foot', to be proactive rather than reactive, to be the driver for a positive ethos rather than succumbing to the pressures of society which are brought into school. This can be very demanding and in some schools a Herculean task, but it is one worth achieving. There is no option if schools wish to succeed – and increasing engagement is the first step, with a continuing challenge to maintain it meaningfully.

Five key principles underpin the recently published *Children's Plan*, which aims to make England the best place in the world for children and young people to grow up:

- Government does not bring up children – parents do – so government needs to do more to support and back up parents and families.
- All children have the potential to succeed and should go as far as their talents can take them.
- Children and young people need to enjoy their childhood as well as grow up prepared for adult life.
- Services need to be shaped by and be responsive to children, young people and families, not designed around professional boundaries.
- It is always better to prevent failure than tackle a crisis later.

(DCSF, 2007)

In ensuring that schools use and meet these principles, it becomes clear that their work will be strengthened by increasing engagement with staff and pupils and indeed parents/carers. The learning school – one that takes *dysgu* to heart in a context of self-reflection and evaluation – will be in a far better position to succeed.

The recent notion of the 21st Century School stresses the need to transform good schools into great schools, and making sure that not just the majority but *all* children get a good education (DCSF, 2009a). The vision confirms a commitment to personalisation – in terms of both tailoring learning for each pupil in the classroom and also making sure wider children's services are tailored to the needs of each child, one of the routes being through schools. This can only happen with more and better collaboration and co-location of services, and it is already possible to see some expressions of this. For example, the Healthy Schools Programme in England – with its emphasis on Personal, Social and Health Education (PSHE), healthy eating, physical activity and emotional health and well-being – is now more closely aligned with the

Extended Schools Programme, which focuses more on the community around the school as well as extending pupil services beyond the usual school day.

Similarly, the Macdonald Review of PSHE called for government to be clearer about the links between the subject, the Healthy Schools Programme and Social and Emotional Aspects of Learning (SEAL) (Macdonald, 2009). This can be seen as part of a general move towards the provision of 'wrap-around' services for both children and their families, as well as for schools themselves. Wrap-around services should mean that both families and schools find that they are supported seamlessly in all their endeavours to improve the *Every Child Matters* outcomes[1] for young people. This means that schools will have to be even more prepared to work in partnerships, to share accountability for outcomes, and be more focused in understanding the needs of their pupils. The idea of the 21st Century School is, in itself, a vision that engages both health and education as it places the learner far more holistically than hitherto, as someone who belongs to and is influenced by the wider community around the school. The attainment of such a goal is supported by a number of English-government Public Service Agreements (PSAs) relating to education and health which have targets for 2011.[2]

Sir Alan Steer's Final Report on behaviour in schools, *Learning Behaviour: Lessons Learned* (Steer, 2009b), stressed the importance of partnerships to focus on improving behaviour and attendance (recommendation 26) and reduce exclusions. This is consistent with the focus on partnerships in the *Children's Plan* (DCSF, 2007). As partnerships were relatively new at the time of publication, the report recommended that consideration be given to consolidating and clarifying their status, as a basis for further development. Key characteristics of partnerships were included in the new guidance outlined in the Apprenticeships, Skills, Children and Learning Bill. These characteristics included a focus on early intervention when behaviour and attendance issues occur; clear arrangements for the placement of 'hard-to-place' pupils and, when appropriate, for the managed move of pupils between schools; the intelligent use of data; an emphasis on improving pupil attendance as well as behaviour; a staff training programme to improve behaviour; and the sharing of resources to enable the partnership to buy in specialist support. Partnerships should also engage with primary schools and further education, and at least one Safer School Partnership police officer. These developments should help to broaden the scope of previous, largely secondary, school-focused partnerships, help to promote early intervention and link different partnership arrangements, in the spirit of the 21st Century School.

There is no doubt that a significant number of children are disengaged from school in England – although the situation appears to be improving. Attendance in secondary schools in England, for example, is the highest ever recorded (DCSF, 2009b). In early 2009, fewer schools had an Ofsted judgement of 'inadequate' or 'unacceptable' behaviour than at any time since Ofsted began inspecting schools[3], reflecting the trends noted in the Chief

Inspector's Report the previous year (Ofsted, 2008a). In the same year, more schools were gaining 'good' or 'outstanding' judgements for behaviour than ever before; and pupil attainment had never been so high (Ofsted, 2008a). All this is greatly to the credit of schools and the pupils and staff who work in them, as well as the wider school community, and flatly contradicts the perception of some public and press commentators that schools are chaotic places full of badly behaved pupils. One of the, usually unspoken, truths about the spate of teenage knife attacks in London in 2007–8 was that these attacks very rarely happened in school, and that London schools had attained particularly good scores for behaviour in Ofsted inspections.

Attendance is obviously a key issue with regard to getting the most from schools – there can be no clearer expression of disengagement from school than not being there. The press and public, popularly and erroneously, pick up on so-called truancy figures, otherwise known as 'unauthorised absence'. The term considered most helpful and in common usage now in schools is persistent absence. Unauthorised absence has increased in recent years as schools have become far stricter in refusing to authorise absence for medical appointments and holidays in term-time,[4] and so may not be an indication of worsening attendance. But there are still over 400,000 pupils who receive fixed-term exclusions each year and over 8,680 who are permanently excluded from school (DCSF, 2008d). Nationally, in England, 6.4 per cent of secondary school pupils are persistently absent and miss 20 per cent or more (one or more days a week) of their schooling – with a consequently deleterious impact on their education and achievement. In primary schools, 2.4 per cent of pupils were reported to be persistently absent in 2007–8. These persistently absent and excluded pupils provide the key indicators of the most heavily disengaged, and they form the statistical baseline by which we can measure progress, particularly in those groups which – nationally – are disproportionally represented. These include Black Caribbean, mixed Black Caribbean/White and Gypsy/Roma/Traveller young people.

Behind every absent, excluded and disengaged pupil lies a complex and often emotionally draining story of wasted time and opportunity; of staff, parents/carers and pupils involved in unsuccessful negotiations or conflict; of low-level disruption in the classroom hindering the learning of others; of efforts needed for reintegration into the classroom after returning from absence; and of attainment being thwarted. The challenge of the 21st Century School provides us with the opportunity to reduce this waste even further.

What is quite clear is that schools are currently performing at very different levels in relation to disengagement and that the deeper the dive to find out why this is, the more complicated the story becomes. For example, some schools have a laudable and much praised zero exclusions policy by which no pupils are ever permanently excluded – and most of these have worked very hard to become more inclusive and offer a highly personalised curriculum and pastoral support system (Field, 2008). However, some schools 'lose' pupils in

teacher + exclusion   students?

a variety of other ways – encouraging withdrawal by the parent/carer to another school; by quite pointedly not meeting specific needs so that withdrawal is inevitable; by promoting education at home; and by accepting sometimes poor-quality alternative provision for the pupil. There is both inter-school variation regarding engagement, and in-school variation such as between year groups and subject areas, to take account of. The genesis of these variations can be found, we believe, in four main factors underlying exclusions, lack of positive behaviour for learning and persistent absence:

1   individual/personal issues of the pupil, such as illness, medical condition, low degree of intra-personal skills, low self-esteem and poor parenting;
2   social and inter-personal skills of the pupil, such as poor decision-making, low communication skills and an overly passive or aggressive demeanour;
3   school-based issues such as inadequate leadership and management, lack of inclusiveness, inappropriate curriculum, poor pastoral support, un-engaging teaching styles and – probably most important and for which the others are symptoms – a poor school ethos;
4   wider social problems that are outside the school's control but which make an everyday impact, such as poverty, sexism, racism, family breakdown and gang culture.

This last point requires further discussion. The tension between, on the one hand, acknowledging that schools can face a very different level of challenge depending on their intake and, on the other, that schools in the most difficult socio-economic situations can and do make a difference is always with us. It is unrealistic to expect schools to tackle the poverty of their community – but they can address some of the negative consequences of that poverty. The best schools manage to get themselves away from being purely reactive by concentrating more on filling their time with being proactive, setting their own agendas and having high expectations (DCSF, 2009c, 2009d). All schools can manage to improve, and the vision of the 21st Century School strongly encourages them to use wider community and professional partnerships to address apparently insuperable social problems.

Responding to the challenge

A multi-component, many-pronged approach is likely to be useful in responding to the challenges described above.

Identifying needs

The first stage of any work involves identifying who and what to focus on. In this respect, available data, such as on segmentation of exclusion, persistent absence and internal school referrals by specific pupil groups, can be used to identify and support pupils who may be at special risk of disaffection. These may include some minority ethnic groups, children looked after, those with special educational needs and those with free school meals eligibility, but this is not an exhaustive list and schools and local authorities need to update their analysis on a regular basis.

In going about this work, a number of issues need to be kept in mind. First, although schools may be getting better at collecting data, much existing data is not used to full potential. With respect to persistent absence, while some schools have rich data on individual pupils, many have not analysed it to see if absence is influenced by ethnicity, gender, day of the week, home location, transport availability, subject, teacher, etc. If absence is high from a particular housing estate, for example, there may be problems to do with transport, local health services or the prevailing culture on the estate. Knowing about this can enable the school to ask more specific questions about the use of wider agencies as well as to consider specific actions to increase the engagement of particular young people.

Effective action nearly always involves discussing the issues with young people themselves, a process by which the school is drawn into increasing engagement as it uses data to learn more about its pupils. An engaged school will have a natural and embedded commitment to teaching and learning in this way.

Planning a response

Having used data to identify who the school should prioritise, the school needs to consider what action to take while concurrently sustaining improvement across the whole school. The necessary actions will always go well beyond a focus on better attendance. Specific groups, and individuals in some cases, will have specific needs. Are working-class White boys bored and disengaged by a starchy and apparently purposeless curriculum? Does the school's reward and sanction system have to be amended to ensure that children from specific minority ethnic communities are not disproportionately subjected to internal exclusion (where they are removed from their usual classes) or external exclusion (where they are removed from school)? Are Black and minority ethnic cultures and histories sufficiently celebrated in the school to raise a sense of belonging for relevant pupils? In other words, what exactly are the barriers to learning? The implications for change leadership and for staff professional development may well be significant.

In this respect, the lead offered by the school's Senior Leadership Team on whole school issues, especially school ethos, will be critical. In early 2009, the National Strategies conducted six 'deep-dive' exercises into local authorities in England to look at inclusive practices, particularly focusing on exclusion, attendance and engagement. The unpublished report showed that in nearly all the most successful primary, middle and special schools and pupil referral

teachers+ inclusion

units visited, senior staff suggested that school ethos was the most important factor behind their success. Ethos is in many ways a difficult concept to measure, but can be clearly felt in a school and is more easily described by its constituent parts. Thus, in a school with a positive and engaging ethos, everyone working in it could explain what their role was, and a focus on 'learning' was often high within that description. In these schools, style of leadership, management systems, teaching styles, opportunities for pupils to participate, the pastoral system, extended services, the involvement of parents/carers, the behaviour and rewards policy and role modelling provided by the senior management team and staff were congruent and consistent, leading to a school ethos which both overtly and tacitly encouraged high levels of engagement by staff and pupils.[5]

Taking action

Lastly, there is the question of taking action. There is a now substantial literature stressing the importance of early intervention in this and other matters (Ramey and Ramey, 1998). Not only is it more cost-effective to intervene early than to have to tackle more ingrained problems later, but it is a sign of an engaged school that it picks up early signals of distress. Successful schools are predominantly proactive, taking the initiative to steer the agenda and experiences for pupils, parents/carers and staff, while at the same time involving them in this. Early intervention needs to be based on good-quality information. Relevant sources of data are numerous and may include transition attainment results (at foundation stage to primary, and primary to secondary and beyond), reported parental/carer issues (e.g. drug/alcohol abuse), present and previous patterns of attendance, time spent on task in lessons, adherence to homework set, levels of engagement in opportunities offered by the school, the involvement of parents/carers in the life of the schools, sickness levels of staff/departments, and behaviour audits conducted by staff and pupils.

In some cases, early intervention may need the support of the wider, multiagency community. This may include child and adolescent mental health services, educational psychologists, the local police, local authority officers and education social workers. But in many cases the school itself will have the means to address the issue, change its focus, strengthen its existing practice, offer support and monitor and assess the impact.

Responding to the needs of individual children and young people

Just as discussion about school ethos reveals a complex web of interweaving elements, so does a consideration of the needs of an individual child or young person. Although it may be hoped that every young person in the school will consider themselves principally as a learner, we recognise that this is not a complete description of that individual. A more holistic analysis captures the subtle interplay between education and health and concludes that the two are intimately inter-connected.

Evidence reveals there are explicit linkages between the social and emotional health of an individual and his or her ability to learn (CASEL, 2008). Issues such as bullying, resilience, mental health, nutrition, physical activity, hydration, social and communication skills – all ostensibly health related – have an impact on the learner's ability to optimise their opportunities. Many of the skills or attitudes championed by health services are also concerns of education. They include skills for learning, motivation, the ability to address challenges, skills to benefit from opportunities, a willingness to participate actively, and the ability to collaborate in school and in wider society.

Given this background, it is small wonder that investment has been put into the Healthy Schools Programme in England (an estimated £22 million in 2008–9) and into counterpart programmes elsewhere in the world (WHO/HBSC, 2008). The Healthy Schools Programme contains a series of criteria designed to support schools to contribute to the five *Every Child Matters* outcomes. Moreover, four key themes are addressed by the programme: physical activity; emotional health and well-being; healthy eating; and Personal, Social and Health Education.

Extended Schools, which offer extended services to both school pupils and the wider school community,[6] provide another example of a national policy trying to capture the multi-levelled approach that research suggests is necessary in order to promote health and educational outcomes concurrently (Warwick *et al.*, 2009). More recently the notion of 'wrap-around support' has given a name to the idea that school support needs to be better coordinated and more complete. Three promising policy initiatives help schools to increase engagement, and at the same time both thrive on and enhance the establishment of wrap-around support. These are SEAL, alternative provision, and Behaviour and Attendance Partnerships.

The social and emotional aspects of learning (SEAL)

SEAL was introduced into English primary schools from 2005, and into secondary schools from 2007. By April 2009 almost 62 per cent of primary schools were using SEAL, along with almost 40 per cent of secondary schools.[7] SEAL offers a whole school approach to promoting concern for the social and emotional aspects of learning, seeing these as essential for more cognitive forms of learning. The skills promoted as part of the programme's work are necessarily linked to promoting positive behaviour. The five social and emotional aspects of learning are respectively focused upon self-awareness, managing feelings, motivation, empathy and social skills.

In primary schools, a comprehensive curriculum package supported by materials to enhance a whole school approach has been developed and made available to schools.[8] In secondary schools, materials have been developed for Years 7, 8 and 9.[9] However, in both phases of education it is important to recognise that curriculum input is one of four possible ways of a school promoting social and emotional aspects of learning. The others are embedding SEAL in the school ethos, ensuring SEAL is reflected in teaching and learning approaches, and professional development for staff to ensure they are confident in teaching social and emotional skills and modelling appropriate behaviours and attitudes. Some schools may find that this work alone is sufficient to gain significant change and measurable impact.[10]

Thus, schools may undertake specific forms of teaching using SEAL learning objectives in mind. These may include the deliberate and specific use of language, group work, games and assessment for learning. Alternatively, whole school activities may be undertaken with the goal of creating a positive and supportive ethos and climate for learning for all staff and pupils. When implemented effectively, SEAL holds the potential to increase the level of engagement in school because it demands staff engagement for it to be successfully introduced; and, second, because its successful introduction will encourage a greater sense of belonging and participation as pupils acquire, apply, develop and consolidate greater skills to enable them to engage.

Systems of alternative provision

In some ways, alternative provision is an unfortunate name for that part of the curriculum which is provided to meet pupils' needs – as in a more perfect world it would be seen as part of a 'mainstream' curriculum, which axiomatically meets all pupils' needs. Some 135,000 pupils a year – mostly of secondary age – currently spend some time in alternative provision (DCSF, 2008e). Roughly one-third are placed in pupil referral units, with the remainder in a range of places including further education colleges and the private and voluntary sectors.

The *Back on Track* White Paper (DCSF, 2008e) built on *Children's Plan* proposals to outline a new strategy for transforming the quality of alternative educational provision for those who are excluded from, or who for some other reason are unable to attend, mainstream school. The document emphasised the key role of schools in the early identification of children with challenging behaviour, and enabling access to the right support before they reach the point of permanent exclusion. As part of this work, schools should be able to make more use of alternative provision as a preventive early intervention. Alternative provision can take many forms including in-school changes to the way in which the curriculum is organised for some pupils, with it being broken down to far more digestible chunks; or teaching some or all of Year 7 in secondary schools through an integrated approach, with one teacher providing continuity of presence.

Learning support units (LSUs) (McSherry, 2005) in schools can also be used to provide for pupils with behavioural difficulties caused by curriculum access issues, learners with school phobia and others for whom the classroom is a difficult place in which to thrive. Most usually, pupils spend part or all of the school week in the LSU, depending on which lessons or subjects were causing difficulty, working on an individual basis with a teacher or teaching assistant – always with the goal of being able to return to the classroom when ready. LSUs should not be confused with exclusion rooms, which are generally punitive and do little to engage pupils.

Alternative out-of-school provision may also be used where typically the school cannot access the equipment or staff to provide the necessary curriculum. This might include the provision of motor vehicle, construction, horticulture, hairdressing and beauty therapy courses – and might take up part of the curriculum, the bulk still being taught in the mainstream school. Finally, pupil referral units (PRUs) may be valuable in providing full-time education for pupils for a limited amount of time while their needs are assessed and prior to re-entry to the school they came from or entry to a new school. PRUs often offer anger management and conflict resolution classes to support pupils who could benefit from them.

Behaviour and Attendance Partnerships

Schools, especially secondary schools, most usually work in partnership with other schools for a variety of reasons. Behaviour and Attendance Partnerships, designed to help schools improve behaviour, reduce exclusions and raise levels of attendance, are an important way for secondary schools to work together to achieve these. They offer schools the chance to use the combined resources provided by all the schools in the local area to achieve both an economy of scale (when, for example, planning alternative provision) and a wider variety of provision to help meet the diverse needs of young people.

Such partnerships do, however, require schools to take responsibility for all the young people in the partnership area and not just those who happen to be on their own roll. This requires a significant change of mindset on the part of some head teachers and staff. It also requires a sense of 'belonging' within the partnership and a willingness to participate in the opportunities offered. In other words, it requires real engagement by a group of schools serving the needs of a local community.

Concluding comments

Although schools are increasingly conscious of the need to engage pupils, and some are more successful at doing so, in moving forward a number of factors need to be thought about. At the policy level, there is a need to clarify the perspective that there is sometimes a tension between different national policy drivers. For example, there is plenty of encouragement to schools to become more inclusive, which is in itself very supportive of increased engagement; but at the same time the National Challenge Programme – which intends to drive up standards in schools by 2011 so that all have 30 per cent or more pupils achieving five A*–C GCSEs (including English and Maths) – can mitigate against inclusion if schools concentrate only on those pupils who are at the borderline of attaining five good GCSEs.

standards against inclusion

At the practice level, there is a need for schools and their school improvement partners to ensure that leadership and management teams maintain an awareness of the need to increase engagement as a high priority, and know about the tools which will allow them to do so. These include policy and programme levers such as SEAL, partnerships to improve behaviour and attendance, alternative provision (as outlined above), as well as professional development activities which promote distributive leadership, such as, for example, the National Programme for Specialist Leaders of Behaviour and Attendance.[11] With respect to future research, there is a need to go beyond existing data as so much of the research in this area is inconclusive, difficult to interpret, or both. Future enquiry should examine the efficacy of the processes that make up the 21st Century School – drawing as much on pupil voice and staff expectations as data on attainment. Quality of engagement may also be revealed through an analysis of the new Ofsted well-being indicators, which were introduced into school inspections in September 2009 (Ofsted, 2008b).

In conclusion, if schools wish to decrease disaffection and increase engagement, they need to devote sufficient time to ensuring that the school community as a whole understands that engagement includes each and every member of the school community – engagement is not simply something that is 'done' to difficult and recalcitrant pupils. This recognition has implications for leadership and management at all levels, for the collection, analysis and use of data, for the professional development of staff, for a careful consideration of the appropriateness of specific strategies, for curricular and pastoral systems and – most important of all – for the overarching ethos of a school. It also raises questions about the breadth of current health and education agendas, viewing health, in particular, as implying much more than a concern to tackle particular health issues or problems, and recognising the multi-faceted ways in which schools, together with their partners, contribute to physical, social and mental well-being.

Notes

1 These are: 1. Being healthy; 2. Staying safe; 3. Enjoying and achieving; 4. Making a positive contribution; and 5. Economic well-being.

2 For further information see www.hm-treasury.gov.uk/pbr_csr07_psaindex.htm (last accessed June 2009).

3 Data held by National Strategies drawing on inspection reports on the Oftsed website and reported to the DCSF in July 2009

4 This has come about as a result of the focus on reducing 'persistent absence' (absent for 20 per cent or more of the school year) caused by any reason. As a consequence, schools are far less likely to give permission for holidays in school terms, thus increasing unauthorised absence, but generally increasing attendance at school. See http://nationalstrategies. standards.dcsf.gov.uk/node/98020 (last accessed July 2009).
5 For fuller discussion about the importance of ethos see McBeath and Myers (2000).
6 See www.teachernet.gov.uk/wholeschool/extendedschools (last accessed July 2009).
7 Internal records held by the National Strategies.
8 See http://nationalstrategies.standards.dcsf.gov.uk/primary/behaviourattendanceandseal/ primaryseal (last accessed July 2009).
9 See http://nationalstrategies.standards.dcsf.gov.uk/secondary/behaviourattendanceandseal/ secondaryseal (last accessed July 2009).
10 See http://nationalstrategies.standards.dcsf.gov.uk/secondary/behaviourattendanceandseal (last accessed July 2009).
11 See www.nationalstrategies.standards.dcsf.gov.uk/npslba (last accessed July 2009).

References

Carter, M., McGee, R., Taylor, B. and Williams, S. (2007) 'Health outcomes in adolescence: Associations with family, friends and school engagement', *Journal of Adolescence*, 30(1): 51–62.

CASEL (2008) *Social and Emotional Learning and Student Benefits: Implications for the Safe School/Healthy Students Core Elements*. Washington, DC: National Center for Mental Health Promotion and Youth Violence Prevention, Education Development Center.

DCSF (Department for Children, Schools and Families) (2007) *The Children's Plan: Building Brighter Futures*. London: The Stationery Office. Available at www.dcsf.gov.uk/ childrensplan (last accessed July 2009).

DCSF (2008a) *Every Child a Reader (ECaR)*. Nottingham: DCSF. Available at http://nationalstrategies.standards.dcsf.gov.uk/node/88927 (last accessed July 2009).

DCSF (2008b) *Every Child a Talker (ECaT)*. Nottingham: DCSF. Available at http:// nationalstrategies.standards.dcsf.gov.uk/node/153355 (last accessed July 2009).

DCSF (2008c) *21st Century Schools: A World-Class Education for Every Child*. Nottingham: DCSF. Available at http://publications.dcsf.gov.uk/default.aspx?PageFunction=productdetails& PageMode=publications&ProductId=DCSF-01044-2008& (last accessed July 2009).

DCSF (2008d) *Permanent and Fixed Period Exclusions from Schools and Exclusion Appeals in England, 2006/07*. London: DCSF. Available at www.dcsf.gov.uk/rsgateway/DB/SFR/ s000793/index.shtml (last accessed July 2009).

DCSF (2008e) *Back on Track: A Strategy for Modernising Alternative Provision for Young People*. London: The Stationery Office. Available at http://publications.dcsf.gov.uk/default.aspx? PageFunction=productdetails&PageMode=publications&ProductId=CM%25207410 (last accessed July 2009).

DCSF (2009a) *Your Child, Your Schools, Our Future: Building a 21st Century Schools System*. Available at www.dcsf.gov.uk/21stcenturyschoolssystem (last accessed July 2009).

DCSF (2009b) *Pupil Absence in Schools in England, Including Pupil Characteristics: 2007/08*. London: DCSF. Available at www.dcsf.gov.uk/rsgateway/DB/SFR/s000832/index.shtml (last accessed July 2009).

DCSF (2009c) *The Extra Mile (Primary): Achieving Success with Pupils from Deprived Communities*. Nottingham: DCSF.

DCSF (2009d) *The Extra Mile (Secondary): Achieving Success with Pupils from Deprived Communities*. Nottingham: DCSF.

Field, E. (2008) 'Understanding the options for school exclusion', *Teaching Expertise*. Available at www.teachingexpertise.com/articles/understanding-options-school-exclusion-4038 (last accessed July 2009).

Fletcher, A., Bonell, C., Sorhaindo, A. and Strange, V. (2009) 'How might schools influence young people's drug use? Development of theory from qualitative case-study research', *Journal of Adolescent Health*, 45:126–132

McBeath, J. and Myers, K. (2000) *Effective School Leaders*. London: Financial Times/Prentice Hall.

Macdonald, A. (2009) *Independent Review of the Proposal to Make Personal, Social, Health and Economic (PSHE) Education Statutory*. Nottingham: DCSF. Available at www.pshe-association.org.uk/pdf/FINAL%20Macdonald%20PSHE%20Ind%20Review.pdf (last accessed July 2009).

McSherry, J. (2005) *Learning Support Units: Principles, Practice and Evaluation*. London: David Fulton Books.

Ofsted (2008a) *The Annual Report of Her Majesty's Chief Inspector of Education, Children's Services and Skills 2007/08*. London: The Stationery Office.

Ofsted (2008b) *Indicators of a School's Contribution to Well-being: Consultation Document*. London: Ofsted. Available at www.ofsted.gov.uk/Ofsted-home/Publications-and-research/Browse-all-by/Documents-by-type/Consultations/Indicators-of-a-school-s-contribution-to-wellbeing (last accessed July 2009).

Ramey, C. T. and Ramey, S. L. (1998) 'Early intervention and early experience', *The American Psychologist*, 53(2): 109–120.

Steer, A. (2009a) *Learning Behaviour: The Report of the Practitioners' Group on School Behaviour and Discipline*. Available at http://www.teachernet.gov.uk/wholeschool/behaviour/steer/ (last accessed July 2009).

Steer, A. (2009b) *Learning Behaviour: Lessons Learned. A Review of Behaviour Standards and Practices in Our Schools*. Nottingham: DCSF. Available at www.teachernet.gov.uk/wholeschool/behaviour/steer (last accessed July 2009).

Warwick, I., Mooney, A. and Oliver, C. (2009) *National Healthy Schools Programme: Developing the Evidence Base*. London: Thomas Coram Research Unit, Institute of Education, University of London.

West, P. (2006) 'School effects research provides new and stronger evidence in support of the health-promoting school idea', *Health Education*, 106(6): 421–424.

West-Burnham, J. and Coates, M. (2005) *Personalizing Learning: Transforming Education for Every Child*. Stafford: Network Educational Press.

WHO/HBSC (2008) *Social Cohesion for Mental Well-being among Adolescents*. Copenhagen: WHO/HBSC. Available at www.euro.who.int/Document/E91921.pdf (last accessed July 2009).

Chapter 5

Tackling obesity
Promoting physical activity and healthy eating in schools

Wendy Wills

Introduction

Since the 1970s, rates of obesity amongst school-aged children have doubled or tripled in economically developed countries such as the UK, USA, Canada and Australia (Wang and Lobstein, 2006). Obesity is defined as excess weight in relation to height (Sproston and Primatesta, 2003) and, although definitions for children vary, being 20 per cent above the ideal weight for height can classify children as obese (Wang and Lobstein, 2006). There is widespread concern about the impact of obesity on children's health and well-being.

Eating a healthy, balanced diet and undertaking regular physical activity can help protect children from becoming obese. Promoting physical activity and healthy eating in a school setting is a complex task, however, because there is no 'proven' formula that works for all children, whatever their age, gender, race, family background or needs.

This chapter summarises evidence on the prevalence and consequences of obesity amongst young people in the UK and considers when and how this sensitive issue can be tackled. This represents an important challenge for schools. Two frameworks which might be helpful for tackling obesity are looked at, both of which place young people's needs and experiences at their centre. The first of these advocates prioritising young people's social and cultural values to ensure that obesity is tackled in a way that has meaning and relevance for local populations. The second focuses on young people's assets – what young people are doing that is positive and how such assets can be utilised to improve diet and activity levels.

The chapter then turns to examine what is meant by eating healthily and being physically active. Factors which influence young people's diet and physical activity are outlined before the chapter asks 'What can schools do?' to tackle obesity. Suggestions are given, drawing on research evidence, to illustrate practical ways that schools can take action through the positive promotion of physical activity and eating healthily.

Childhood obesity

Body Mass Index (BMI[1]) is often used to define when weight is excessive in relation to height (Cole et al., 2000), but defining obesity in children is more complex than in adults, because of the changes to height and weight that occur during standard age-related growth development (Jotangia et al., 2006). BMI thresholds for obesity in children therefore have to take account of gender and age.[2]

Data from the English National Child Measurement Programme (NCMP) show that 18.3 per cent of Year 6 children (aged 10–11 years) and 9.6 per cent of Reception Year children (aged 4–5 years), measured in 2007–8, were classified as obese (NHS, 2008), meaning they were over the 95th percentile for their height/weight. Current projections suggest that one in four children and young people in the UK could be obese by 2050 (Foresight, 2007), although there is some evidence that obesity trends are starting to flatten out (NHS Information Centre, 2007). It is too early to confirm, however, if the upward trend has been permanently slowed down or reversed. Table 5.1 shows current obesity rates amongst boys and girls. Overall, there are no significant differences by gender.

Obesity is evident across all social groups, but children whose parents have manual jobs, rather than non-manual or professional occupations, are more likely to be obese. In addition, children living in economically deprived areas are also at greater risk of becoming obese compared with those living in more affluent areas (Jotangia et al., 2006). In general, inner city areas tend to have higher rates of childhood obesity compared with other area types (Wang and Lobstein, 2006). Children whose parents are obese have a significantly higher

Table 5.1 Prevalence of obesity in England amongst boys and girls aged 2–15 years, 2001–02

Age (years)	Boys (%)	Girls (%)	All (%)
2–3	–	–	12.7
4–5	–	–	13.4
6–7	–	–	13.6
8–10	–	–	19.5
2–10	14.9	12.5	–
11	22.0	18.1	–
12	17.5	19.3	–
13	18.7	19.8	–
14	15.4	18.7	–
15	17.9	15.6	–

Source: Health Survey for England (adapted from Jotangia et al., 2006). The HSE uses the UK National BMI Percentile Classification of obesity whereby children over the 95th percentile for height/weight are classified as obese.

risk of being obese themselves; boys aged 2–15 years are 12 times more likely to be obese and girls 10 times more likely, if they have two obese parents (Sproston and Primatesta, 2003). Black Caribbean children and Indian boys tend to be heavier whilst Bangladeshi children tend to weigh less than children in the general population (Erens *et al.*, 2000).

Is (tackling) obesity harmful for children? The challenge for schools

The health consequences of being obese as an adult are clear. In summary, obese adults have a significantly greater risk of developing type 2 diabetes, cardiovascular disease, some cancers, joint problems and other life-limiting long-term conditions (Reilly *et al.*, 2003). There is a 50 per cent likelihood that a person who is obese in adolescence will remain obese into adulthood (Steinbeck, 2001). Obesity in childhood has also been directly linked with later disease risk, regardless of weight in adulthood (Reilly *et al.*, 2003). Being obese in adolescence is associated with the concurrent risk of developing high blood pressure, asthma or type 2 diabetes (Sproston and Primatesta, 2003). In addition, obesity in childhood is associated in some children with low self-esteem, bullying, emotional distress and an increased incidence of disordered eating (skipping meals, for example) (O'Dea, 2004).

Despite these physical, social and emotional consequences, there is a risk that tackling obesity will stigmatise obese children and do more harm than good. Obesity is not a straightforward indicator of a child's poor health, just as being a healthy weight is not an indication that a child is in good health. Intensive surveillance of young people's activities and bodies often leads children to feel marginalised and disengaged from efforts to improve their health (O'Dea, 2004; Brooks and Magnusson, 2006). Any health-promotion initiative or message must be concerned with avoiding negative or harmful outcomes, and schools must avoid promoting body image concerns, dieting and disordered eating (O'Dea, 2004). Obesity has become associated in society with laziness, greed, shame and other negative images, even amongst health professionals (Hankey *et al.*, 2003), and children are often well aware of the 'thin is good, fat is bad' message. Tackling obesity as an abnormal bodily state instils it with a sense of morality, that there is a 'right' and a 'wrong' when it comes to body size (Evans, 2006; Evans and Colls, 2009), even though many obese children do not see their own bodies in this negative way (Wills *et al.*, 2006).

The English National Child Measurement Programme requires that all consenting children in Reception and Year 6 are weighed and measured. A recent change means that all consenting parents of children measured will receive details about their child's weight. Despite providing evidence about obesity prevalence, the NCMP raises two challenges for schools. First, reporting children's weight reinforces the idea to children that they are being monitored and that their body size, *per se*, is indicative of something sinister. This does little to encourage young people to critically engage with issues about weight and health (Burrows and Wright, 2007). Second, giving parents information about their child's weight does little to overcome popular beliefs about what an obese child 'looks' like (many parents do not recognise or acknowledge obesity in their own child (Jeffrey *et al.*, 2005)), making it harder for schools to engage parents to positively address diet and physical activity.

Positive frameworks for tackling obesity

Tackling obesity mindfully, through the promotion of a healthy lifestyle, is likely to produce benefits for children, in terms of developing positive health promotion messages, preventing the marginalisation or stigmatisation of (obese) children and reducing the likelihood that young people will develop disordered eating and poor body image (whatever their weight). Two frameworks conducive to a positive, child-centred approach are a grounded socio-cultural framework and an assets-based approach.

Socio-cultural frameworks

The popular mantra 'you are what you eat' symbolises a framework which takes into account young people's social and cultural beliefs, experiences and habits. The social groups that young people belong to, including those determined by where they live, their socio-economic status (SES) and their ethnicity, help to shape and form their perceptions about healthy eating, tastes, preferences and attitudes to weight, exercise and obesity. Peers and extended family often help to compound these 'normalised' beliefs and behaviours. Experiences and beliefs become so firmly grounded that they are difficult to shift; they are also so taken for granted (Williams, 1995) that most people are not aware of how or why, for example, they choose to eat brand 'x' rather than brand 'y'.

It is important that schools see the social and cultural values of specific groups as different, but not inferior, to the values of others. So, for example, schools need to examine what young people gain from avoiding salad at lunchtime or from continually bringing in a 'sick note' to avoid physical education lessons. Do these behaviours help them to fit in with friends; to eat the way their family has taught them to eat; to not be marked out as 'sporty'? Would changing these behaviours represent a significant 'cost' to young people from different social or ethnic groups? Adopting a socio-cultural framework would help schools to understand and more positively challenge young people's eating and physical activity behaviours.

The National Institute of Health and Clinical Excellence (NICE) has identified socio-cultural approaches as effective frameworks for behaviour change, if they are planned in partnership with, and take account of, community needs and experiences (NICE, 2007).

Assets-focused frameworks

Problem-focused or deficit models of health promotion have not been entirely successful. Focusing on what people do 'wrong' has not eliminated inequalities in health-related behaviours, and an assets-focused, positive framework, which looks at what people do 'right', may be useful for school-based health promotion. Assets frameworks work with the notion that people are co-creators of good health and not just responsible for illness and disease (Lindström and Eriksson, 2006). Assets can be factors or resources (physical, material, emotional or social) that young people have which can be utilised for the good of their health (Morgan and Ziglio, 2007). Instead of looking at why young people are not more physically active, for example, an assets framework would suggest looking at how and when young people *do* undertake some form of activity and working with this to increase activity levels.

Assets can be explored at the individual (e.g. self-esteem, competence or the ability to learn), community (e.g. peer and friendship networks and community cohesion) or institutional level (Morgan and Ziglio, 2007), so there is considerable scope for schools to utilise an assets framework for promoting diet and physical activity. At the community level, school-based peer and class groups can be used as a force for creating positive food and activity choices. Most schools already possess at least some of the assets needed at the institutional level to promote physical activity or healthy eating, through their commitment to the National Healthy Schools Programme.

This approach is advocated for by the World Health Organization (WHO) European Office for Investment in Human Development on the grounds that it will promote health and support the development of healthier communities (Morgan and Ziglio, 2007).

What does it mean to eat healthily and to be physically active?

Current UK guidance for eating a healthy diet includes eating at least five portions of fruit and vegetables daily, two portions of fish each week (one to be oily fish), plenty of starchy foods (preferably whole grains) and cutting down on fat, saturated fat and salt (see www.eatwell.gov.uk/healthydiet). A healthy diet is known to be protective against cancer and cardiovascular disease (Sproston and Primatesta, 2003), and eating a diet that contains the right amount of food is conducive to not gaining weight. Eating healthily is also suggested as promoting better well-being in children as well as facilitating adequate growth and cognitive and emotional development (Shepherd *et al.*, 2001). Few people in the UK, however, follow official guidance to consume a healthy diet. One estimate suggests that only seven adults per thousand are eating a diet that meets most or all of the guidance (Lobstein, 2008). Children and young people's diets tend to contain large amounts of sugar and lower-nutrient baked goods (Food Standards Agency, 2000).

As most children and young people spend a considerable amount of time in school, the food that is provided there, through school lunches but also through breakfast clubs, break-time tuck shops and vending machines, contributes significantly to young people's dietary intake. Nutrient and food-based standards for schools are currently being implemented across the UK (for example, see www.schoolfoodtrust.org.uk). The standards advise schools how often they should serve specific foods and the minimum nutrient content required for school lunches. As the guidance relates to all food served in schools (including vending machines and breakfast clubs), this represents a significant challenge. This also represents an opportunity, however, to ensure that a healthy diet is advocated and supplied whilst taking account of young people's socio-cultural beliefs, experiences and assets to help promote healthier choices.

Factors which influence young people's eating habits reflect structural elements of the school dining experience as well as pupil preferences. Teachers are often not perceived as helping young people to make healthier food choices (Ludvigsen and Sharma, 2004; Shepherd *et al.*, 2006). Gender is an important factor, as teenage girls prioritise spending time with friends during the lunch break whereas boys prioritise undertaking activities (attending clubs or playing football, for example) (Wills, 2005; Wills *et al.*, 2005; Scottish Consumer Council, 2008).

Young people consistently report preferring the taste and texture of fast food (O'Dea, 2003; Ludvigsen and Sharma, 2004; Shepherd *et al.*, 2006) and many link eating 'unhealthy' food with being with friends (Chapman and Maclean, 1993; Shepherd *et al.*, 2006). In research conducted by Barnardo's, primary and secondary school students were asked who would eat a meal consisting of rye bread, cottage cheese, milk, yogurt and an apple. Many children, who found it difficult to imagine any child eating such foods, said the food would be eaten by girls who were 'posh', 'sporty', 'brainy', a 'goody goody' and someone who was thin or skinny (Ludvigsen and Sharma, 2004).

Children report disliking queuing for food, the lack of choice/consultation about menus/facilities, the perceived lack of availability (food running out before the end of the lunch break, for example), the lack of opportunities to sit with friends (particularly those who take a packed lunch and those from different year groups) and a shortage of time to eat and be with their friends (Wills, 2005; Wills *et al.*, 2005; Scottish Consumer Council, 2008). Purchasing food outside school is seen by some children as a positive choice because it allows them to make their own decisions and to be treated as young adults (Scottish Consumer Council, 2008). For many young people, improving food in schools will not overcome the social factors which determine where and what they eat. These choices and beliefs need to be viewed as opportunities to work with young people, rather than as problems which need solving by adults.

Physical activity in childhood and adolescence

The Department of Health in England recommends that children and young people undertake at least 60 minutes of moderate-intensity physical activity every day (Department of Health, 2005). Activities to promote bone health and muscle strength (e.g. through skipping, dancing or football – activities which put stress on the bones) should take place at least twice a week, particularly during adolescence (Department of Health, 2004, 2005). Being physically active helps combat weight gain, improves well-being (including mental health) and, in the long term, helps to prevent the onset of chronic illness (Department of Health, 2005). Physical activity also aids children's social relationships (Department of Health, 2004).

A large proportion of children are already physically active, according to data from the Health Survey for England (NHS Information Centre, 2007). Almost three-quarters of boys aged 2–15 years (72 per cent) and almost two-thirds of girls (63 per cent) are active for at least 60 minutes per day. The number of girls achieving this amount of daily physical activity decreases with age.

There are ambitious plans for increasing access and availability to physical activity provision through schools. These include encouraging flexibility for providing non-traditional sports and activities; asking schools to try harder to engage disabled children, looked after children and those excluded from mainstream education in physical activities; and extending the amount of time children spend on PE and sport (Department of Health, 2005). Plans also include reversing the decline in the numbers of pupils who walk or cycle to school (Department for Education and Skills, 2003).

So what encourages and supports young people to participate in regular physical activity in school? As with healthy eating, factors facilitating physical activity operate at school and individual levels. Young people who participate in PE believe that being offered a wide choice of activities is important (Brunton et al., 2005; Brooks and Magnusson, 2006; Rees et al., 2006), particularly non-traditional activities like cycling and aerobics. Girls, in particular, welcome such choices (Rees et al., 2006). Receiving support from peers, teachers and parents to continue with physical activity is reported as important by some young people, especially during the transition to secondary school (Allender et al., 2006). Girls often say they find it difficult to continue with physical activity without the support of friends (Wills et al., 2006).

Girls are more motivated if the changing facilities are attractive (Brooks and Magnusson, 2006) and if they have PE uniforms over which they have some choice (in the design, for example, or over what they can wear for each activity) (Flintoff and Scraton, 2001; Brooks and Magnusson, 2006). Single-sex PE lessons are viewed positively and encourage participation and motivation (Mulvihill *et al.*, 2000; Flintoff and Scraton, 2001). Young people who view team-based activities positively feel that such activities take the pressure off them to perform as individuals (Mulvihill *et al.*, 2000), and young people who engage in a lot of sport like the feeling of comradeship and competitiveness that this provides (Brunton *et al.*, 2005). Younger children prefer not to be forced to compete with each other, or to win (Allender *et al.*, 2006).

The benefits that young people say they gain from undertaking regular physical activity highlight the type of assets that schools can work with to promote physical activity. Several studies show that young people are aware of the positive impact that physical activity has on their well-being, including improvements to self-esteem, energy levels, confidence and the ability to overcome problems (Mulvihill *et al.*, 2000; Flintoff and Scraton, 2001; O'Dea, 2003). Socialising and spending time with friends, enjoyment, improving skills and weight control (girls only) are also benefits cited by young people (Mulvihill *et al.*, 2000; Flintoff and Scraton, 2001; O'Dea, 2003; Brunton *et al.*, 2005; Brooks and Magnusson, 2007). Flintoff and Scraton's study found, however, that most of these benefits related to physical activity outside of the school setting. School-based PE was seen as boring and unmotivating (Flintoff and Scraton, 2001).

The case study school in Brooks and Magnusson's study highlights how PE provision can be turned around in consultation with young people (Brooks and Magnusson, 2006). The changes the school made required a radical overhaul of staff and the curriculum and accepting that the school would not win as many trophies. Young people who started to undertake physical activity after the changes were made said that changing the school culture to one which encouraged and rewarded participation rather than winning was crucial. For girls, this increased their confidence and allowed them to find activities that they enjoyed. For boys, many were relieved that the sporting culture had become less aggressive and intimidating. Some previously non-participating young people also said they had started to seek out further opportunities to participate in physical activity, outside school.

What can schools do?

To be effective, a child-focused positive approach to tackling obesity is needed which promotes both healthy eating and physical activity. Carefully planned initiatives should use a socio-cultural framework to work with children's backgrounds, experiences and needs. In addition, schools should seek to explore the assets that children have, at the individual, community and institutional level, in order to help young people create and sustain their own good health and well-being. These elements of good practice are now discussed in more detail.

The delivery of health promotion to tackle obesity in schools

A whole-school training programme can help to address the mixed messages that are sometimes inadvertently delivered across the school setting, and to ensure that a whole school engages in integrated thinking and action to tackle obesity. One example of such a programme is the 'Growing through Adolescence' (GTA) resource, developed as part of the activities of the European Network of Health Promoting Schools.[3] GTA is designed for training teachers at upper primary and lower secondary school level and it can also be used with other school staff, like nurses and the catering team. The resource sets out the scientific evidence relating to topics associated with young people and healthy eating along with suggested training activities for staff. The resource is not intended for direct use with young people but it encourages staff to reflect on their own perceptions and experiences about, for example, the factors that drive obesity and body image. This can lead to a more well-rounded appreciation of the impact that both formal and informal teaching have on young people's health-relevant choices and decisions.

NHS Health Scotland initiated and positively evaluated GTA training courses across Scotland (Leven, 2008) but little use so far has been made of the resource in other parts of the UK.

Engaging schools, parents and young people

A systematic review of the barriers and facilitators to healthy eating suggests that school-wide approaches can be effective at improving diet, if they involve parents, teachers and young people working in partnership (Shepherd et al., 2001). This is in line with the ethos of an inclusive, health-promoting school. NICE guidance on obesity suggests that older children (from around 12 years) must be approached in ways which acknowledge their growing autonomy (NICE, 2006); this raises certain challenges for schools. Recruiting and engaging older children in obesity initiatives can be difficult, for example (Aicken et al., 2008), but the benefits for young people, when they are successfully consulted and engaged, can be immense (Wills et al., 2008).

Schools need to be willing to learn from the communities where they are based by engaging with parents and the wider community. Schools can consider events or other ways to find out what parents think about obesity, diet and physical activity and build these findings into the initiatives and resources that they develop. Newsletters, peer-led sessions and regular information updates have been found to be effective (Shepherd et al., 2001). Ignoring the socio-cultural backdrop within and surrounding schools is counter-productive as any subsequent attempt to tackle obesity will have little meaning for those it is trying to target. Similarly, schools need to look at what young people, their parents and communities are already doing that either (a) are positive assets or (b) could be turned into positive assets. Table 5.2 provides some suggestions, drawing on the research evidence cited in this chapter, but schools need to find ways to consult with young people in order to build an inventory of socio-culturally grounded assets of relevance to their students. This means regularly engaging with young people in schools and not just those involved with, for example, school councils.

Table 5.2 Suggestions for tackling obesity in school through the positive promotion of diet and physical activity

Area for change	Examples of initiatives drawing on socio-cultural and assets frameworks
Choice and availability of sports/activities	'Just for fun' activities to enhance enjoyment/pleasure and sociability
	Offer team and individual sports/activities whenever possible Consider 'taster' sessions of traditional and non-traditional activities on offer both within and outside PE
Sporting/activity culture	Consider how to balance winning and excellence with encouraging/rewarding participation
	Address divisions between cliques and stereotypes (e.g. participating vs. non-participating students)
	Consider how staff (not just PE teachers) can support young people to participate in physical activity
	Develop peer-led/mentoring schemes between older/ younger children (within schools and across secondary/ primary clusters) to promote inclusion and participation
Promoting healthy food in schools	Consider regular 'taster' sessions to promote the taste and texture of different foods
	Involve young people in the development and promotion of menus and snacks
	Promote benefits other than generic 'health' benefits, e.g. foods give a natural energy boost, good for nails/hair, etc.
	Develop sustainable food policies/agendas and encourage young people to become active, ethical consumers
Food/eating culture	Develop 'buddy' systems to encourage children to support each other to try new foods
	Boost the social aspects of eating through addressing the dining environment
	Consider giving young people more choice about where to eat, e.g. healthy food vans
Positive culture of body acceptance and health promotion	Deliver training, like 'Growing through Adolescence', to all school staff to ensure that mixed messages about weight are not given to children and young people
	Invite parents and communities into schools to discuss their own experiences of weight, diet and physical activity

Conclusion

Obesity has become a priority issue for public health, and schools are increasingly expected to assist in tackling it. Whilst some obese children suffer concurrent emotional, social and physical problems, many do not. Eating a healthy diet and undertaking regular physical activity are, however, conducive to good health and well-being for all children. Schools can make a positive impact in these areas of health promotion by utilising socio-cultural and assets-based frameworks to identify what it is within their own school communities that will have the greatest impact. Taking a whole school approach and working with parents and young people means that schools can make significant and sustainable changes which will assist young people in achieving good mental, physical and social well-being. Developing a body-positive culture within which children can flourish and develop assets for good health is a constructive way forward for schools to tackle obesity.

Notes

1 BMI = weight (kg)/height $(m)^2$.
2 The 'cut-off' for defining obesity in children by age and gender is subject to continuing academic and clinical debate. For a discussion of current methods and thinking see Cole *et al.* (2000) and Sproston and Primatesta (2003).
3 GTA is funded by the European Commission, the WHO Regional Office for Europe and the Council of Europe. The resource is freely available through the publications/manuals database on the Schools for Health in Europe website (www.schoolsforhealth.eu; accessed 8 June 2009).

References

Aicken, C., Arai, L. and Roberts, H. (2008) *Schemes to Promote Healthy Weight among Obese and Overweight Children in England*. London: EPPI-Centre, Social Science Research Unit, Institute of Education, University of London.

Allender, S., Cowburn, G. and Foster, C. (2006) 'Understanding participation in sport and physical activity among children and adults: A review of qualitative studies', *Health Education Research*, 21(6): 826–835.

Brooks, F. and Magnusson, J. (2006) 'Taking part counts: Adolescents' experiences of the transition from inactivity to active participation in school-based physical education', *Health Education Research*, 21(6): 872–883.

Brooks, F. and Magnusson, J. (2007) 'Physical activity as leisure: The meaning of physical activity for the health and well-being of adolescent women', *Health Care for Women International*, 28: 69–87.

Brunton, G., Thomas, J., Harden, A., Rees, R., Kavanagh, J., Oliver, S., Shepherd, J. and Oakley, A. (2005) 'Promoting physical activity amongst children outside of physical education classes: A systematic review integrating intervention studies and qualitative studies', *Health Education Journal*, 64(4): 323–338.

Burrows, L. and Wright, J. (2007) 'Prescribing practices: Shaping healthy children in schools', *International Journal of Children's Rights*, 15: 83–98.

Chapman, G. and Maclean, H. (1993) '"Junk food" and "healthy food": Meanings of food in adolescent women's culture', *Journal of Nutrition Education*, 25: 108–113.

Cole, T., Bellizzi, M., Flegal, K. and Dietz, W. (2000) 'Establishing a standard definition for child overweight and obesity worldwide: International survey', *British Medical Journal*, 320: 1–6.

Department for Education and Skills (2003) *Travelling to School: An Action Plan*. Nottingham: DfES.

Department of Health (2004) *At Least Five a Week: Evidence on the Impact of Physical Activity and Its Relationship to Health*. London: The Stationery Office.

Department of Health (2005) *Choosing Activity: A Physical Activity Action Plan*. London: Department of Health.

Erens, B., Primatesta, P. and Prior, G. (2000) *Health Survey for England '99: The Health of Minority Ethnic Groups*. London: Department of Health.

Evans, B. (2006) '"Gluttony or sloth": Critical geographies of bodies and morality in (anti)obesity policy', *Area*, 38(3): 259–267.

Evans, B. and Colls, R. (2009) 'Measuring fatness, governing bodies: The spatialities of the Body Mass Index (BMI) in anti-obesity politics', *Antipode*, 41(5): 1051–1083.

Flintoff, A. and Scraton, S. (2001) 'Stepping into active leisure? Young women's perceptions of active lifestyles and their experiences of school physical education', *Sport, Education and Society*, 6(1): 5–21.

Food Standards Agency (2000) *National Diet and Nutrition Survey of Young People Aged 4–18 Years*. London: Food Standards Agency.

Foresight (2007) *Tackling Obesities: Future Choices – Project Report*. London: Government Office for Science.

Hankey, C., Eley, S., Leslie, W., Hunter, C. and Lean, M. (2003) 'Eating habits, beliefs, attitudes and knowledge among health professionals regarding the links between obesity, nutrition and health', *Public Health Nutrition*, 7(2): 337–343.

Jeffrey, A. N., Voss, L. D., Metcalf, B. S., Alba, S. and Wilkin, T. J. (2005) 'Parents' awareness of overweight in themselves and their children: Cross sectional study within a cohort (EarlyBird 21)', *British Medical Journal*, 330: 23–24.

Jotangia, D., Moody, A., Stamatakis, E. and Wardle, H. (2006) *Obesity amongst Children under 11*. London: Joint Health Surveys Unit.

Leven, T. (2008) *Evaluation of Growing through Adolescence Resource and Associated Training for Trainers Course*. Edinburgh: NHS Health Scotland.

Lindström, B. and Eriksson, M. (2006) 'Contextualizing salutogenesis and Antonovsky in public health development', *Health Promotion International*, 212(3): 238–244.

Lobstein, T. (2008) 'Child obesity: What can be done and who will do it?', *Proceedings of the Nutrition Society*, 67: 301–306.

Ludvigsen, A. and Sharma, N. (2004) *Burger Boy and Sporty Girl: Children and Young People's Attitudes towards Food in School*. Ilford: Barnardo's.

Morgan, A. and Ziglio, E. (2007) 'Revitalising the evidence base for public health: An assets model', *IUHPE Promotion and Education*, 14(Suppl. 2): 17–22.

Mulvihill, C. B., Rivers, K. and Aggleton, P. (2000) 'Views of young people towards physical activity: Determinants and barriers to involvement', *Health Education*, 100(5): 190–199.

NHS (2008) *National Child Measurement Programme 2007/08 School Year Headline Results*. London: NHS Information Centre for Health and Social Care.

NHS Information Centre (2007) *Health Survey for England 2007: Latest Trends*. London: NHS Information Centre.

NICE (2006) *Guidance on the Prevention, Identification, Assessment and Management of Overweight and Obesity in Adults and Children*. London: NICE.

NICE (2007) *Behaviour Change at Population, Community and Individual Levels*. London: NICE.

O'Dea, J. A. (2003) 'Why do kids eat healthful foods? Perceived benefits of and barriers to healthful eating and physical activity among children and adolescents', *Journal of the American Dietetic Association*, 103(4): 497–500.

O'Dea, J. A. (2004) 'Prevention of child obesity: "First, do no harm"', *Health Education Research*, 20(2): 259–265.

Rees, R., Kavanagh, J., Harden, A., Shepherd, J., Brunton, G., Oliver, S. and Oakley, A. (2006) 'Young people and physical activity: A systematic review matching their views to effective interventions', *Health Education Research*, 21(6): 806–825.

Reilly, J. J., Methven, E., McDowell, Z. C., Hacking, B., Alexander, D., Stewart, L. and Kelnar, C. J. (2003) 'Health consequences of obesity', *Archives of Disease in Childhood*, 88: 748–752.

Scottish Consumer Council (2008) *Out to Lunch?* Glasgow: Scottish Consumer Council.

Shepherd, J., Harden, A., Rees, R., Brunton, G., Garcia, J., Oliver, S. and Oakley, A. (2001) *Young People and Healthy Eating: A Systematic Review of Research on Barriers and Facilitators*. London: EPPI-Centre, Social Science Research Unit, Institute of Education, University of London.

Shepherd, J., Harden, A., Rees, R., Brunton, G., Garcia, J., Oliver, S. and Oakley, A. (2006) 'Young people and healthy eating: A systematic review of research on barriers and facilitators', *Health Education Research*, 21(2): 239–257.

Sproston, K. and Primatesta, P. (2003) *Health Survey for England 2002: The Health of Children and Young People*. London: The Stationery Office.

Steinbeck, K. (2001) 'The importance of physical activity in the prevention of overweight and obesity in childhood: A review and an opinion', *Obesity Reviews*, 2: 117–130.

Wang, Y. and Lobstein, T. (2006) 'Worldwide trends in childhood overweight and obesity', *International Journal of Pediatric Obesity*, 1(1): 11–25.

Williams, S. (1995) 'Theorising class, health and lifestyles: Can Bourdieu help us?', *Sociology of Health and Illness*, 17(5): 577–604.

Wills, W. J. (2005) *Food, Eating, Health and Fatness: The Perceptions and Experiences of Young Teenagers from Disadvantaged Families*. Edinburgh: RUHBC, University of Edinburgh.

Wills, W. J., Backett-Milburn, K., Gregory, S. and Lawton, J. (2005) 'The influence of the secondary school setting on the food practices of young teenagers from disadvantaged backgrounds in Scotland', *Health Education Research*, 20(4): 458–465.

Wills, W. J., Backett-Milburn, K., Gregory, S. and Lawton, J. (2006) 'Young teenagers' perceptions of their own and others' bodies: A qualitative study of obese, overweight and "normal" weight young people in Scotland', *Social Science & Medicine*, 62(2): 396–406.

Wills, W. J., Appleton, J. V., Magnusson, J. E. and Brooks, F. (2008) 'Exploring the limitations of an adult-led agenda for understanding the health behaviours of young people', *Health and Social Care in the Community*, 16(3): 244–252.

Chapter 6

The role of schools in reducing alcohol-related harm among young people

Willm Mistral and Lorna Templeton

Introduction

> Of all drugs, the use of alcohol has shown the greatest recent growth and causes the most widespread problems among young people in the UK today. It is also the least regulated and the most heavily marketed.
>
> (Advisory Council on the Misuse of Drugs, 2006: 6)

There is compelling evidence of the negative impact of excessive drinking by young people, not only on their own short- and long-term health, but also as a major contributory factor to much anti-social behaviour (DCSF, 2008). Also, 'binge'[1] or 'extreme' drinking (Martinic and Measham, 2008) during youth and early adulthood has been shown to correlate highly with alcohol problems, drug use, low educational attainment and criminal behaviour later in life (Viner and Taylor, 2007).

This chapter will summarise the prevalence of alcohol use among young people, outline the main motivations underlying this, and review the key harms, risks and protective factors for problematic alcohol use among young people. The chapter will then examine the role that schools can play in the prevention of alcohol-related harm, emphasising the place of the education sector within broader 'multi-component' initiatives which are now commonly recognised as the most productive way forward.

Prevalence of alcohol use among young people

The 2003 European Schools Project on Alcohol and other Drugs (ESPAD[2]: Hibell *et al.*, 2004) reported data from over 100,000 young people aged 15 to 16 years from 35 countries. Young people in the UK reported some of the highest levels of lifetime use, frequent drinking in the last 30 days, drunkenness and binge-drinking. The English Alcohol Needs Assessment Research Project (Department of Health, 2005) reported that one-third of young people aged 16 to 24 years were hazardous or harmful drinkers (hazardous defined as drinking above the recommended sensible levels of drinking; harmful defined as drinking at those levels and experiencing harm), with a further 8 per cent reported as alcohol dependent. Patterns of lifetime drinking, and of experiences of alcohol consumption and drunkenness, are broadly similar across England, Scotland, Wales and Northern Ireland (Chief Medical Officers of England, Wales and Northern Ireland, 2009).

However, in the UK there is growing consensus that there is an increasing 'polarisation of drinking patterns amongst young people' (Measham, 2007: 207). Evidence suggests that the average weekly consumption of 11 to 15-year-olds who drink doubled in the 1990s (Fuller, 2007) and has remained at those increased levels in the early twenty-first century. A survey conducted by *Positive Futures* (a social inclusion programme supported by the Home Office) with 1,250 young people aged 10 to 19 years indicated that 42 per cent of the sample started drinking when they were 13 years old or younger and a further 23 per cent when they were 14 or 15 years old. Across the UK, age 13 has been identified as the 'tipping point' (Talbot and Crabbe, 2008) when most young people report having had their first alcoholic drink. The evidence is mixed as to whether alcohol consumption by young women is increasing and similar to levels seen in young men, but what is clear is that consumption among younger children is a growing concern.

On the other hand, what surveys also show, but which is often ignored in media reports quick to highlight problems and demonise young people, is that there are large numbers of children and young people who do not drink, have never been drunk, nor experienced any alcohol-related problems. For example, data from one recent survey (Lynch, 2008) of 7,831 11 to 15-year-olds from 272 English secondary schools reported a rise in the number of adolescents who have never had an alcoholic drink, from 39 per cent in 2003 to 46 per cent in 2007, and also a decline in the number of young people who have drunk alcohol in the previous seven days from 26 per cent in 2003 to 20 per cent in 2007.

Likewise, the Ofsted 'TellUs3' survey (Ofsted, 2008) reported that 25 per cent of 8 to 16-year-old respondents had never had an alcoholic drink, and 35 per cent had never been drunk. Moreover, many of these young people do not belong to those cultural groups usually associated with moderate or no alcohol consumption. We do not yet know enough about the reasons these young people give for not drinking or the strategies they employ to avoid drinking or getting drunk, and further research in this area might usefully inform the harm prevention agenda.

Information on alcohol use by young people comes primarily from school-based surveys which are able to include very large numbers. However, many of these surveys do not capture the most prolific users, because alcohol (or drug) use is strongly correlated with temporary or permanent school exclusion. Furthermore, surveys often use different methodologies, definitions, time-frames and data collection tools, making it difficult to draw summative conclusions from the findings. Nevertheless, what such work highlights is that a substantial number of young people are drinking at a young age, regularly and at high levels.

Why young people drink

Young people mainly drink socially, in friendship groups, and the most common reason given for drinking alcohol is 'to get drunk' (Brain et al., 2000; Talbot and Crabbe, 2008). Other reasons for drinking include 'for fun'; to impress the opposite sex; to 'fit in'; to improve confidence in a group; to get a 'buzz' from doing something 'illegal'; to experiment; to fill in time; to be 'numb'; to escape; and 'to have something to do' (Coleman and Cater, 2005; Sheehan and Ridge, 2001).

Conforming to perceived social norms about the drinking behaviour of other young people and adults also affects alcohol use. Anderson and Baumberg (2006) report that young people actively seek to learn about alcohol from family and peers, as well as cultural sources such as television, which may present only a distorted view of alcohol use. The Academy of Medical Sciences (2004) reports that among young people, exposure to alcohol advertising increases positive beliefs about drinking, reduces perception of risk, shapes perceptions about acceptable levels of alcohol intake, and increases consumption. Further, some young people drink to mirror family drinking behaviour, or to cope with family problems.

There have been several recent reviews of the risks and harms[3] associated with alcohol use among young people (Chief Medical Officers of England, Wales and Northern Ireland, 2009; Newbury-Birch et al., 2009; Templeton, 2009). The next sections will look at the key conclusions which can be drawn from these reviews, before moving on to look at what is known about the factors which protect against alcohol consumption and its associated risks and harms.

Alcohol-related harms

There is a wealth of evidence of the negative impact of excessive drinking by young people, not only on their own short- and long-term health, but also through its being a contributory factor to a range of other problems. Young people who drink to excess are more likely to be involved in a range of risky behaviours, with heavy drinkers more likely to initiate sex earlier, have more partners and not use contraception, thereby risking pregnancy and sexually transmitted diseases; be involved in, and injured from, fights; take illicit drugs or smoke cigarettes; indulge in 'dare-type' behaviours; and take less care by walking home alone or getting into the car of a drink-driver or stranger (Jones et al., 2007; Newburn and Shiner, 2001).

The updated Scottish *Plan for Action on Alcohol Problems* (Scottish Executive, 2007) states that drinking among children is associated with a range of problems such as accidents, anti-social behaviour, truancy and poor educational attainment, as well as longer-term harms. Evidence suggests that 10 to 15-year-olds who have been drunk once or more a month in the past year were over twice as likely to commit an offence as those who had not (Wilson *et al.*, 2005). Among 15-year-olds who first drank alcohol at 10 years or younger, 17 per cent report having taken Class A drugs at the age of 14, compared with 2 per cent of those who first drank when they were 14 years old (Advisory Council on the Misuse of Drugs, 2006). Nearly 10,000 children aged 11 to 17 are admitted to hospital each year in the UK as a result of their alcohol consumption (Chief Medical Officers of England, Wales and Northern Ireland, 2009). Data for 2007–8 from the National Drug Treatment Monitoring System in England indicate that 8,589 young people under 18 years received specialist treatment for a primary alcohol problem. This is just over one-third of the total receiving treatment for alcohol or drug problems in that time (NTA, 2009).

Contrary to the discourse of professionals, young people who drink to get drunk only rarely consider 'harm' as an outcome of drinking, and balance the risks of extreme drinking with the desire to have a good time with their friends, in a way that has been described as 'calculated hedonism' (Szmigin *et al.*, 2008). Many young people see extreme drinking in friendship groups as a normal part of their brief journey through adolescence, which they will abandon as they get older:

> Problematic alcohol consumption was associated with drinking alone, so in most cases the group-based nature of our participants' drinking insulated them against the possibility that they (or their friends) might be an 'alcy'.
>
> (Griffin *et al.*, 2008: 2)

Risk factors for problematic alcohol use

Figure 6.1 summarises the most commonly cited individual, familial and environmental risk factors for problematic alcohol use. Early age of onset of alcohol consumption and parental or familial use of alcohol (Velleman *et al.*, 2005) are the most commonly cited factors associated with alcohol use and subsequent related problems among young people. In recent years there has been an increasing trend among UK adults toward home-based alcohol consumption, and family practices governing when and how much young people can drink appear to vary greatly (DCSF, 2008). School pupils' propensity to drink reflects their beliefs about their families' attitudes to their drinking, and children tend to follow their parents' consumption patterns. Among parents who never drink, 10 per cent have children who drink regularly, while among parents who drink three or more times a week, 31 per cent have children who

Early age of onset of consumption

Parental approval of drinking, or lax rules and discipline associated with drinking

Use and modelling of drinking by other family members

Living with parental alcohol misuse. Genetic susceptibility if parent(s) have alcohol problems/dependency

Family structure, e.g. permanent separation from a biological parent

Childhood physical/sexual abuse

Other parental psychopathology such as mental health problems

Socio-economic status, living in areas of high social deprivation

Parental education and economic/employment status

Use of other substances

Childhood conduct problems, truancy, deviant/offending behaviour, aggression

Mental health problems, e.g. depression, anxiety, ADHD, sleeping problems

Personality characteristics, e.g. sensation seeking, poor coping, low social competence

School-related factors, including low aspiration, low functioning/achievement, truancy, bullying

Peer influence – drinking, use of other substances, peer relations, quality and reciprocity of the friendship

Unsupervised drinking and/or drinking in public places

Lack of religious affiliation

Night time economy factors

Media exposure and imagery

Figure 6.1 Risk factors for young people's problematic use of alcohol

drink frequently (Harrington, 2000). Fuller (2007) found that 11 to 15-year-old pupils whose families did not mind them drinking as long as they did not drink too much were around three and a half times more likely to have drunk in the previous seven days, compared with pupils whose families did not like them to drink. Young people whose families let them drink as much as they liked were over nine times as likely to have drunk alcohol in the previous seven days. Of the young people who drank 14 or more units in the previous week, 48 per cent reported being given alcohol directly by their parents whilst 42 per cent admitted taking it without their parents' consent.

Protective factors

It is increasingly recognised that not everyone is at the same risk of experiencing alcohol-related harm. A clearer picture is emerging of protective factors, both general and specific, which operate at the individual, family or wider environmental levels. Separately or together, these protective factors are believed to promote 'resilience', and there are a number of indicators for resilience to alcohol-related problems (Velleman and Templeton, 2007).

Protective factors can influence the initiation of consumption and subsequent levels and patterns of consumption, as well as future exposure to risk. Importantly, it is not necessarily the case that a protective factor is simply the absence of, or opposite of, a risk factor. Protective factors include, but are not confined to, individual characteristics and family-related factors (e.g. Velleman *et al.*, 2005); a young person's involvement in community activities, sport or other diversionary activities; government policy measures to control use (Mistral, 2009); and the role of educational establishments. Being part of a non-white, minority ethnic group has also been identified as a protective factor against excessive or problematic alcohol consumption (Fuller, 2008).

Family factors are believed to be a particularly important set of protective influences. Seven familial domains have been defined: relations versus structure, cohesion, communication, behaviour modelling, management, supervision and the influence of parents and peers (Velleman *et al.*, 2005). Velleman *et al.* (2005) conclude that the relational aspects of families (e.g. cohesion, discipline, communication) seem to have a much greater influence than structural aspects (e.g. single-parent families, family size, birth order) in how children learn about alcohol. More specifically, it is believed that family-related characteristics such as stability of care, consistency, safety, lack of conflict and positive family harmony are more important for younger children. With increasing age, the domains of school, peers and other external factors become more influential. It has been recommended that consideration should be given to work with families before young people are first introduced to alcohol:

> In general, results [. . .] showed that providing clear alcohol-specific rules lowers the likelihood of drinking initiation, regardless of the age of the youngsters. Once adolescents have established a drinking pattern, the impact of parental alcohol-specific rules declined or even disappeared.
>
> (Van Der Vorst *et al.*, 2007: 1064)

The UK Government response to alcohol-related harm

Interventions for problematic alcohol use among young people have been developed to operate at the individual, school, family and community levels; and to be delivered through a number of avenues, including the education sector, the family, the media, the alcohol industry and peer groups. The UK Government response to alcohol use in young people has become increasingly visible, grounded in the five core outcomes of the *Every Child Matters* agenda

(HMSO, 2003), namely being healthy, staying safe, enjoying and achieving, making a positive contribution, and economic well-being. However, each of the devolved administrations in England, Scotland, Wales and Northern Ireland has its own individual strategy tailored to local circumstances (Chief Medical Officers of England, Wales and Northern Ireland, 2009). For example, young people under 18 years, binge drinkers aged 18 to 24 years and harmful drinkers are target groups in the revised English national alcohol strategy, *Safe, Sensible, Social*, whilst the *Children's Plan*, the *Youth Alcohol Action Plan* and the *Youth Matters Review* all include a focus on the management of alcohol use. In Scotland, for example, a *Youth Commission on Alcohol and Young People* has been established. The prevention of misuse and harm in young people is also central to the Welsh Substance Misuse Strategy 2008–18 (Welsh Assembly Government, 2008).

Importantly, within this raft of policy initiatives there is a move towards recognition of the existence of a complex problem which needs to be tackled by involving a range of different sectors within the community. For example, alongside enforcement of laws relating to sales to under-age young people, the *Youth Alcohol Action Plan* (DCSF *et al.*, 2008) also promises to take action regarding young people drinking in public places; work with the alcohol industry and young people; develop a national consensus in relation to young people and alcohol; develop partnerships with parents; and support young people to make sensible choices about alcohol.

The role of schools

In the UK, alcohol harm prevention in schools is often part of wider drugs education, and aims to intervene with young people well before patterns of regular drinking become established. All young people need to be informed about the harm that can result from excessive use of alcohol, and the reach of school-based programmes can be high because of the availability of captive audiences. However, a great deal of research over many years has shown that although school-based *information* programmes can increase knowledge and change attitudes, alcohol use remains largely unaffected (Anderson and Baumberg, 2006; Elder *et al.*, 2005). It has been suggested that the emphasis and mode of delivery of substance use education programmes have often been too narrow, and a review by the Advisory Council on the Misuse of Drugs (2006) reported that school-based interventions often fail because the information is out of date, and staff ill-prepared to deliver such lessons. Subsequently, a report by the Advisory Group on Drug and Alcohol Education (2008) recommended that parents' knowledge and skills about drug and alcohol education and prevention should be enhanced; that the quality of drug and alcohol education should be improved by inclusion in Personal, Social and Health Education (PSHE) and making this a statutory subject; and schools and colleges should be supported to better identify and intervene early with young people who are particularly vulnerable to substance misuse. A review of PSHE, ordered by the UK Government, was due to be published in April 2009.

As well as providing information, *multi-component* interventions aim to enhance the social and problem-solving skills of young people, include interventions which engage the wider family, and appear to be more effective in reducing alcohol use and alcohol-related problems. The National Institute for Health and Clinical Excellence (NICE, 2007a) recommends that schools should ensure alcohol education is an integral part of the national science and PSHE curriculum, taking into account different age groups and learning needs in line with guidance from the Department for Children, Schools and Families. Schools should aim to encourage children not to drink; to delay the age at which young people start drinking; and to reduce the harm it can cause among those who do drink. Education programmes should increase knowledge of the potential physical, mental and social damage alcohol use can cause; provide opportunities to explore attitudes to, and perceptions of, alcohol use; help develop self-esteem, decision-making, assertiveness and coping skills; and increase awareness of how the media, advertisements, role models and the views of parents, peers and society can influence alcohol consumption. Schools should also seek to reduce harm among those who do drink by offering brief, one-to-one advice on the harmful effects of alcohol use and, where appropriate, referring pupils to external services.

NICE (2007a) recommends the adoption of a 'whole school' approach, involving staff, parents and pupils in the development of policy in the school environment, as well as professional development of, and support for, staff. Where appropriate, parents or carers should be offered information about where they can get help to develop their parenting skills, including problem-solving and communication skills, advice on setting boundaries for their children, and teaching them how to resist peer pressure. Recommendations also include the need to maintain and develop partnerships with children's services, primary care trusts, drug and alcohol action teams, crime and disorder reduction partnerships, youth services, drug and alcohol services, the police and community organisations. These partnerships should support alcohol education in schools, and ensure school programmes and interventions on alcohol use are integrated with community activities introduced as part of the *Children's Plan* (DCSF, 2008).

Hence, there is an emerging consensus for the value of a multi-component approach. This more programmatic style of intervention comprises a range of elements targeting different spheres (e.g. school, family, alcohol industry), and involving multiple stakeholders framed within locally developed strategies evolving from national directives. Some work has summarised the key features of such programmes (Cuijpers, 2003; Thom and Bayley, 2007; Wagner et al., 2004), and it has been suggested that the effectiveness of schools-based initiatives can be enhanced if they are part of such multi-component programmes.

Examples of school-based programmes

One example of a multi-component school-based initiative in England is *Blueprint* (Baker, 2006). Led by three government departments, a pilot programme was launched in 2003 in 23 secondary schools. *Blueprint* aims to target several risk and protective factors in order to slow the rate of substance use during early adolescence, and reduce the harm caused. *Blueprint* has five integral parts:

1 *Schools*: Fifteen lessons are given over a two-year period, using a 'normative' approach to show to pupils that rates and approval of substance use are lower than they think, and to consider social influence within peer groups and the media.
2 *Parents*: Materials have been specifically designed to involve parents in the programme, and parenting skills workshops are offered.
3 *Community*: Coordination with other organisations working in a similar field seeks to create a coherent preventive approach.
4 *Media*: Efforts are made to raise awareness of *Blueprint* and its key messages in the surrounding communities.
5 *Policy*: Efforts are made to develop local strategies to reduce the supply of alcohol, tobacco and volatile substances.

Another UK example of a multi-component initiative is *Positive Futures*, a national social inclusion programme working with schools and other community organisations, using sport, arts, leisure and educational activities to engage disadvantaged and socially marginalised young people. *Positive Futures* aims to deliver more cohesive communities, greater participation in sport, and reductions in crime, disorder and substance misuse (Talbot and Crabbe, 2008).

The most widely implemented and promising school-based prevention programme in Europe is the *Healthy School and Drugs Project* (HSDP) used in over two-thirds of Dutch secondary schools. This high level of implementation has been achieved by involving schools closely in the development of the intervention and by building strong relationships with local prevention specialists and local authorities (Cuijpers *et al.*, 2002). The HSDP involves a coordinating committee of representatives from school staff, local health services and parents; the involvement of parents in formulation of school policy on substance use; identification of pupils with problems and provision of appropriate support; and nine teacher-led sessions including interactive activities and videos for all 12 to 15-year-olds, delivered over three years. The first three lessons are on tobacco; the next three are on alcohol; and the final three in the third year are on marijuana, ecstasy and gambling. The first lesson of each group gives basic information about the substance, while the second and third sessions focus on attitudes, behaviours and training in making choices, refusal skills and increasing self-esteem. Evaluation has shown a reduced prevalence of alcohol use at the end of three years, although effects were less pronounced among those who disliked school.

In Perth, Western Australia, the *School Health and Alcohol Harm Reduction Project* (SHAHRP: McBride, 2008) was initially undertaken in six schools, involving 1,111 students, while 1,232 students in eight other schools acted as a comparison group. Core components of SHAHRP included teacher training, a teacher manual, student workbooks and video. The first phase, implemented at age 13 years (Talbot and Crabbe's 'tipping point'), consisted of 17 skill-based activities conducted over eight to ten lessons. The second phase comprised 12 activities delivered over five to seven weeks. Student interaction was emphasised and included delivery of information, skill rehearsal, individual and small group decision making, and discussions based on scenarios suggested by students, all focused on identifying and reducing alcohol-related harm. Evaluation demonstrated that participating students, compared with the control group who received generic alcohol education, had greater alcohol-related knowledge, consumed less alcohol and experienced less alcohol-related harm. Follow-up evaluation suggested that the impact on harm was maintained, although the impact on alcohol consumption itself weakened over time (McBride, 2008).

Thinking family

In recent years, a wealth of research has highlighted the pivotal role that families play as both a risk for, but also a protection against, alcohol-related problems (Velleman *et al.*, 2005). Guidance issued by the Chief Medical Officers of England, Wales and Northern Ireland (2009) suggests that advice should be made available to parents and carers on young people's alcohol use, and that more targeted support, including structured parenting training groups, should be provided at a local level to meet the needs of families facing additional difficulties. The initiatives described below show that schools can play a very important part in delivering advice, support and skills training.

Foxcroft *et al.* (2003), in a systematic review of 56 studies of initiatives for the prevention of alcohol use in young people, reported the *Strengthening Families Programme* (SFP: Spoth *et al.*, 2001) in the USA as the most promising, with positive outcomes in both the short and the long term. The SFP has been widely implemented in schools, as well as family and youth service agencies, community mental health centres, substance misuse treatment centres, and prisons. The programme comprises seven two-hour sessions for parents and children, separated for the first hour and then together in supervised activities. Four booster sessions, six months to one year later, reinforce the skills gained. Youth sessions focus on goal setting, dealing with stress and strong emotions, communication, responsible behaviour, and dealing with peer pressure. Parents discuss the importance of nurturing while, at the same time, setting rules, monitoring compliance and applying appropriate discipline to protect against substance use. Promising findings from the application of this model to the UK context have now been reported (Coombes *et al.*, 2009).

Two other multi-component family interventions in the USA appear positive. The *Seattle Social Development Program* (Hawkins *et al.*, 1999) involves both classroom instruction and parent interventions. Over five years, starting in their first year of school, children receive training in cognitive, social and problem-solving skills, including communication, decision-making, negotiation and conflict resolution. Parents receive an annual offer of training workshops appropriate to the developmental level of their child. In an area with a low-income, multi-ethnic population, this has been found to reduce heavy drinking at age 18 years.

Linking the Interests of Families and Teachers (LIFT: Eddy *et al.*, 2003) is also a classroom-based programme for primary-age children comprising both child social and problem-solving skills training and parent management training, and targeting substance misuse alongside other problematic behaviours. Implemented among mainly white populations in areas with high youth crime, four years after completion young people who did not do the programme were more likely to report regular drinking of alcohol than those who had done LIFT.

What can teachers and schools do?

Responding to alcohol use and alcohol-related harm is not reducible to resolution in one area. There is no one thing that a teacher or other school professional can do. However, there are a number of activities which might be useful to consider depending on local circumstances and resources.

One area of activity includes awareness and implementation of national guidance (for example, Chief Medical Officers of England, Wales and Northern Ireland, 2009; DfES, 2004; NICE, 2007b). It is the responsibility of all schools, on their own and in partnership with other local stakeholders, to consider how best to integrate the details of such guidance into their PSHE agendas and other curricula. Further, schools can ensure that they are active members of local, multi-agency partnerships which are endeavouring to development intervention strategies in their areas. Through this, schools can find out what is on offer in their area and become involved in the development and implementation of initiatives. Encouraging the establishment of multi-component programmes, such as those mentioned above, may be a useful starting point (although the transferability of initiatives from other countries will need to be carefully considered). Ensuring that staff are adequately and regularly trained to deliver these messages will be a key consideration.

Another area of activity is to ensure that each school has a library of easily accessible information resources for students, teachers and parents. This information should include leaflets, phone numbers of local organisations, and website addresses (for example, *talktofrank*, which is a national website about drug use aimed at young people).

Finally, it is important to remember that all school personnel have a pastoral responsibility to the children in their care for the duration of their engagement in primary and secondary education. For some young people, alcohol misuse will be a problem in its own right, whereas for others it will be a symptom of other problems which the young person is experiencing (for example, bullying, ill health or problems at home). School policy should not judge alcohol use by a pupil as punishable misconduct, but teachers and other school personnel should be sufficiently trained and knowledgeable to feel confident in approaching pupils to help them understand the risks of alcohol use, and to offer skills training, advice and support in overcoming any ignorance, pressures or problems which might be pushing them towards excessive use of alcohol.

Conclusion

Many young people do not drink alcohol or do not experience any adverse consequences if they do. Further, many young people who do drink will respond positively to attempts made by schools, in partnership with parents and community organisations, to provide information, skills training and support which could reduce the likelihood of problematic alcohol consumption and negative consequences. As many formative years are spent in the education sector, schools have a crucial role to play in harm prevention and in the broad multi-component initiatives which are now recognised as the way forward in reducing alcohol-related harm.

Notes

1 There is ongoing debate as to how to define 'binge' drinking. Some define it according to the number of drinks or units which are consumed during a drinking episode, whilst others define or measure it more subjectively according to subsequent drunkenness or the presence of other problems. The definition commonly used in many research studies is 'five consecutive drinks in one sitting more than three times in the last thirty days', suggested by Midanik (1999), while others use 8 or more units in a single session for men and 6 or more for women. For an exploration of this confused concept, see Herring *et al.* (2008). However, for the most part such definitions are relative to adult levels of drinking/problems; there are as yet no suggested levels of 'non-binge' or 'sensible' drinking by children or young people.
2 More information on this project can be found at www.espad.org (accessed 12 March 2009).
3 Risks in this case are defined as the predictors, related to both alcohol consumption and situational factors, which, if present, increase the likelihood of a young person drinking or drinking problematically. Harms are defined as the negative consequences of such use of alcohol.

References

Academy of Medical Sciences (2004) *Calling Time: The Nation's Drinking as a Major Public Health Issue*. London: Academy of Medical Sciences. Online. Available at www.acmedsci.ac.uk (accessed 12 March 2009).

Advisory Council on the Misuse of Drugs (2006) *Pathways to Problems: Hazardous Use of Tobacco, Alcohol and Other Drugs by Young People in the UK and Its Implications for Policy*. London: Advisory Council on the Misuse of Drugs.

Advisory Group on Drug and Alcohol Education (2008) *Drug Education: An Entitlement for All*. A report to the Government by the Advisory Group on Drug and Alcohol Education. Online. Available at http://publications.dcsf.gov.uk/eOrderingDownload/Advisory%20Group%20Report%20-%20Drug%20&%20Alcohol%20Education%20Review.pdf (accessed 12 March 2009).

Anderson, P. and Baumberg, B. (2006) *Alcohol in Europe: A Public Health Perspective. A Report for the European Commission*. London: Institute of Alcohol Studies.

Baker, P. J. (2006) 'Developing a Blueprint for evidence-based drug prevention in England', *Drugs: Education Prevention and Policy*, 13(1): 17–32.

Brain, K., Parker, H. and Carnwath, T. (2000) 'Drinking with design: Young drinkers as psychoactive consumers', *Drugs: Education, Prevention and Policy*, 7(1): 5–20.

Chief Medical Officers of England, Wales and Northern Ireland (2009) *Draft Guidance on the Consumption of Alcohol by Children and Young People from the Chief Medical Officers of England, Wales and Northern Ireland*. London: Department for Children, Schools and Families.

Coleman, L. and Cater, S. (2005) 'Underage "binge" drinking: A qualitative study into motivations and outcomes', *Drugs: Education, Prevention and Policy*, 12(2): 125–136.

Coombes, L., Allen, D., Marsh, M. and Foxcroft, D. (2009) 'The Strengthening Families Programme (SFP) 10–14 and substance misuse in Barnsley: The perspectives of facilitators and families', *Child Abuse Review*, 18: 41–59.

Cuijpers, P. (2003) 'Three decades of drug prevention research', *Drugs: Education, Prevention and Policy*, 10(1): 7–20.

Cuijpers, P., Jonkers, R., de Weerdt, I. and de Jong, A. (2002) 'The effects of drug abuse prevention at school: The "Healthy School and Drugs" project', *Addiction* 97(1): 67–73.

Department for Children, Schools and Families (DCSF) (2008) *The Children's Plan: Building Brighter Futures – Summary*. London: The Stationery Office.

Department for Children, Schools and Families (DCSF), the Home Office and the Department of Health (2008) *Youth Alcohol Action Plan*. London: The Stationery Office.

Department for Education and Skills (DfES) (2004) *Drugs: Guidance for Schools*. Nottingham: DfES Publications.

Department of Health (2005) *Alcohol Needs Assessment Research Project (ANARP): The 2004 National Alcohol Needs Assessment for England*. London: Department of Health.

Eddy, J. M., Reid, J. B., Stoolmiller, M. and Fetrow, R. (2003) 'Outcomes during middle school for an elementary school-based preventive intervention for conduct problems: Follow-up results from a randomized trial', *Behavior Therapy*, 34(4): 535–552.

Elder, R. W., Nichols, J. L., Shults, R. A., Sleet, D. A., Barrios, L. C. and Compton, R. (2005) 'Effectiveness of school-based programs for reducing drinking and driving and riding with drinking drivers: A systematic review', *American Journal of Preventive Medicine*, 28(5): 288–304.

Foxcroft, D., Ireland, D., Lister-Sharp, D., Lowe, G. and Breen, R. (2003) 'Longer-term primary prevention for alcohol misuse in young people: A systematic review', *Addiction*, 98(4): 397–411.

Fuller, E. (2007) *Smoking, Drinking and Drug Use among Young People in England in 2006*. London: National Centre for Social Research, National Foundation for Educational Research.

Fuller, E. (ed.) (2008) *Drug Use, Smoking and Drinking among Young People in England in 2007*. London: National Centre for Social Research, National Foundation for Educational Research.

Griffin, C., Szmigin, I., Hackley, C., Mistral, W., Bengrey-Howell, A., Clark, D. and Weale, L. (2008) *Branded Consumption and Social Identification: Young People and Alcohol*. Milton Keynes: ESRC Identities and Social Action Programme. Online. Available at www.open.ac.uk/socialsciences/identities/findings/Griffin.pdf (accessed 12 March 2009).

Harrington, V. (2000) *Underage Drinking: Findings from the 1998–99 Youth Lifestyles Survey*. Home Office Research, Development and Statistics Directorate Research Findings No. 125. London: Home Office.

Hawkins, J. D., Catalano, R. F., Kosterman, R., Abbott, R. and Hill, K. G. (1999) 'Preventing adolescent health-risk behaviors by strengthening protection during childhood', *Archives of Pediatrics & Adolescent Medicine*, 153(3): 226–234.

Herring, R., Berridge, V. and Thom, B. (2008) 'Binge drinking: An exploration of a confused concept', *Journal of Epidemiology and Community Health*, 62: 476–479.

Hibell, B., Anderson, B., Bjarnason, T., Ahlstrom, S., Balakireva, O., Kokkevi, A. and Morgan, M. (2004) *The ESPAD Report 2003: Alcohol and Other Drugs Use among Students in 35 European Countries*. Stockholm: Swedish Council on Information on Alcohol and Other Drugs.

HMSO – Her Majesty's Stationery Office (2003) *Every Child Matters*. Crown Copyright. Cm 5860. Norwich: The Stationery Office.

Jones, L., James, M., Jefferson, T., Lushey, C., Morleo, M., Stokes, M., Sumnal, H., Witty, K. and Belis, M. (2007) *A Review of the Effectiveness and Cost-Effectiveness of Interventions Delivery in Primary and Secondary Schools to Prevent and/or Reduce Alcohol Use by Young People under 18 Years Old: Final Report*. London: National Institute for Health and Clinical Excellence.

Lynch, S. (2008) 'Drinking alcohol', in E. Fuller (ed.) *Drug Use, Smoking and Drinking among Young People in England in 2007*. London: Office for National Statistics.

McBride, N. (2008) *International Bulletin: The School Health and Alcohol Harm Reduction Project (SHAHRP). An Evidence-Based Program to Reduce Alcohol Related Harm in Young People*. Perth: National Drug Research Institute, Curtin University.

Martinic, M. and Measham, F. (eds) (2008) *Swimming with Crocodiles: The Culture of Extreme Drinking*. International Center for Alcohol Policies: Series on Alcohol in Society. New York: Routledge.

Measham, F. (2007) 'The turning tides of intoxication: Young people's drinking in Britain in the 2000s', *Health Education*, 108(3): 207–222.

Midanik, L. (1999) 'Drunkenness, feeling the effects and 5+ measures', *Addiction*, 94: 887–897.

Mistral, W. (2009) *Effectiveness of National Policies and Initiatives to Reduce Alcohol-Related Harm among Young People*. Paper prepared for the Young People and Alcohol Project. London: Thomas Coram Research Unit, Institute of Education, University of London/Department for Children, Schools and Families.

Newburn, T. and Shiner, M. (2001) *Teenage Kicks? Young People and Alcohol: A Review of the Literature*. York: Public Policy Research Unit for the Joseph Rowntree Foundation.

Newbury-Birch, D., Walker, J., Avery, L., Beyer, F., Brown, N., Jackson, K., Lock, C. A., McGovern, R., Kaner, E., Gilvarry, E., McArdle, P., Ramesh, V. and Stewart, S. (2009) *The Impact of Alcohol Consumption on Young People: A Systematic Review of Published Reviews*. Research Report No. DCSF-R067 for the Department for Children, Schools and Families. Online. Available at www.dcsf.gov.uk/research/data/uploadfiles/DCSF-RR067.pdf (accessed 12 March 2009).

NICE – National Institute for Health and Clinical Excellence (2007a) *Interventions in Schools to Prevent and Reduce Alcohol Use among Children and Young People. NICE Public Health Guidance 7*. London: National Institute for Health and Clinical Excellence.

NICE – National Institute for Health and Clinical Excellence (2007b) *Interventions to Reduce Substance Misuse among Vulnerable Young People. NICE Public Health Intervention Guidance 4: Quick Reference Guide*. London: National Institute for Health and Clinical Excellence.

NTA – National Treatment Agency for Substance Misuse (2009) *Getting to Grips with Substance Misuse among Young People: The Data for 2007/08*. London: National Institute for Health and Clinical Excellence.

Ofsted (2008) *TellUs3 National Report*. London: Ofsted. Online. Available at www.ofsted.gov.uk/Ofsted-home/Publications-and-research/Browse-all-by/Documents-by-type/Statistics/TellUs3-National-Report (accessed 12 March 2009).

Scottish Executive (2007) *Plan for Action on Alcohol Problems: Update*. Produced by R. R. Donnelley, B43835 02/07. Edinburgh: Scottish Executive.

Sheehan, M. and Ridge, D. (2001) '"You become really close . . . you talk about silly things you did, and we laugh." The role of binge drinking in female secondary students' lives', *Substance Use and Misuse*, 36(3): 347–372.

Spoth, R. L., Redmond, C., Trudeau, L. and Shin, C. (2001) 'Longitudinal substance initiation outcomes for a universal preventive intervention combining family and school programs', *Psychology of Addictive Behaviors*, 16: 129–134.

Szmigin, I., Griffin, C., Mistral, W., Bengry-Howell, A., Weale, L. and Hackley, C. (2008) 'Re-framing "binge-drinking" as calculated hedonism: Empirical evidence from the UK', *International Journal of Drug Policy*, 19: 359–366.

Talbot, S. and Crabbe, T. (2008) *Binge Drinking: Young People's Attitudes and Behaviour*. London: Crime Concern.

Templeton, L. (2009) *Alcohol-Related Problems Facing Young People in England: Risks, Harms and Protective Factors*. Paper prepared for the Young People and Alcohol Project. London: Thomas Coram Research Unit, Institute of Education, University of London.

Thom, B. and Bayley, M. (2007) *Multi-component Programmes: An Approach to Prevent and Reduce Alcohol-Related Harm*. York: Joseph Rowntree Foundation.

Van Der Vorst, H., Engels, R., Dekovic, M., Meeus, W. and Vermulst, A. (2007) 'Alcohol-specific rules, personality and adolescents' alcohol use: A longitudinal person–environment study', *Addiction*, 102(7): 1064–1075.

Velleman, R. (2009) *How do children learn about alcohol?* York: Joseph Rowntree Foundation.

Velleman, R. and Templeton, L. (2007) 'Understanding and modifying the impact of parents' substance misuse on children', *Advances in Psychiatric Treatment*, 13: 79–89.

Velleman, R., Templeton, L. and Copello, A. (2005) 'The role of the family in preventing and intervening with substance use and misuse: A comprehensive review of family interventions, with a focus on young people', *Drug and Alcohol Review*, 24: 93–109.

Viner, R. M. and Taylor, B. (2007) 'Adult outcomes of binge drinking in adolescence: Findings from a UK national birth cohort', *Journal of Epidemiology and Community Health*, 61: 902–907.

Wagner, E., Tubman, J. and Gil, A. (2004) 'Implementing school-based substance abuse interventions: Methodological dilemmas and recommended solutions', *Addiction*, 99(S2): 106–119.

Welsh Assembly Government (2008) *Working Together to Reduce Harm: The Substance Misuse Strategy for Wales 2008–2018*. Cardiff: Welsh Assembly Government.

Wilson, D., Sharp, C. and Patterson, A. (2005) *Young People and Crime: Findings from the 2005 Offending, Crime and Justice Survey*. London: Home Office.

Chapter 7

The role of schools in drug education and wider substance misuse prevention

Martine Stead and Robert Stradling

Education in schools is a major plank of the current drug prevention strategy in the UK. By informing young people about the risks of substance misuse and equipping them with skills to deal with drug-offer situations, schools are expected to play a leading role in protecting children and young people from substance-related harm. However, this can be a difficult issue for schools to address, and guidance is needed on how to deliver engaging and effective drug education. This chapter examines the evidence base for effective curricular and whole school approaches to substance misuse, looks at some of the conflicting expectations surrounding school-based drug education, and argues for a more realistic assessment of schools' role within broader substance misuse prevention efforts. The focus is on illicit substances, although we make reference to tobacco and alcohol where appropriate.

Young people and substance use

Young people grow up in a society in which the use of potentially harmful substances is widespread, and most forms of substance use, including smoking, begin in adolescence. Substance use by children and young people can harm the healthy development of the body, brain and behaviour, and can contribute to suicide, homicide, injuries, poisoning and the spread of infectious diseases (Toumbourou *et al.*, 2007). There are also social and legal consequences for young people, such as restrictions on work and travel as a result of conviction for possession.

In 2007, 17 per cent of 11–15-year-olds in England said they had taken illegal drugs in the last year and 10 per cent that they had taken them in the last month; among 15-year-olds, the proportions were 31 per cent and 17 per cent (Fuller, 2008). Most of this drug use is accounted for by cannabis, tried or used by 22.7 per cent of 15-year-olds in 2006 (AGDAE, 2008). The prevalence of drug use is similar among boys and girls, and increases with age. Pupils of mixed and Asian ethnicity are more likely than white pupils to have taken drugs in the last month, but there are no differences by ethnicity for drug use in the last year (Fuller *et al.*, 2008). Levels of cannabis use are broadly similar across all the countries of the UK, but vary widely across Europe (for example, from 3 per cent to 30 per cent in 2005/2006) (Currie *et al.*, 2008).

However, it is important to set young people's substance use in context. Illegal drug use is infrequent, with only 5 per cent of pupils overall taking drugs once a month or more (Fuller, 2008). In 2007, no single Class A[1] drug had been taken by more than 2 per cent of 11–15-year-olds in the previous year. Moreover, the overall trend in use, for both legal and illegal substances, is downwards. The proportion of young people who had tried drugs at least once fell from 29 per cent in 2001 to 25 per cent in 2007, and there were similar falls in the proportions of pupils who had taken drugs in the last year and the last month. Fewer young people – 36 per cent – reported being offered drugs in 2007, compared with 42 per cent in 2001 (Fuller, 2008).

This downward trend may be attributable to various factors, including changes in social norms, drug re-classification, media campaigns, news coverage, drug education in schools,[2] or a combination of all of these. What the trend confirms is the importance of continuing to inform and educate about drugs and of continuing to provide young people with the skills to deal with drug-offer situations.

Schools as a setting for drug education

Since the early 1980s, schools have been seen to have an important role to play in the implementation of national drug prevention strategies (Department for Education and Skills, 2004). There have been a number of reasons for this. First, schools offer the most systematic and efficient way of reaching almost all young people (Faggiano *et al.*, 2005). Second, four out of five drug users try various substances before the onset of adulthood (Faggiano *et al.*, 2008). Third, the early initiation into drug use is a good predictor of later dependency (Agrawal *et al.*, 2004; Gfroerer *et al.*, 2002). Fourth, peer group influence is an important factor in persuading young people to start to use various substances and continue using them (Hall and Valente, 2007). Finally, since schools have a duty of care which includes creating a safe and healthy environment for pupils and staff alike, they are also required to take appropriate action if pupils or others bring potentially harmful substances on to school sites.

While the main focus in development and evaluation has been on the contribution that schools can make to primary drug prevention programmes – that is, those which are universal and aimed at non-users – there has been a recent and growing recognition that schools can also make a contribution to secondary prevention programmes aimed at young people who have tried drugs or who are generally more vulnerable and in need of additional support from children's services (UNODCCP, 2003).

How effective is school drug education?

Several reviews have brought together evidence on the effectiveness of drug education programmes (e.g. Faggiano *et al.*, 2008; Tobler and Stratton, 1997; Tobler *et al.*, 2000; White and Pitts, 1998). Effectiveness is usually measured in terms of substance use outcomes – age of first use, regular use – and sometimes also impact on mediating variables, such as skills, norms and knowledge, which are known to be protective against, or to increase the risk of, drug use. Many reviews also compare different *approaches* to drug education, typically summarised as 'skills-based' programmes, 'affective' programmes and 'knowledge-based' programmes (Stead and Angus, 2004). Broadly speaking, 'skills-based' approaches are those which teach young people to deal with direct and indirect social influences from peers and the media. They usually include a focus on resistance skills – skills to deal with drug-offer situations – and normative education, which seeks to correct young people's tendency to overestimate the extent of drug use by their peers and to show that not using drugs is acceptable and normal behaviour (Botvin, 2000; Donaldson *et al.*, 1994; Hansen, 1992). 'Affective' approaches, on the other hand, which were particularly popular in the 1980s, were based on an assumption that drug use results from low self-esteem and sought to enhance personal and social development. 'Knowledge-based' approaches assume that increased knowledge of the consequences of drug use will deter young people from using them.

As with any kind of evidence, there are problems with assessing effectiveness, including discrepancies between individual studies in their methods and measures, insufficient sample sizes, lack of appropriate control or comparison groups, and so on. There are also difficulties in comparing different approaches because many programmes, particularly since the 1990s, have combined elements of several different approaches. Despite these limitations, there is reasonable consensus from the evidence that some drug education programmes can impact on uptake, age of onset and prevalence of substance use, at least in the short term. Not all programmes are effective, however, and a small minority of programmes have counter-productive effects. It is also clear that interactive drug education programmes are nearly always more effective than non-interactive programmes (e.g. Tobler and Stratton, 1997; Tobler *et al.*, 1999, 2000). Likewise, skills-based approaches are more effective than affective and knowledge-based approaches (Faggiano *et al.*, 2008; Thomas, 2004; Tobler and Stratton, 1997). Indeed, one of the few programmes to show consistent and moderately long-lasting effects is Life Skills Training (Botvin *et al.*, 1990, 2000), consisting of three components: drug resistance skills for dealing with peer and media pressure to engage in substance use; personal self-management skills such as setting goals, analysing problems and making decisions; and general social skills such as effective communication and making or refusing requests.

Affective approaches are generally ineffective in terms of drug use behaviour, although there is some evidence of effects on 'mediating variables' – that is, factors which are associated with a greater likelihood of progressing to or desisting from substance use, such as drug knowledge, attitudes and self-efficacy (Faggiano et al., 2008; Tobler, 1986; Tobler et al., 1999). Drug education programmes which are primarily designed to give information about the negative consequences of drugs are generally less effective than other approaches at influencing drug use behaviour (Faggiano et al., 2008; Rundall and Bruvold, 1988; Thomas, 2004; Tobler, 1986). However, information provision can form part of the curriculum in effective programmes (e.g. Lister-Sharp et al., 1999; White and Pitts, 1998). The key factor seems to be that programmes relying only on knowledge-giving are unlikely to change behaviour.

Although much is now known about the various approaches likely to be effective, the design of appropriate curricula is not an exact science. The ways in which these approaches are translated into lessons and learning activities, the amount of exposure necessary, the structure and sequence of the lessons and activities, the appropriateness of the language level employed and so forth are decisions which are still relatively untested (Stradling et al., 2008). Most UK school drug education programmes are allocated fewer hours than is typical of the best-evaluated drug education curricula. This raises important practical questions about whether sufficient time is being allocated to enable evidence-based approaches to have the desired impact.

Commentators draw differing conclusions from the evidence on drug education effectiveness. The Advisory Council on the Misuse of Drugs noted in September 2006:

> The extensive published research on school-based preventive initiatives makes disappointing reading. While many of the evaluations were poorly designed, those that were conducted to an acceptable standard found that even carefully designed, resourced and implemented programmes resulted in, at best, small and short-lived delays in the use of tobacco, alcohol or other drugs by pupils.
>
> (ACMD, 2006: 81)

Other reviewers and commentators are more optimistic. Faggiano and colleagues in the USA conclude their review: 'Despite these limits, the review suggested a consistent pattern of results: school-based programs based on life skills seem the most effective in reducing incidence of drug use' (Faggiano et al., 2008: 394). From an analysis of results from four randomised controlled trials involving over 7,000 pupils, they suggest that implementing such programmes would result in around 3.3 per cent of young people refraining from trying marijuana. White and Pitts' (1998) meta-analysis suggests that the proportion of young people who would be persuaded against early drug use by drug education programmes is around 3.7 per cent. They note that, while this seems a small effect size, in a pharmaceutical trial it would be considered sufficient evidence that a treatment can work. Nearly all reviewers, however, caution that effects do not generally last beyond the short term.

Any discussion about the value of school drug education needs to be clear about what is meant by effectiveness. The stated aim of drug *education* is to provide opportunities for pupils to develop their knowledge, skills, attitudes and understanding about drugs and appreciate the benefits of a healthy lifestyle. In contrast, the stated aims of drug *prevention* in the UK are to 'minimize the number of young people engaging in drug use; delay the age of onset of first use; reduce the harm caused by drugs; and enable those who have concerns about drugs to seek help' (AGDAE, 2008: 11). It is clear there is a mismatch here. Although drug education in schools does not aim explicitly to impact on behaviour, the expectations surrounding drug education programmes are that they will help deliver on the behavioural goals of drug prevention – to reduce and delay drug use. Consequently, interventions and approaches are deemed to be ineffective if they do not impact on behaviour – even if they deliver other benefits such as engaging young people's interest and trust (Hastings *et al.*, 2002). Other areas of education are not expected to impact on behaviour in the same way, and tend not to be loaded with such high expectations (Ofsted, 2005: 28).

Putting evidence into practice

The challenge of doing drug education

Drug education is not easy for schools. Teachers who are not specialists in Personal, Social and Health Education (PSHE), the context in which much drug education takes place, may feel uncomfortable using interactive techniques and may worry about their lack of specialist drug knowledge (Stead *et al.*, 2007a). The importance of teachers receiving training and support to develop their confidence to teach drug education is supported by the Blueprint study, an evaluation of a large Home Office drug education programme implemented in four English local authority areas between 2003 and 2006 (Baker, 2006; Stradling *et al.*, 2008). Surveys of drug education in Scotland have found that although the majority of teachers involved in drug education have received related staff development or training in the past three years, this is more often concerned with drug awareness and information than with methods and skills (Stead *et al.*, 2009; Stradling and MacNeil, forthcoming).

Schools are encouraged to use evidence-based approaches in their drug education, but may feel overwhelmed by the plethora of different programmes on offer, or may find it difficult to keep up to date with the latest thinking on effective approaches. Several studies suggest that there is often a mismatch between evidence and practice. Lowden and Powney's (2000) examination of drug education provision in Scotland between 1996 and 1999 found that although the majority of schools claimed to provide some form of drug education, this teaching tended to be largely concerned with information acquisition, driven by resources and packages rather than based on clear theories and approaches, and relied considerably on external agencies such as the police. A review of drug education carried out by the UK school inspection service Ofsted, based on a survey of 60 schools and 200 inspection reports, noted that the quality of teaching about drugs had improved since 1997 but was not as high in secondary as in primary schools (Ofsted, 2005). In particular, it tended to be poorest in secondary schools, where it was often taught by teachers with no specialist training or experience in delivering PSHE.

Should tobacco, alcohol and drugs be treated separately or together?

There are several arguments for teaching about smoking, drinking and illegal drug use together. There is a tendency for risk behaviours to cluster together – if a pupil smokes, drinks alcohol or takes drugs, he or she is more likely to do one of the other two as well – and they share several common risk factors, including a tendency to overestimate peer prevalence and poor parent–child relationships. The odds of all three behaviours are increased if a pupil has truanted or been excluded from school (Fuller, 2008). This suggests that it may be more efficient to address smoking, drinking and drugs in combination. It may also be more acceptable to schools, when struggling with an already crowded curriculum, to develop and teach just one programme rather than several. It could also be argued that the approach to substance misuse needs to be integrated so that messages reinforce each other and linkages are made between transferable skills such as decision-making, coping with social influence and so on.

There are also arguments for treating the substances differently. While integration is valuable, learning progression probably dictates that late primary and early secondary years (10–13) will probably need to focus more on tobacco, alcohol and volatile substances because these are the substances which young people are more likely to encounter at this age. In addition, the substances have different legal status, with alcohol and tobacco being age-restricted but otherwise socially sanctioned products. There are also different public health goals for each behaviour. While the message concerning tobacco is unequivocally negative, messages surrounding alcohol are much less clear-cut. Effective alcohol education programmes in schools are ones which adopt a harm minimisation rather than a prevention approach (e.g. McBride et al., 2004, but see also Chapter 6, this volume). Devising a programme or curriculum which can embrace all the different messages and objectives for different substances, both legal and illegal, can be challenging.

How should drug education fit into the wider PSHE curriculum?

Although some aspects of drug education can be covered in secondary school science teaching, the main curriculum area for covering tobacco, alcohol and drugs education is PSHE. Many of the component areas of PSHE reflect shared objectives and concepts. Shared objectives include enabling pupils to make informed choices, recognise and understand their strengths and the pressures they are facing, develop strategies for coping with these pressures, and understand the risks and consequences involved in different actions and social situations. Shared concepts include self-awareness, self-esteem, confidence, independence, risk awareness, resilience, respect for self and others, and social responsibility.

Given this degree of commonality, there is a strong case for arguing that PSHE is the most appropriate 'home' for drug education and that there is real scope for synergy of learning here. However, synergy depends on consistency of approach. Continuity of learning and progression are also important. Generally, there tends to be clear progression in the choice of topics to be covered in PSHE for different age groups, and this reflects the guidance provided on PSHE by education authorities. However, an evaluation of drug education in Scottish schools (Stead *et al.*, 2005, 2009) found there is not necessarily a consensus in schools about when certain substances should be introduced, and a number of drug education topics covered in the last years of primary schooling were repeated in the first two years of secondary school without taking into account pupils' increased maturity and different needs.

Who should teach school drug education?

Drug education can be taught by regular classroom teachers (sometimes known as form tutors), by specialist PSHE teachers, by other staff within a school such as a school nurse, by external agencies, or by same-age or older peers. Peer approaches aim to harness the social interactions between peers to promote health-related behaviours and reduce drug use. The approach rests on the assumption that messages (information, norms, attitudes, behavioural models) are better and more credibly delivered by trusted sources, i.e. young people (not necessarily the same age as the target audience). Peer approaches vary widely in their goals and methods, making effectiveness difficult to ascertain (Parkin and McKeganey, 2002).

There is no clear evidence from the drug education research literature to suggest that one group is more effective than another. Involvement of peer educators may improve the effectiveness of drug education (e.g. Bangert-Drowns, 1988; Gottfredson and Wilson, 2003; Lister-Sharp *et al.*, 1999), but the evidence is not conclusive or clear-cut, and trained teachers and health professionals can also be effective deliverers of drug education

(Rooney and Murray, 1996; Tobler and Stratton, 1997; Tobler *et al.*, 2000). The effectiveness of a particular delivery agent is likely to be strongly bound up with programme type, training, implementation quality and the perceived credibility of the deliverer in the eyes of programme participants (Coggans *et al.*, 2003).

The 2005 Ofsted report claimed that 'the quality of teaching is unsatisfactory in twice as many lessons taught by tutors (non-specialist form teachers) as by specialist teachers' (Ofsted, 2005: 16). In the inspectorate's view, the key issue is 'the variable level of subject knowledge and enthusiasm of the tutors that is quickly apparent to the pupils, who react negatively or are simply embarrassed by their tutor's reluctance to teach the subject' (p. 16). The Home Office Blueprint study found few differences in the quality of Blueprint teaching between teachers with prior expertise in PSHE and drug education and teachers new to these areas, after both groups had participated in Blueprint training. This suggests that, with appropriate training, materials and support, non-specialist teachers can be equipped to teach drug education to a high level (Stead *et al.*, 2007b).

There are both benefits and challenges in using external contributors such as youth workers, police and theatre groups. They can bring specialist knowledge, first-hand experiences and credibility to drug education lessons (Ofsted, 2005). Young people often enjoy the novelty of someone new in the classroom and appreciate the opportunity to discuss drugs in a more 'adult' way, beyond the usual teacher–pupil relationship; they engage particularly well with drama and real-life stories (Stead *et al.*, 2001). However, it is extremely important that schools use the expertise of external contributors appropriately (Buckley and White, 2007) – for example, using the police to contribute to pupils' knowledge about the law, but not relying on them to deliver all aspects of a programme. The most effective inputs are those which are matched to the needs of pupils and are an integrated part of a school's drug education programme, rather than a stand-alone session with no follow-up. Training is as important for external contributors as for teachers.

How can children and young people's diverse needs best be met?

In the UK, the favoured approach to drug education has been a 'universal' one – that is, targeting activities at a whole year group or school population. However, the diversity in young people's needs and experiences poses many challenges for the designers and teachers of universal drug education programmes.

First, the degree of variation in knowledge and experience among young people can be considerable. In the same classroom there are likely to be young people with hardly any knowledge about drugs alongside peers who know the local street names, may have already experimented with various substances, or have parents or older siblings who are users. The Blueprint evaluation found that young people who were particularly knowledgeable about drugs looked forward to their drugs education lessons and, according to their teachers, participated more actively in these lessons than in the rest of the curriculum (Stead *et al.*, 2007a). On the other hand, they were also more likely to challenge some of the information in the resources and to question the teacher's credibility as a source of information. Young people are also likely to differ in how comfortable they feel talking about drugs; some will be reluctant to expose their naïveté and limited knowledge to potential ridicule from their peers, while others may be nervous about revealing to teachers the extent of their knowledge and experience (Stead *et al.*, 2005).

Another challenge posed by the diversity of experience among young people is how best to meet the needs of those who are particularly at risk of initiating substance misuse. These include children whose parents or carers misuse drugs, young offenders, looked after children, particularly those accommodated away from home, those excluded from school and school phobics and poor attenders. Universal prevention programmes appear to be less effective for these higher-risk young people (Windle and Windle, 1999).

This raises important questions about the potential contribution that schools can make to secondary prevention with high-risk groups. It was observed earlier that schools are required to take appropriate action if pupils bring illegal and potentially harmful substances on to school sites, and education authorities in the UK, and indeed in much of Europe, have issued guidelines on how schools should deal with such incidents. However, as yet, most evaluations of school-based substance misuse prevention have focused on universal curriculum initiatives, with relatively little research attention paid to the impact of policies and actions specifically aimed at young people found on site with drugs or other banned substances.

In the 1990s, some education authorities and individual schools introduced zero tolerance policies whereby students found with illegal drugs on school premises were permanently excluded. There is a lack of reliable evidence on whether such a strategy reduced the risk of others being encouraged to experiment, but there is evidence that zero tolerance did not reduce the use of illegal drugs by excludees themselves (Munro and Midford, 2001). Similarly, Pentz *et al.* (1989) found that punitive school policies on smoking were far less effective than policies which emphasised prevention and offered support to help young people quit. Currently in the UK the number of young people temporarily or permanently excluded from mainstream schooling for possession of sanctioned substances is relatively small (averaging around 2 per cent of excludees; the majority are excluded for persistent disruptive, abusive or violent behaviour). However, some UK education authorities have recently sought to reduce exclusions, as studies have shown that young excludees are four times more likely to have used illicit substances and five times more likely to be current drug users than their counterparts in mainstream schooling (Goulden and Sondhi, 2001).

Within many schools there will also be children and young people from ethnic and cultural minorities where topics relating to alcohol and illegal drugs are highly sensitive. This highlights the importance of ensuring that parents are informed and consulted about the school's PSHE programme. This can help allay any fears parents have that drug education may encourage their children to experiment; at the same time, teachers can explain how even children from communities where the use of alcohol and other substances is prohibited still need to know how to cope with social influences and peer group pressure.

There is very little research evidence specifically related to substance misuse by children and young people with special needs, and even less evidence on their drug education needs (McNair, 1996). Children and young people requiring regular medication may need a specific focus on the appropriate uses of medicine, including not sharing it with others and the consequences of taking it in combination with other drugs. Children with low literacy levels and poor communication skills may need specifically designed resources which are more visual, have less text and use larger font sizes.

How should the whole school and wider community be involved?

All schools in the UK are now encouraged to have a substance misuse policy including a protocol for managing drug-related incidents. Most schools also recognise that teaching and non-teaching staff are potential role models and respond to this by encouraging all staff to support the policy in practical ways, such as by making the whole school site a non-smoking area, no alcohol consumption at staff gatherings on site, and so on.

There is a growing body of research evidence to indicate that the ethos of the school can have a positive impact on the effectiveness of drug education (Bonell et al., 2007). West et al.'s (2004) longitudinal study of the effects of school on health behaviours in Scotland found that drug, alcohol and tobacco use were lower in schools with a positive school ethos, even allowing for the potentially confounding effects of family socio-demographics, parental behaviour and neighbourhood. There is evidence that health-promoting school approaches may improve outcomes for a range of health behaviours, although there have been too few studies to specify the most effective mix of ingredients or their relative importance (Lister-Sharp et al., 1999).

Moving beyond the school itself, there is some evidence to suggest that drug education programmes may be more effective when they work with other agencies to target young people's wider environment – by, for example, strengthening family resilience (Velleman et al., 2005) and tackling the availability of substances in the local community – than when they involve only classroom education (Bruvold, 1993; Tobler and Stratton, 1997; Tobler et al., 2000; Wilson et al., 2001). However, the evidence base is limited, and again it is not clear exactly what mix of activities is needed in such programmes for effectiveness. These sorts of multi-component community programmes bring many challenges, including overcoming parents' reluctance to participate in school-based drug education programmes (Stead *et al.* 2007a; Velleman *et al.*, 2000).

Conclusion

Recently in the UK there has been a growing emphasis on the school's role in promoting health and well-being. This builds on the whole school approach underpinning initiatives such as Health Promoting Schools, Healthy Schools and the National Healthy Schools Programme.[3] This approach emphasises the scope for substance misuse education across the curriculum rather than solely through PSHE programmes. The one concern here, however, is that this might be accompanied by even more emphasis on knowledge transmission through different school subjects while the most effective approaches, aimed at developing life skills and social strategies, will be neglected.

Although evidence of drug education's long-term impact on drug use behaviour is unclear, there is evidence to suggest that it can have important short-term effects in terms of reducing and delaying uptake of substances. A large number of reviews and studies point to certain types of school drug education being more effective than others, and these approaches are recommended in evidence-based guidance. However, it can be challenging to put this evidence into practice, not least because of the anxieties and stigma surrounding the subject, because many teachers lack specialist training to teach drug education effectively, and because PSHE continues to be a relatively low-status subject in schools. In response to this, the Department for Children, Schools and Families (DCSF), which is responsible for education in England, announced in October 2008 an intention to make PSHE a statutory subject. An independent review was commissioned which recommended that PSHE should become part of the statutory National Curriculum for primary and secondary schools (MacDonald, 2009). Traditionally, this is an area of the curriculum where assessment has been weak or non-existent and this has contributed to its low status. The independent review adopted the view that assessment should be an integral part of teaching and learning PSHE but this did not necessitate the development of examination standards and qualifications. At the time of writing, a public consultation on the proposal was under way and if legislation is introduced it is likely that PSHE will become a statutory school subject in 2011–12. More guidance, information, training and support are needed to help schools continue to improve their drug education and whole school action on drugs. It is also important not to place an over-reliance on schools as the key mechanism for addressing young people's drug use; as discussed elsewhere in this book, the consumption of harmful substances is a society-wide problem which requires integrated action and collective responsibility.

Notes

1 Illegal drugs are divided in the UK into three different classes (A, B and C) which carry different levels of penalty for possession and dealing. Class A drugs, which are considered to be most likely to cause harm and attract the severest penalties, include heroin, cocaine, ecstasy and LSD; Class B includes cannabis and amphetamines; and Class C includes tranquillisers, some painkillers and ketamine. Source: Home Office (2009).
2 Throughout the chapter, we use the term 'drug education' to cover education about all substances, both illegal and legal.
3 See, for example, documentation on health and well-being experiences and outcomes within the Curriculum for Excellence in Scotland. For further information see www.ltscotland.org.uk/curriculumforexcellence/healthandwellbeing (accessed June 2009).

References

ACMD (Advisory Council on the Misuse of Drugs) (2006) *Pathways to Problems: Hazardous Use of Tobacco, Alcohol and Other Drugs by Young People in the UK and Its Implications for Policy.* London: Home Office. Online. Available at http://drugs.homeoffice.gov.uk/publication-search/acmd/pathways-to-problems/Pathwaystoproblems.pdf?view=Binary (accessed February 2009).

AGDAE (Advisory Group on Drug and Alcohol Education) (2008) *Drug Education: An Entitlement for All. A Report to Government by the Advisory Group on Drug and Alcohol Education.* London: AGDAE. Online. Available at www.teachernet.gov.uk/_doc/13032/ACFE3AC.pdf (accessed February 2009).

Agrawal, A., Neale, M. C., Prescott, C. A. and Kendler, K. S. (2004) 'A twin study of early cannabis use and subsequent use and abuse/dependence of other illicit drugs', *Psychological Medicine*, 34(7): 1227–1237.

Baker, P. J. (2006) 'Developing a Blueprint for evidence-based drug prevention in England', *Drugs: Education, Prevention and Policy*, 13(1): 17–32.

Bangert-Drowns, R. L. (1988) 'The effects of school-based substance abuse prevention: A meta-analysis', *Journal of Drug Education*, 18(3): 243–264.

Bonell, C., Fletcher, A. and McCambridge, J. (2007) 'Improving school ethos may reduce substance misuse and teenage pregnancy', *British Medical Journal*, 334: 614–616.

Botvin, G. J. (2000) 'Preventing drug abuse in schools: Social and competence enhancement approaches targeting individual-level etiologic factors', *Addictive Behaviors*, 25(6): 887–897.

Botvin, G. J., Baker, E., Dusenbury, L., Tortu, S. and Botvin, E. M. (1990) 'Preventing adolescent drug abuse through a multimodal cognitive-behavioral approach: Results of a 3-year study', *Journal of Consulting and Clinical Psychology*, 58(4): 437–446.

Botvin, G. J., Griffin, K. W., Diaz, T., Scheier, L. M., Williams, C. and Epstein, J. A. (2000) 'Preventing illicit drug use in adolescents: Long-term follow-up data from a randomized control trial of a school population', *Addictive Behaviours*, 25(5): 769–774.

Bruvold, W. H. (1993) 'A meta-analysis of adolescent smoking prevention programs', *American Journal of Public Health*, 83: 872–880.

Buckley, E. J. and White, D. G. (2007) 'Systematic review of the role of external contributors in school substance use education', *Health Education*, 107(1): 42–62.

Coggans, N., Cheyne, B. and McKellar, S. (2003) *The Life Skills Training Drug Education Programme: A Review of Research.* Edinburgh: Scottish Executive Drug Misuse Research Programme, Effective Interventions Unit.

Currie, C., Nic Gabhainn, S., Godeau, E., Roberts, C., Smith, R., Currie, D., Picket, W., Richter, M., Morgan, A. and Barnekow, V. (2008) *Inequalities in Young People's Health: HBSC International Report from the 2005/06 Survey*. WHO Policy Series: Health Policy for Children and Adolescents, Issue 5. Copehagen: WHO Regional Office for Europe. Online. Available at www.emcdda.europa.eu/stats08/eyetab8 (accessed June 2009).

Department for Education and Skills (2004) *Drugs: Guidance for Schools*. England: DfES.

Donaldson, S. I., Graham, J. W. and Hansen, W. B. (1994) 'Testing the generalizability of intervening mechanism theories: Understanding the effects of adolescent drug use prevention interventions', *Journal of Behavioral Medicine*, 17(2): 195–216.

Faggiano, F., Vigna-Taglianti, F. D., Versino, E., Zambon, A., Borraccino, A. and Lemma, P. (2005) 'School-based prevention for illicit drugs use', *Cochrane Database of Systematic Reviews*, 2: CD003020.

Faggiano, F., Vigna-Taglianti, F. D., Versino, E., Zambon, A., Borraccino, A. and Lemma, P. (2008) 'School-based prevention for illicit drugs use: A systematic review', *Preventive Medicine*, 46(5): 385–396.

Fuller, E. (ed.) (2008) *Drug Use, Smoking and Drinking among Young People in England in 2007*, NHS IC (Information Centre). Online. Available at www.ic.nhs.uk/webfiles/publications/sdd07/SDD%20Main%20report%2007%20%2808%29-Standard.pdf (accessed February 2009).

Gfroerer, J., Wu, L. and Penn, M. (2002) *Initiation of Marijuana Use: Trends, Patterns and Implications*. Bethesda, MD: Substance Abuse Mental Health Services Administration.

Gottfredson, D. C. and Wilson, D. B. (2003) 'Characteristics of effective school-based substance abuse prevention', *Prevention Science*, 4(1): 27–38.

Goulden, C. and Sondhi, A. (2001) *At the Margins: Drug Use by Vulnerable Young People in the 1998/99 Youth Lifestyles Survey*, Home Office Research Study 228. London: Home Office.

Hall, J. A. and Valente, T. W. (2007) 'Adolescent smoking networks: The effects of influence and selection on future smoking', *Addictive Behaviors*, 32(12): 3054–3059.

Hansen, W. B. (1992) 'School-based substance abuse prevention: A review of the state of the art in curriculum', *Health Education Research*, 7(3): 403–430.

Hastings, G. B., Stead, M. and MacKintosh, A. M. (2002) 'Rethinking drugs prevention: Radical thoughts from social marketing', *Health Education Journal*, 61(4): 347–364.

Home Office (2009) *Drugs and the Law: Class A, B and C Drugs*. Online. Available at www.homeoffice.gov.uk/drugs/drugs-law/Class-a-b-c (accessed June 2009).

Lister-Sharp, D., Chapman, S., Stewart Brown, S. and Sowden, A. (1999) 'Health promoting schools and health promotion in schools: Two systematic reviews', *Health Technology Assessment*, 3(22): 1–209.

Lowden, K. and Powney, J. (2000) *Drug Education in Scottish Schools 1996–1999*. SCRE Research Report No. 95, March. Glasgow: Scottish Centre for Research in Education (SCRE).

McBride, N., Farringdon, F., Midford, R., Meuleners, L. and Philip, M. (2004) 'Harm minimisation in school drug education: Final results of the School Health and Alcohol Harm Reduction Project (SHAHRP)', *Addiction*, 99: 278–291.

MacDonald, A. (2009) *Independent Review of the Proposal to Make Personal, Social, Health and Economic Education Statutory*. London: Department for Children, Schools and Families (DCSF).

McNair, L. (1996) *Substance Abuse and Learning Disability: Conference Report*. Edinburgh: Health Education Board for Scotland.

Munro, G. and Midford, R. (2001) 'Zero tolerance and drug education in Australian schools', *Drug and Alcohol Review*, 20: 105–109.

Ofsted (2005) *Drug Education in Schools: A Report from the Office of Her Majesty's Chief Inspector of Schools*. HMI 2392. Online. Available at www.ofsted.gov.uk/Ofsted-home/Publications-and-research/Browse-all-by/Education/Key-stages-and-transition/Key-Stage-1/Drug-education-in-schools-2005 (accessed February 2009).

Parkin, S. and McKeganey, N. (2002) 'The rise and rise of peer education approaches', *Drugs: Education, Prevention and Policy*, 7(3): 294–310.

Pentz, M. A., Dwyer, J. H., MacKinnon, D. P., Flay, B. R., Hansen, W. B., Wang, E. Y. and Johnson, C. A. (1989) 'A multi-community trial for primary prevention of drug abuse: Effects on drug use prevalence', *Journal of the American Medical Association*, 261: 3259–3266.

Rooney, B. L. and Murray, D. M. (1996) 'A meta-analysis of smoking programs after adjusting for error in the units of analysis', *Health Education Quarterly*, 23(1): 48–64.

Rundall, T. G. and Bruvold, W. H. (1988) 'A meta-analysis of school-based smoking and alcohol-use prevention programs', *Health Education Quarterly*, 15(3): 317–334.

Stead, M. and Angus, K. (2004) *Literature Review into the Effectiveness of School Drug Education: Conducted for Scottish Executive Education Department*. Edinburgh: Scottish Executive. Online. Available at www.scotland.gov.uk/Resource/Doc/96342/0023318.pdf (accessed February 2009).

Stead, M., MacKintosh, A. M., Eadie, D. and Hastings, G. (2001) 'Preventing adolescent drug use: The development, design and implementation of the first year of "NE Choices"', *Drugs: Education, Prevention and Policy*, 8(2): 151–175.

Stead, M., MacKintosh, A. M., McDermott, L., Eadie, D., MacNeil, M., Stradling, R. and Minty, S. (2005) *Evaluation of the Effectiveness of Drug Education in Scottish Schools*. ISBN 0 7559 2939 X (Web-only publication). Online. Available at www.scotland.gov.uk/Publications/2006/03/14135923/0 (accessed February 2009).

Stead, M., Stradling, R., MacKintosh, A. M., MacNeil, M., Minty, S., Eadie, D. and the Blueprint Evaluation Team (2007a) *Delivery of the Blueprint Programme – Delivery Report*. London: Home Office. Online. Available at http://drugs.homeoffice.gov.uk/publication-search/blueprint/dpreports (accessed February 2009).

Stead, M., Stradling, R., MacNeil, M., MacKintosh, A. M. and Minty, S. (2007b) 'Implementation evaluation of the Blueprint multi-component drug prevention programme: Fidelity of school component delivery', *Drug and Alcohol Review*, 26(6): 653–664.

Stead, M., Stradling, R., MacNeil, M., MacKintosh, A. M., Minty, S., McDermott, L. and Eadie, D. (2009) 'Bridging the gap between evidence and practice: A multi-perspective examination of real world drug education', *Drugs: Education, Prevention and Policy*. Epub 2009 Jul 7. DOI: 10.1080/09687630802228341.

Stradling, R. and MacNeil, M. (forthcoming) *A Review of Substance Misuse Resources Used in Scottish Schools*. Edinburgh: NHS Scotland.

Stradling, R., MacNeil, M., Cheyne, B., Scott, J. and Minty, S. (2008) *Delivering Drug Education in the Classroom: Lessons from the Blueprint Programme – Practitioners' Report*. London: Home Office. Online. Available at http://drugs.homeoffice.gov.uk/publication-search/blueprint/dpreports (accessed February 2009).

Thomas, R. (2004) 'School-based programmes for preventing smoking (Cochrane Review)', in *The Cochrane Library*, Issue 1. Chichester: John Wiley & Sons.

Tobler, N. S. (1986) 'Meta-analysis of 143 adolescent drug prevention programs: Quantitative outcomes results of program participants compared to a control or comparison group', *Journal of Drug Issues*, 16(4): 537–567.

Tobler, N. and Stratton, H. (1997) 'Effectiveness of school-based drug prevention programs: A meta-analysis of the literature', *Journal of Primary Prevention*, 18(1): 71–128.

Tobler, N. S., Lessard, T., Marshall, D., Ochshorn, P. and Roona, M. (1999) 'Effectiveness of school-based drug prevention programs for marijuana use', *School Psychology International*, 20(1): 105–137.

Tobler, N. S., Roona, M. R., Ochshorn, P., Marshall, D. G., Streke, A. V. and Stackpole, K. M. (2000) 'School-based adolescent drug prevention programs: 1998 meta-analysis', *Journal of Primary Prevention*, 20(4): 275–336.

Toumbourou, J. W., Stockwell, T., Neighbors, C., Marlatt, G. A., Sturge, J. and Rehm, J. (2007) 'Interventions to reduce harm associated with adolescent substance use', *The Lancet*, 369(9570): 1391–1401.

UNODCCP (United Nations Office for Drug Control and Crime Prevention) (2003) *School-Based Drug Education: A Guide for Practitioners and the Wider Community*. February 2003. United Nations Office for Drug Control and Crime Prevention. Online. Available at www.unicef.org/lifeskills/files/School-basedDrugEducation03.doc (accessed February 2009).

Velleman, R., Mistral, W. and Sanderling, L. (2000) *Taking the Message Home: An Evaluation of 5 Projects Involving Parents in Drugs Prevention*. DPAS Paper 5. London: Home Office.

Velleman, R. D. B., Templeton, L. J. and Copello, A. G. (2005) 'The role of the family in preventing and intervening with substance use and misuse: A comprehensive review of family interventions, with a focus on young people', *Drug and Alcohol Review*, 24(2): 93–109. Informa Healthcare (0959-5236, 10.1080/09595230500167478).

West, P., Sweeting, H. and Leyland, A. (2004) 'School effects on pupils' health behaviours: Evidence in support of the health promoting school', *Research Papers in Education*, 19(3): 261–291.

White, D. and Pitts, M. (1998) 'Educating young people about drugs: A systematic review', *Addiction*, 93(10): 1475–1487.

Wilson, D. B., Gottfredson, D. C. and Najaka, S. S. (2001) 'School-based prevention of problem behaviors: A meta-analysis', *Journal of Quantitative Criminology*, 17: 247–272.

Windle, M. and Windle, R. C. (1999) 'Adolescent tobacco, alcohol and drug use: Current findings', *Adolescent Medicine: State of the Art Reviews*, 10(1): 153–163.

Chapter 8

Promoting sexual health

Roger Ingham and Julia Hirst

On 28 October 2008, Jim Knight, the Minister for Schools in England, announced that Personal, Social, Health and Economic (PSHE) Education, including Sex and Relationships Education (SRE),[1] would become a statutory part of the curriculum at all key stages in all state-maintained schools from 2010. This news was greeted with immense enthusiasm from many quarters, including members of the Sex Education Forum[2] and the Independent Advisory Group of the Government's Teenage Pregnancy Unit.[3]

But why was this announcement felt to be important? What role can, or should, schools play in teaching about this area? Surely, some say, this should be the sole responsibility of parents, not the state? Further, so say many of the same people, teaching about sex at young ages will only encourage experimentation and 'promiscuity'; young people should be helped to protect their 'innocence' for as long as possible. Indeed, some amongst these critics might also argue that SRE is not required; instead, society should instruct, urge, implore, advise, or whatever, young people to save sex until they are married. In this context, they do not need education about contraceptives or other details since it will simply not be required.

In this chapter, we outline some aspects of SRE and what role schools can play to increase the contribution that it can make to health outcomes. First, we consider what healthy sex and relationships involve and briefly elaborate on some of the disputes in the area. Second, national and international evidence is summarised alongside a discussion of the methodological challenges facing research in the area. Third, the policy background in England[4] is described and some of the implications of recent changes are discussed. Fourth, some key components of a good SRE curriculum will be outlined alongside consideration of some wider issues. Finally, some future directions are considered.

What are healthy sex and relationships?

In thinking about healthy sex and relationships, and how these relate to SRE, it is useful to clarify what we understand by the term 'sexual health'. The

World Health Organization's unofficial working definition provides a useful starting point since many national and regional sexual health documents tend to draw on this:

> Sexual health is a state of physical, emotional, mental and social well-being in relation to sexuality; it is not merely the absence of disease, dysfunction or infirmity. Sexual health requires a positive and respectful approach to sexuality and sexual relationships, as well as the possibility of having pleasurable and safe sexual experiences, free of coercion, discrimination and violence. For sexual health to be attained and maintained, the sexual rights of all persons must be respected, protected and fulfilled.
>
> (WHO, 2006: 5)

This definition offers a framework for thinking about sexual health which is comprehensive, positive and holistic. It draws emphasis away from preoccupations with more negative aspects such as the prevention of sexually transmitted infections (STIs) and unplanned pregnancy, and instead places these within a broader context of relationships, well-being and the potential for pleasure, safety and respect for rights. Equally, it is a realistic and useful starting point for discussion with young people in its implicit recognition of the vulnerabilities (such as coercion, discrimination and violence) which can be – and often are – experienced.

The National Strategy for Sexual Health and HIV in England (DH, 2001) echoes the WHO definition in acknowledging the physical, social, emotional and relationship aspects of sexual health, and similarly upholds the entitlement to specific human rights:

> Sexual health is an important part of physical and mental health. It is a key part of our identity as human beings together with the fundamental human rights to privacy, a family life and living free from discrimination. Essential elements of good sexual health are equitable relationships and sexual fulfilment with access to information and services to avoid the risk of unintended pregnancy, illness or disease.
>
> (DH, 2001: 5)

Recognition of sexual health as 'a key part of our identity', if taken literally, offers a mandate for privileging sexual health education in all aspects of young people's schooling. Similarly, the 'rights to privacy, a family life and living free from discrimination' indirectly signal what the wider aspects of sexual health and relationships education might include, such as issues of bullying, homophobia, religious intolerance and, more specifically, whether legal equality (over issues such as age of consent, rights to parenthood and civil partnerships) equates with social equality and equality of opportunity, irrespective of sexual identity.

While the reference to 'sexual fulfilment' in the DH 2001 definition is a development on previous, more negative, definitions that were more disease and problem focused, it does not go as far as the WHO definition, which 'requires a positive . . . approach' and the 'possibility of having pleasurable' sexual experiences. Research evidence suggests this is an important issue in the design of sexual health curricula. More traditional programmes which restrict content to physical/biological/disease/reproduction are said not to be effective in bringing about safer sexual outcomes, whereas successful initiatives are those underpinned by more positive conceptions of sexual health which acknowledge the positive and pleasurable aspects of sexual identity and practice (Boyce *et al.*, 2007; Hogarth and Ingham, 2009).

The latter is referred to as a 'sex positive' approach, and underpins the approach adopted in this chapter, with a central tenet being the right to pleasure, alongside physical, emotional, mental and social well-being. By 'physical' we mean issues such as pregnancy and STIs. In parallel, mental, emotional and social well-being refer to issues that young people routinely flag up as important, such as self-esteem, regret, concern for their reputation, coercion, dealing with bullying and attitudes to diversity and acceptance of difference.

While these definitions offer a basis for designing sexual health curricula, it is important that young people and educators have opportunities to discuss the various meanings and understanding of 'sexual health' since these should underpin what their SRE programme is trying to achieve. However, irrespective of what young people might wish from SRE, decisions over content are often influenced by some disputed issues.

There have been a number of grounds for objection to greater provision of SRE in schools. Mention was made earlier about the reservations of those who argue on religious and/or cultural grounds that sex education is likely to be harmful. In addition to these objections, however, there seem to be some that are rather more pragmatic (or less ideological) in nature. The unease that many teachers feel about dealing with the topics involved has led to a range of supposed barriers being erected. For example, whilst the infamous Section 28 was in force,[5] many teachers allegedly refused to mention same-sex attraction and behaviour for fear of falling foul of this legislation, even though educational purposes were specifically excluded from the prohibition. Again anecdotally, some schools and governors argue that parents do not wish schools to deal with SRE, despite evidence to the contrary.

What is important to understand is that sex and relationships education – and discussions thereof – does not take place in a context of universal acceptance. Whereas presumably everyone would agree on the need for support to reduce obesity, or to improve mental health (even if there is less agreement on how best to achieve these), this is not the case for SRE. Some commentators suggest that even mentioning 'peripheral' issues relating to the area (in this case the correct names for body parts in a booklet aimed at 6 and 7-year-olds)[6] can cause harm to children and young people; for example:

I am sure that most parents will agree the truth is the very best answer but it is the degree of detail that is so important . . . It's unfair to burden very young children with explicit details and then wonder why they say words and do things not acceptable in schools or in society. We cannot expect small children to cope with the amount of information government want primary schools to implant into childish minds. One wonders how the 'experts' reconcile themselves with the statistic the more we have offered detailed sex education the quicker teenage pregnancies and diseases have spread.[7]

(Margaret Morrissey, Parents Out Loud)

This quotation nicely illustrates a curious logic: that the correct names may subsequently lead to the use of terms that are 'not acceptable'. Further, the final sentence implies that increases in sex education can be directly blamed for increased STIs and under-18 pregnancies (even though the latter have been reducing steadily in England, Wales and Scotland over recent years).[8]

A further example is provided by discussions that occurred in a school in Torbay concerning the planned use of a video in an SRE class:

Governors at a primary school in Devon will have the final say on whether children will be able to watch a sex education DVD made by Channel 4 following concerns by two parents that it is too explicit. The Living and Growing programme is the fourth best seller in educational DVDs produced by Channel 4's learning and education arm. But when the programme was shown to a group of 160 parents at Sherwell Valley Primary School, Torbay, to seek their permission to show the DVD to pupils, two parents objected complaining that it encouraged children to touch themselves.

(Andalo, 2007)

One would have thought that it is not normal in a democratic society for two objectors to overrule the wishes of 158 others!

The impact of the lack of a consensus on how to respond to the SRE needs of young people is well illustrated by various compromises that have been reached over the years in relation to policies. For example, the last time there was a major UK parliamentary debate on sex education in schools, the position was reached that, apart from the biological aspects covered in the National Curriculum for science, secondary schools should include SRE but parents had the right to withdraw their children on religious and/or cultural grounds. This compromise was arrived at in an effort to please those on both sides of the debate, although, in practice, probably neither side was actually satisfied. Although only a very small minority of children have, in fact, been withdrawn, the general effect on schools of the *threat* of parents withdrawing children (and/or the threat of negative media coverage) almost certainly puts a brake on SRE development. Further, the impact of the Government not having made the subject a statutory part of the curriculum (prior to the recent announcement) may well have signalled to teachers and governors that it is not really to be taken seriously, despite the supposed official encouragement. Recent developments should lead to changes in this respect.

Evidence overview

There are, in theory, two major means of justifying the inclusion of SRE within school curricula. The first concerns the rights of young people to adequate information and support to enable them to make informed decisions regarding their health. These rights are enshrined in the UN Convention on the Rights of the Child, to which the UK is a signatory.

The other justification is somewhat more pragmatic – that SRE is effective in improving sexual health. Despite the strength of conviction of those pressing for greater SRE provision, however, the actual strength of the evidence on effectiveness is not particularly strong. This is not actually very surprising, given the wide range of factors that affect young people and their sexual activity, as well as the wide variation in SRE programmes in terms of delivery, focus, length, timing, ages covered, topics included, teaching methods adopted, teacher qualities, how linked they are with other agencies, and other issues.

Additionally, what is actually meant by 'improvement' in sexual health may not be universally agreed upon; for example, many will suggest that reduced teenage pregnancy rates or STI prevalence are crucially important outcome measures, while others would suggest that delayed sexual activity is equally or more important. Which of these is afforded greater priority in education lessons will have a large impact on content and delivery, and may reflect underlying moral approaches (see, for example, Ingham, 2007a). Other potential outcome measures could be knowledge, gender attitudes, acceptance of diversity, self-esteem, enjoyment of sexual activity (solo and/or joint), improved confidence to use services, and so on.

There have been a number of approaches to evaluation over recent years. Given the wide range of styles of programme and delivery, a popular approach has used systematic reviews, whereby a large number of studies are considered against a set of standards to ensure scientific rigour. Only studies that reach the required criteria are included, ensuring a level of quality and faith in the conclusions.

Perhaps the best-known advocate of this approach has been Douglas Kirby, who has been carrying out such reviews for around twenty years (Kirby, 1997, 2001, 2007; Kirby et al., 2007). In general terms, Kirby's conclusions are positive towards sex education, with results indicating that education prior to first intercourse does appear to help to delay this event, and that increased contraceptive use arises from programmes after sexual debut. He highlights various criteria that seem to characterise effective programmes (although it should be acknowledged that these have not all been subject to careful evaluation in all the various potential combinations!). Amongst the key criteria are:

- The process of developing the curriculum involved a range of experts, assessed the needs of the relevant target group, used a clear model of goals and processes required to achieve these, designed suitable and practical activities, and pilot-tested the programme.
- There was a focus on clear health goals and specific behaviours required to achieve these, and the programmes provided clear messages, covered skills and competencies to avoid risk, and dealt with psychosocial risk factors.
- The teaching methods created safe environments for young people to participate, included multiple activities to target each of the risk and protective factors, used sound instruction methods that involved participation, made the material relevant to the young people's cultures and development, and covered topics in a logical sequence.
- Support was obtained from administrative authorities, trained and motivated educators were used, methods were adopted (and adapted) to maintain young people's involvement, and the full range of activities was covered.

A similar exercise, albeit with less stringent scientific criteria for inclusion, was carried out for the World Health Organization by Grunseit and colleagues, with basically similar results; this drew more substantially on research carried out in poorer countries than the USA and Canada (Grunseit et al., 1997). Similarly, the Health Development Agency (HDA) and National Institute for Health and Clinical Excellence (NICE) in the UK have carried out reviews of reviews and reached similar conclusions (Swann et al., 2003; Ellis and Grey, 2004; Downing et al., 2006; Trivedi et al., 2007). Downing et al. (2006) included the following conclusions:

> There is sufficient review-level evidence to conclude that school-based sex education can be effective in reducing the sexual risk behaviours of young people. (p. 38)

> There is tentative review-level evidence to conclude that sex education is more effective if begun before the onset of sexual activity. (p. 38)

> ... there is sufficient review-level evidence to conclude that small group work involving skills-building activities can be effective at reducing the sexual risk behaviour of all target groups. (p. 40)

Two large studies have been carried out over recent years in the UK to try to address the issue of whether SRE 'works' or not. Both adopted a comparative design in which matched schools were randomly allocated to a group and either received the new programme (the intervention arm) or continued to receive what they had before (the control arm). Both programmes were allegedly designed according to the best principles of behaviour-change theories, with one relying on teacher-led delivery (the SHARE programme) and the other using peers as educators (the RIPPLE programme).

The SHARE programme was assessed through 25 schools in Scotland, randomly allocated to intervention or control conditions. Specialist teachers were extensively trained in a one-week course, and the programme ran for 20 weeks (in theory, at least) for pupils aged between 13 and 14 years. The main outcome measures were condom use, age at first intercourse and, as a result of longer-term follow-up and pupil matching to NHS records, numbers of conceptions and abortions up to age 20. None of the major outcome measures showed any differences between conditions, although there were small differences in reported enjoyment of sex education, and slightly lower-reported regret about sexual encounters amongst young people who had received the intervention (Wight et al., 2002; Henderson et al., 2007).

The RIPPLE project used peer educators instead of teachers. Twenty-nine schools were involved, and pupils in Year 9 (aged 13–14 years) of the intervention arm (13 schools) received three sessions of peer contact. The key outcome measure selected in advance was condom use at first intercourse; this showed no variation between trial arms, but there was a slight increase in age at first intercourse amongst the women in the intervention arm of the study (Stephenson et al., 2004; Strange et al., 2006).

A third large-scale SRE programme was developed in the mid-1990s, and has attracted support from a number of local authorities in England and Wales that have bought into the package of training and materials. The APAUSE project (Mellanby et al., 1996, 2001) uses a mix of teacher and peer-led approaches and was initially developed from lessons learned from studies of successful US programmes. Although this approach has never been subject to a formal controlled trial, an external evaluation based on the data collected from recipients reported some degree of success (Blenkinsop et al., 2004).

Other approaches have also been used to explore the possible impact of sex education, albeit in a less direct manner. For example, using data from the first UK National Survey of Sexual Attitudes and Lifestyles (NATSAL), Wellings et al. (1995) showed that respondents who reported that their school was a major source of sex education were more likely to report safer early sexual activity on a number of indices.

Although much of the evidence clearly points in a similar direction, it is difficult to find clear unequivocal evidence as to how best to deliver SRE in schools. This may not, in fact, be surprising. Sexual activity is a complex behaviour, and it is unlikely that one form of intervention alone will have a clearly measurable impact. This is not, however, to imply that school-based SRE is unimportant; rather, that all the different agencies involved need to work together to create a culture for young people which supports choice, respect and responsibility. For many years, it seems that the 'blame' for poor sexual health outcomes in the UK has been attributed to others – parents blame schools and/or their 'children's friends', schools blame health authorities, everybody blames the media, and so it has gone on. Potentially effective programmes in one area of young people's lives could easily be undermined by conflicting approaches in another.

Perhaps the most important lesson to be learned from the many reviews of studies, taken together, is that there is no evidence that SRE leads to earlier or riskier sexual activity. Normally, non-significant results gain little attention; in this case, however, this clear (non-) finding has served to persuade some policy-makers that the harm forecast by the conservative thinkers does not, in fact, pose a genuine threat.

A further source of support for SRE is what young people themselves think about it. Various studies using a range of methods, over many years (for example, Schofield, 1965; Allen, 1987; Kehily, 2002; Hirst, 2004), have led to the same conclusion – that SRE provision is patchy, that much of it is too late for many young people, that it tends to deal with biological issues to the detriment of social and emotional issues, and so on. The UK Youth Parliament collected the views of over 21,000 young people from across the UK, and reported that 40 per cent felt that their SRE was poor or very poor, with a further 33 per cent reporting it as being average. Over 60 per cent overall reported having no discussion of personal relationships and only half knew where their local sexual health clinic was located (UK Youth Parliament, 2007).

Further, and despite what the spokespeople for certain parents' organisations may say, surveys consistently show that the vast majority of parents do want schools to play more part in SRE delivery (NFER, 1994; Stone and Ingham, 1998).

The policy position in England

As mentioned earlier, the policy position in England is currently in a state of change. The Education Act (1996) and the Learning and Skills Act (2000) had divided secondary age (Key Stages 3 and 4) coverage into compulsory (puberty, reproduction and virus transmission as part of the science National Curriculum) and non-compulsory (other aspects) and enshrined the parental right of withdrawal (OPSI, 1996, 2000). Schools could include as much or as little as they liked in the non-statutory parts – some hold regular classes in each school year, whilst others hold 'drop-down' days once a year at which local health and related agencies and services are invited in to display their wares. Some schools have specialist and trained PSHE education teachers, whilst others rely on (sometimes completely untrained) form tutors and/or subject specialists in other disciplines (PE appears to be a frequent one). The Government issued guidance on SRE in 2000 (DfEE, 2000) and the Qualifications and Curriculum Agency published (optional) key stage statements in 2007 (QCA, 2007).

Primary schools need to have a policy on SRE, but the policy can simply state that they do not deal with the subject matter.

This situation leads to great unevenness in provision across the country. The level of input received by pupils often depends on whether individuals in particular schools (teachers and/or governors) feel that the topic is important, and then being encouraged (or, in some cases, tolerated) by their managers and colleagues to devise a programme. Training is patchy; relevant issues are not covered in Initial Teacher Training courses, and there is no PSHE education specialism in teacher training institutions. A national PSHE education certification programme[9] was introduced in 2001 and as of December 2008 over 8,000 teachers and community nurses had gained accreditation. An early evaluation of the pilot phase was encouraging (Warwick et al., 2005).

The various calls for changes in provision, as well as increasing concern being recorded by Ofsted inspectors (Ofsted, 2002, 2005, 2007) and the recently introduced obligations on schools to improve their pupils' well-being, all contributed to the Schools Minister, Jim Knight, agreeing to a review of PSHE education, including SRE, in early 2008. A Review Steering Group was established, comprising representatives of various interested organisations including different faith groups, young people, sexual health charities, researchers, and others. The group's report and recommendations were submitted to the Government in October and the Government response was published shortly afterwards.[10] The Minister used the occasion of the twenty-first birthday party of the Sex Education Forum to announce the change in status of PSHE education/SRE in England as from 2010, along with changes in the way alcohol education is managed.[11]

The change has a number of far-reaching implications. First, considerably more training in PSHE/SRE will need to be provided, with suggestions for some statutory programmes of study to be included in all initial teacher training courses as well as PSHE education becoming a specialist subject. Second, all state schools will need to cover the curriculum to be determined for all key stages, although there will be some flexibility to enable individual schools to tailor their teaching 'to reflect the ethos of the school' (para. 8 of Government response) and faith schools will be able to develop supplementary material if they wish to. Third, whether the right of parents to withdraw their children from classes should be maintained is to be considered further. Above all, the review and response stress the need to place more emphasis on the relationships aspects of SRE, and work should be 'within a clear and explicit values framework of mutual respect, rights and responsibilities, gender equality and acceptance of diversity' (page 2 of Government response).

The mention of the importance of values in the proposed new programmes of study is vitally important. One of the common criticisms from the moral right is that sex education takes place within a moral vacuum, and is somehow value-free. Through an emphasis on the need for a value framework based on mutual respect, rights and responsibilities, it will be more widely realised that values are not the sole preserve of particular narrow religious organisations and their adherents.

Curriculum issues

So, what will or should SRE look like? If programmes are shaped by what young people say they need and want, then the only certainty is that they will all look quite different. School students, researchers, policy-makers and school inspectors alike are agreed that there is no 'one size fits all' programme. To be meaningful to real lives, the actual detail of the curriculum should evolve through consultation with young people. At present, it appears that 'too many schools do not base their curriculum' on students' needs (Ofsted, 2007: 2) and rely on more traditional approaches which were designed years ago and not for or with the specific students whose needs it aims to serve.

Before looking in detail at what SRE might look like, it is worth reminding ourselves of young people's main criticisms of SRE. In brief, they include the following: emphasis is on the risks and dangers of sexual acts and outcomes of pregnancy and/or STIs; input does not match the realities of young people's experience; relationships tend to be ignored or not taken seriously; where sex is discussed, content is restricted to vaginal penetration; sexual behaviour is addressed in isolation from other issues such as relationships and the social circumstances in which sex might take place; heterosexual identity is assumed with little or no acknowledgement of lesbian, gay, bisexual, trans or questioning (LGBTQ) young people; and there are too few opportunities for developing skills that could help in achieving desires, whether these be no sex at all, sexual activities which do not involve penetration and/or other safer sexual practices.

So, having suggested what young people's centred programmes should *not* be like, we will consider a way forward. We consider four broad (but closely connected and overlapping) areas as key. The first involves values, rights and responsibilities. Values here refers to the principles, standards, morals and ideals that we live by and these naturally overlap with our human and social rights and responsibilities to one another and the societies in which we live. This element underpins the entire PSHE and SRE curriculum in that the approach adopted should mirror principles of upholding rights and fair standards for all. The Citizenship curriculum (now part of PSHE in some schools) should address much of the 'rights' agenda, but there is one specific aspect which we touch on here because of the significance to promoting sexual health; namely, education on the workings of power. By this we mean discussion on how power is not distributed equally, that certain groups and individuals have more power than others, which results in some people's rights being honoured and having better quality of life and opportunities than others; in the particular area covered by SRE, the crucial importance of gendered power needs to be highlighted and challenged.

This dovetails into the second area, which is emotional well-being and relationships. A starting point here is to ask students for their views on what useful input would address, but we envisage it would incorporate discussion on relationships (not having/having a girlfriend or boyfriend, breaking up, going 'too far', choosing not to have sex, etc.); managing one's parents/ guardians and negotiating levels of freedom and trust; and identity, appearance, self-esteem, feeling good about oneself (and not), reputation, and gender and sexuality stereotypes of 'acceptable' appearance and behaviour. Here, it is important to pick up on power again and specifically gender and sexuality politics and the power imbalances that can exist between males and females, and heterosexual and LGBTQ young people, and that can lead to infringement of rights and abuses of power. The main aim is to promote the importance of politeness and respect, of good manners, and of negotiation and respecting choices.

The third area is the more traditional content which focuses on biological, physical and practical issues. These include, in no particular order, input and discussion on: puberty; a range of sexual practices (including non-penetrative and penetrative); pregnancy, gestation and birth; transmission routes, symptoms and treatment of STIs; methods of preventing STIs and methods of contraception; sexual health services (including genito-urinary medicine); and pregnancy and termination services.

In this area, it is particularly important to attend to young people's criticisms of SRE, as summarised above. To assist this, we offer a list of things to avoid:

- Do not assume heterosexuality; instead, assume there are gay, lesbian, bisexual and trans or unsure/questioning young people in the group. References to sexual acts should be inclusive (see next point).
- Do not restrict discussion or images of sexual behaviour to vaginal penetration or the missionary position (man on top) because this restricts sexual acts to the most risky, is heterosexist, reinforces stereotypes of women as sexually passive, and offers least chance of pleasure for women.
- Do not adopt an alarmist approach and/or solemn tone which emphasises only the risks and dangers of sexual acts (i.e. pregnancy and/or STIs); instead emphasise safer non-penetrative practices which are more inclusive of LGBTQ young people and have greater potential for enjoyment through stroking and mutual masturbation and removing the worry of STIs or pregnancy.

- Do not de-contextualise sex from relationships; instead explore the types and range of relationships and family that young people experience and acknowledge their importance (positives and negatives) in the pathways to adulthood. This embraces same-sex attracted and bisexual youths and those with same-sex parents or non-traditional families.
- Do not ignore the realities of young people's experience; rather, ask young people to talk about their socialising, where and what takes place (drugs, alcohol, etc.), and the potential impact on sexual practices and ways of staying safe. In our experience, young people relish the opportunity to do this if a safe and trusting 'classroom' climate is in place.
- Do not ignore the need to support skills development and enhance the potential for achieving desires, whether these involve no sex at all, or safer sexual practices.

Last but not least are skills and competencies, which obviously relate to the previous content areas. Arguably, one of the most important competencies for SRE is to enable young people to feel sufficiently equipped to choose to be involved or not in sexual relationships and, if they are sexually active, that their actions are consensual and safe. In other words, their SRE should contribute towards their potential for having and maintaining positive sexual health. It is useful to consider the desired *outcomes* and *processes*. A positive sexual health *outcome*, if we return to the WHO definition of sexual health, is one that does not threaten sexual health in the physical sense of avoiding sexually transmitted infections and which allows one to exercise choices over conception; and in the emotional sense of having enjoyed the experience and having minimal or no regret.

The *processes* involved in achieving positive outcomes would be practices that are chosen – choosing either not to have sex or to have sex. If the latter, that it is satisfying, involves emotional connection and negotiation on how far to go, and, if necessary, involves the effective use of condoms. Overall, such processes would meet the desired outcomes and honour the rights of all involved. A 'positive' outcome would also exclude post-sex worries over contracting an STI and/or conception, having no regrets over the person with whom, or the circumstances under which, sex took place, and having not been coerced or acted against one's will. The latter naturally overlaps with earlier discussion in PSHE or SRE on power, respect and responsibility in relationships and provides an important opportunity to openly condemn sexual acts which are non-consensual either through the use of force, fear or drugs (including alcohol), through large age differentials, or in other ways.

To develop the notion of sexual competence a little further, skills for, and factors which influence, safer sex are necessary inclusions in SRE. Discussion could include factors which influence the reliable use of contraception and/or condoms, the influence of perceptions of peer practices (likely to be exaggerated; Perkins *et al.*, 2005), and contextual factors such as where sex takes place (often not at home or indoors for UK youth) and the place of alcohol and/or other drugs. While sex educators can do little directly to influence the contexts for sex, they can acknowledge – and consider the implications of the reality – that it is often furtive, clandestine and rushed and, together with alcohol, that these contexts can and do influence sexual negotiation and decision-making and young people's sense of self (Hirst, 2008).

Another important competency in protecting sexual health is knowledge and skills to use sexual health services effectively. This would include guidance on 'youth-friendly' sexual health services (where they are, what to expect, rights and confidentiality vis-à-vis contraceptives and emergency contraception). Encouraging young men's involvement is crucial here, given that boys are typically more resistant to SRE and have less access to sources of information and support than girls (Hilton, 2001). Accompanied visits to sexual health services, and role play on requesting sexual health advice from an external agency, are useful to this end. Indeed, an increasing number of schools and colleges are now incorporating sexual health services on their premises in order to make access easier and more normalised for those who need support (Emmerson, 2008).

The issue of regret is complex, and worthy of more space than is available here (but see Hirst, 2008). Irrespective of how regret is conceptualised, however, it is vital to have conversations in SRE about ways of minimising the potential for regret.

Open and honest discussions with young people on the issues are important not just in terms of honouring the rights of young people to accurate knowledge and skills on sexuality and relationships but also because it signals our recognition of young people's sexuality and their capacity to experience it in ways not unlike older counterparts (teachers, parents, youth workers, carers, etc.). In other words, it signals a normalised conception of teenage sexuality which is a vital and necessary endorsement from trusted adults in young people's pathways to sexual maturity.

Although much of what we have covered relates to relationship contexts for sexual activity, aspects of self-exploration should not be ignored. Although acknowledgement of, and discussion about, masturbation poses many challenges for educators, there are ways of normalising the practice to try to avoid the guilt that is often created (Ingham, 2005). Indeed, recent work has tentatively suggested that comfort with one's own body may be protective for young women in that they may not feel the need to seek pleasure from others with whom they may not be completely comfortable (Hogarth and Ingham, 2009).

Finally, it is almost certainly important not to assume in advance that the issues need to be taken too seriously unless, of course, seriousness is warranted in, for example, the case of discussing abusive relationships. In general, SRE is anticipated with excitement but often then experienced with disappointment. It is important to capitalise on this eagerness to enjoy discussion of sexualities and relationships by embracing the humour of sex alongside discussion which is useful and meaningful to current and future lives. Of course, it is important to acknowledge the potential for embarrassment, and the need to take content – and each other – seriously and to honour confidentiality, but if it is honest and realistic, young people are more likely to engage and to find it memorable.

A particular dilemma for schools is how to deal with differences. Young people develop at different rates, physically as well as socially. This can pose challenges for teachers when working with a class made up of pupils of the same age band but with quite different knowledge and experience. In our experience, the later SRE is provided, the more acute is the challenge. Conversely, if SRE input, particularly on issues of puberty and sexual practices, takes place early enough (that is, before any – or at least the vast majority – of the class has reached puberty, or engaged in sexual practices, respectively), this is rarely a significant problem if the approach is sensitive and capitalises on teachers' skills in managing a variety of needs, experiences and abilities, irrespective of curriculum subject context.

In recognition of this, delivery is perhaps best offered through a combination of whole and small group work, mixed and single-sex work, and with ample opportunities for one-to-one sessions if desired by a student or deemed necessary (e.g. if the 'teacher' has concerns or observes heightened responses such as anger, withdrawal or tears). Planning should also build in flexibility of time (that is, not be restricted to a fixed number of lessons for covering the curriculum) to facilitate variations in pace of delivery which befit emergent needs. For example, if an issue stimulates lots of questions or discussions, it is important that the 'timetable' does not sabotage opportunities to address these adequately. A good planning option is one that timetables a specified individual to be 'on call' at the same time as the SRE classes, so that they can be called upon to provide one-to-one support – or to take over the class – should an unexpected need or event arise.

Wider contexts

In addition to the inclusion of these important issues in the programmes of study, other, more nebulous features of schools may have important implications for young people's general understanding of sex and relationship issues; a few will be briefly considered here to serve as examples.

Amongst the main predictors of teenage pregnancy is a lack of aspirations regarding future activities (see, for example, Berrington et al., 2005). Schools can be in a difficult position in this area; on the one hand, efforts are being made to improve performance overall in schools through publication of examination league tables, more regular inspections, and so on. On the other hand, pupils who are unmotivated, and/or receive little support from home, and/or have mental health problems, may need more targeted and specialist support than many schools can manage within their normal resources. Realistic employment opportunities for young people in some geographical areas may be lacking, and it is unreasonable to expect a school to be able to resolve such structural shortcomings on their own. Similarly, some communities have a long history of early child-rearing. Close inter-agency working between schools and other local government departments is essential to deal with these wider contextual challenges.

Second, a school's general approach to bullying, and, in particular, bullying on the grounds of sexuality and sexual experience, can affect the discourses of sexuality that prevail and dominate. Phoenix *et al.* (2003), for example, observed that in some inner-city schools there was pressure on young men to have sex (with a young woman) in order to prove to their friends that they were not 'gay'. Amongst the many reasons why young people have early sex, this is not one that would rank high on many people's list of 'good' ones!

Third, the extent to which parents or carers are aware of, and involved in, school SRE programmes can have a major impact on their effectiveness. Although, as mentioned earlier, the majority of parents want schools to do more and earlier than they do at present, this is not to imply that they do not wish to have any involvement. Rather, many parents see the task as a joint venture in which schools provide knowledge and skills, and parents can attempt to ensure that suitable values are in place that reflect their religious and/or cultural preferences. There has been a recent growth in approaches that support parents and carers in communicating about sexual matters (see, for example, Parentline Plus[12] and Speakeasy[13] at the national level, and the Sheffield-based Parent to Parent peer education scheme[14]).

Finally, there is an issue of who is best placed to deliver sex and relationships education. There is almost certainly no easy answer to this question – a lot will depend on the qualities and expertise of the teachers and any visitors used. Currently, there is probably a greater reliance on outside speakers for some topics but this may simply reflect a lack of adequate training for teachers. There are certainly advantages in using outside experts to help 'signpost' young people to external services, or to share specific experiences such as being a young parent, or living with HIV.

What we would certainly wish to warn against is the use of outsiders to present a specific ideological or moral position which is intended to increase feelings of guilt and/or shame. For example, abortion is a legal act in Great Britain under certain specified circumstances, and yet some schools choose to 'teach' it solely as a moral issue (which may involve outside organisations showing pictures of aborted fetuses). This is perhaps understandable (though maybe not defensible) in schools with strong faith backgrounds, but seems to be wholly inappropriate in secular schools.

Any outsiders brought in to help present sections of the SRE curriculum should agree to follow the school's policy guidelines, as well as agreeing to present objective and evidence-informed material.

Towards the future and changing cultural discourses

In addition to the development of programmes of study suitable for different stages, work needs to be carried out to try to change the general culture regarding sex and sexuality education in the UK. This could help to ensure that challenges to schools' programmes – be they substantive or petty – do not serve to sidetrack the efforts and enthusiasm of those involved. Altering the views of those who are bigoted is never easy. There are, however, many who feel nervous about change but who are open to persuasion through evidence as well as having matters explained to them rather than their relying on sensationalist media coverage of issues. Time and effort will be needed to engage in this activity.

Fundamental clashes of faith potentially pose greater challenges. Bartz (2007) has written about the situation in Norway, where a traditionally liberal approach to SRE may be challenged by recent increases in the numbers of Muslim immigrants. A particular issue that will need to be addressed revolves around the situation where young people are behaving in a way that their culture and/or religion does not tolerate. The official policy that schools and parents should work together in developing programmes is seriously stretched in these cases. In a somewhat different context, Goldman (2008) writes on how to respond to some typical objections from parents regarding sexuality education in schools. These objections were gleaned from a range of newspapers and other media in Australia, but almost certainly reflect many of those heard on a global level.

We end with two quotations that illustrate cultural approaches to sex and relationships education in two countries, each with teenage conception rates considerably lower than those in the UK. Admittedly, these countries are economically somewhat different from the UK too, so we are not suggesting that SRE is alone responsible for variations in sexual health. But policies do lay down a marker of how those in positions of responsibility in societies wish to treat their young people in relation to this most important of areas of development.

The first is part of a personal communication to R.I. from Katarina Lindahl, from the RFSU (Swedish Association for Sexuality Education), and the second comes from a paper on the Dutch approach to sex education:

> The guiding stars are knowledge instead of ignorance, openness with regards to facts instead of mystifying and an acceptance of young people's sexuality (or sexual emotions), relationships and love, with or without a partner. The idea is that the sex education should support and prepare young people for a responsible present and/or future sexual life . . . Sexual enjoyment is also regarded as a value in itself . . . There is no opposition to sex education in Sweden.
>
> (Lindahl, 2006, personal communication)

Dutch sexuality education emerges from an understanding that young people are curious about sex and sexuality and that they need, want, and have a right to accurate and comprehensive information about sexual health . . . it encourages young people to think critically about their sexual health, including their desires and wishes . . . attention is paid on discussing values, establishing personal boundaries, communicating wishes and desires, and developing assertiveness . . . What are often considered taboo or sensitive topics, such as sexual orientation and masturbation, are common themes in Dutch materials.

(Ferguson *et al.*, 2008, various pages)

Given the considerably lower levels of teenage pregnancy in these countries (Ingham, 2007b), it is clear that such 'open' approaches do not lead to disastrous consequences for young people's sexual health; indeed, just the opposite! Although no one would claim that SRE on its own is responsible for these variations (for example, family communication, economic contexts and gender relations are also important), it is surely a crucial component. This kind of evidence should encourage those charged with developing and delivering SRE in the UK that it is indeed a crucially important activity in which schools and colleges have a major role to play.

Notes

1 This is the expression currently favoured in England; other countries use different terms. An earlier period in the UK parliament's deliberations referred to 'relationship' in the singular. We prefer to use the plural as being more realistic.

2 The Sex Education Forum is an umbrella organisation, comprising around 50 varied agencies and interest groups, established in 1987 to provide policy guidance to the Government; see www.ncb.org.uk/sef (accessed 13 February 2009).

3 A non-departmental public body that monitors the implementation of the Government's Teenage Pregnancy Strategy; see www.everychildmatters.gov.uk/health/teenagepregnancy/tpiag (accessed 13 February 2009).

4 Education is a devolved responsibility in the UK parliamentary system, such that Scotland has its own national parliament, and Wales and Northern Ireland each have their own national assemblies. In practice, legislation in educational matters is broadly similar; see, for example, National Assembly for Wales (2002). England is used as the policy example in this chapter for no other reason than size.

5 Section 28 (sometimes referred to as Clause 28) of the Local Government Act 1988 was introduced during Mrs Thatcher's time as Prime Minister and sought to prevent local authorities from 'intentionally promoting homosexuality' or 'promote the teaching . . . of the acceptability of homosexuality as a pretended family relationship'.

6 The terms used in the booklet are 'nipples', 'vagina', 'penis' and 'testicles', as well as 'ear', 'mouth', 'eye', 'hair', 'foot', 'hand', etc. In a spirit of equal treatment, both the boy and the girl are shown to have nipples, as well as ears, feet, etc.

7 www.parentsoutloud.com (accessed 20 October 2008). The resource being referred to is *Let's Grow with Nisha and Joe*, published by the fpa (formerly the Family Planning Association) in London.

8 Accurate rates of conception for Northern Ireland are hard to obtain due to the different legal status of abortion in that country.

9 See www.pshe-cpd.com (accessed 13 February 2009).
10 See www.teachernet.gov.uk/publications (search using reference DCSF-00860-2008) (accessed 13 February 2009).
11 See www.dcsf.gov.uk/speeches/search_detail.cfm?ID=835 (accessed 13 February 2009).
12 www.parentlineplus.org.uk (accessed 13 February 2009).
13 www.fpa.org.uk/Inthecommunity/Speakeasy (accessed 13 February 2009).
14 www.sexualhealthsheffield.nhs.uk/projects/5-7.php (accessed 13 February 2009).

References

Allen, I. (1987) *Education in Sex and Personal Relationships*. London: Policy Studies Institute.

Andalo, D. (2007) 'Sex education DVD "too explicit"', *The Education Guardian*, 27 February.

Bartz, T. (2007) 'Sex education in multicultural Norway', *Sex Education*, 7(1): 17–33.

Berrington, A., Diamond, I., Ingham, R. and Stevenson, J. with Borgoni, R., Cobos Hernández, M. I. and Smith, P. W. F. (2005) *Consequences of Teenage Parenthood: Pathways Which Minimise the Long Term Negative Impacts of Teenage Childbearing. Final Report – November 2005*. Final report to the Department of Health. Southampton: University of Southampton Statistical Sciences Research Institute.

Blenkinsop, S., Wade, P., Benton, T., Gnaldi, M. and Schagen, S. (2004) *Evaluation of the APAUSE Sex and Relationships Education Programme*. London: DfES.

Boyce, P., Huang Soo Lee, M., Jenkins, C., Mohamed, S., Overs, C. and Paiva, V. (2007) 'Putting sexuality (back) into HIV/AIDS: Issues, theory and practice', *Global Public Health*, 2(1): 1–34.

DfEE (Department for Education and Employment) (2000) *Sex and Relationship Education Guidance*. London: DfEE.

DH (Department of Health) (2001) *Better Prevention, Better Services, Better Sexual Health: The National Strategy for Sexual Health and HIV*. London: DH.

Downing, J., Jones, L., Cook, P. A. and Bellis, M. A. (2006) *Prevention of Sexually Transmitted Infections (STIs): A Review of Reviews into the Effectiveness of Non-clinical Interventions. Evidence Briefing Update*. Liverpool: Centre for Public Health, Liverpool John Moores University, for NICE.

Ellis, S. and Grey, A. (2004) *Prevention of Sexually Transmitted Infections (STIs): A Review of Reviews into the Effectiveness of Non-clinical Interventions. Evidence Briefing*. London: Health Development Agency.

Emmerson, L. (2008) *National Mapping Survey of On-Site Sexual Health Services in Education Settings: Provision in FE and Sixth-Form Colleges*. London: Sex Education Forum, National Children's Bureau.

Ferguson, R., Vanwesenbeeck, I. and Knijn, T. (2008) 'A matter of facts . . . and more: An exploratory analysis of the content of sexuality education in the Netherlands', *Sex Education*, 8(1): 93–106.

Goldman, J. (2008) 'Responding to parental objections to school sexuality education: A selection of 12 objections', *Sex Education*, 8(4): 415–438.

Grunseit, A., Kippax, S., Aggleton, P., Baldo, M. and Slutkin, G. (1997) 'Sexuality education and young people's sexual behavior: A review of studies', *Journal of Adolescent Research*, 12(4): 421–453.

Henderson, M., Wight, D., Raab, G., Abraham, C., Parkes, A., Scott, S. and Hart, G. (2007) 'The impact of a theoretically based sex education programme (SHARE) delivered by teachers on NHS registered conceptions and terminations: Final results of cluster randomised trial', *British Medical Journal*, 334: 133–135.

Hilton, G. (2001) 'Sex education: The issues when working with boys', *Sex Education*, 1(1): 31–41.

Hirst, J. (2004) 'Researching young people's sexuality and learning about sex: Experience, need, and sex and relationship education', *Culture, Health and Sexuality*, 6(2): 115–129.

Hirst, J. (2008) 'Developing sexual competence? Exploring strategies for the provision of effective sexualities and relationships education', *Sex Education*, 8(4): 399–413.

Hogarth, H. and Ingham, R. (2009) 'Masturbation amongst young women and associations with sexual health: An exploratory study', *Journal for Sex Research*, DOI: 10.1080/002 4490902878993.

Ingham, R. (2005) '"We didn't cover that at school": Education *against* pleasure or education *for* pleasure', *Sex Education*, 5(4): 375–390.

Ingham, R. (2007a) 'Some reflections on encouraging abstinence and delay as possible approaches to reducing ill health among young people', in P. Baker, K. Guthrie, R. Kane, C. Hutchinson and K. Wellings (eds) *Teenage Pregnancy and Reproductive Health*. London: Royal College of Obstetricians and Gynaecologists, pp. 115–131.

Ingham, R. (2007b) 'Variations across countries: The international perspective', in P. Baker, K. Guthrie, R. Kane, C. Hutchinson and K. Wellings (eds) *Teenage Pregnancy and Reproductive Health*. London: Royal College of Obstetricians and Gynaecologists, pp. 17–29.

Kehily, M. J. (2002) *Sexuality, Gender and Schooling: Shifting Agendas in Social Learning*. London: RoutledgeFalmer.

Kirby, D. (1997) *No Easy Answers*. Washington, DC: National Campaign to Prevent Teen Pregnancy.

Kirby, D. (2001) *Emerging Answers: Research Findings on Programs to Reduce Teen Pregnancy*. Washington, DC: National Campaign to Prevent Teen Pregnancy.

Kirby, D. (2007) *Emerging Answers 2007: Research Findings on Programs to Reduce Teen Pregnancy and Sexually Transmitted Diseases*. Washington, DC: National Campaign to Prevent Teen and Unplanned Pregnancy.

Kirby, D., Laris, B. and Rolleri, L. (2007) 'Sex and HIV education programs: Their impact on sexual behaviors of young people throughout the world', *Journal of Adolescent Health*, 40: 206–217.

Lindahl, K. (2006) 'Sexuality education in Sweden: A brief description', email (10 May).

Mellanby, A. R., Phelps, F. A., Crichton, N. J. and Tripp, J. H. (1996) 'School sex education. A process for evaluation: Methodology and results', *Health Education Research*, 11(2): 205–214.

Mellanby, A. R., Newcombe, R. G., Rees, J. and Tripp, J. H. (2001) 'A comparative study of peer-led and adult-led school sex education', *Health Education Research*, 16(4): 481–492.

National Assembly for Wales (2002) *Sex and Relationships Education in Schools*. Circular number 11/02. Cardiff: Department for Training and Education, Welsh Assembly Government.

NFER (National Foundation for Educational Research in England and Wales) (1994) *Parents, Schools and Sex Education: A Compelling Case for Partnership*, prepared for the Health Education Authority. London: HEA.

Ofsted (2002) *Sex and Relationships Education in Schools*, HMI 433. London: Ofsted. Available at www.ofsted.gov.uk (accessed 13 February 2009).

Ofsted (2005) *Personal, Social and Health Education in Secondary Schools*, HMI 2311. London: Ofsted. Available at www.ofsted.gov.uk (accessed 13 February 2009).

Ofsted (2007) *Time for Change? Personal, Social and Health Education*, HMI 070049. London: Ofsted. Available at www.ofsted.gov.uk (accessed 13 February 2009).

OPSI (Office of Public Sector Information) (1996) *Education Act 1996*. London: OPSI. Available at www.opsi.gov.uk/acts/acts1996/Ukpga_19960056_en_1 (accessed 13 February 2009).

OPSI (Office of Public Sector Information) (2000) *Learning and Skills Act 2000*. London: OPSI. Available at www.opsi.gov.uk/acts/acts2000/ukpga_20000021_en_1 (accessed 13 February 2009).

Perkins, H. W., Haines, M. P. and Rice, R. (2005) 'Misperceiving the college drinking norm and related problems: A nationwide study of exposure to prevention information, perceived norms and student alcohol misuse', *Journal of Studies on Alcohol*, 66(4): 470–478.

Phoenix, A., Frosh, S. and Pattman, R. (2003) 'Producing contradictory masculine subject positions: Narratives of threat, homophobia and bullying in 11–14 year old boys', *Journal of Social Issues*, 59(1): 179–195.

QCA (Qualification and Curriculum Authority) (2007) *National Curriculum*. London: QCA. Available at http://curriculum.qca.org.uk (accessed 13 February 2009).

Schofield, M. (1965) *The Sexual Behaviour of Young People*. London: Longman.

Stephenson, J., Strange, V., Forrest, S., Oakley, A., Copas, A., Allen, E., Babiker, A., Black, S., Ali, M. and Monterio, H. (2004) 'Pupil-led sex education in England (RIPPLE): Cluster-randomised intervention trial', *The Lancet*, 364: 338–346.

Stone, N. and Ingham, R. (1998) *Exploration of the Factors That Affect the Delivery of Sex and Sexuality Education and Support in Schools*. Southampton: Centre for Sexual Health Research, University of Southampton. Available at http://eprints.soton.ac.uk/40486/01/FinalReport.PDF (accessed 13 February 2009).

Strange, V., Forrest, S., Oakley, A. and Stephenson, J. and the RIPPLE team (2006) 'Sex and relationships education for 13–16 year olds: Evidence from England', *Sex Education*, 6(1): 31–46.

Swann, C., Bowe, K., McCormick, G. and Kosmin, M. (2003) *Teenage Pregnancy and Parenthood: A Review of Reviews. Evidence Briefing*. London: Health Development Agency.

Trivedi, D., Bunn, F., Graham, M. and Wentz, R. (2007) *Update on Review of Reviews on Teenage Pregnancy and Parenthood: Submitted as an Addendum to the First Evidence Briefing 2003*. Hatfield: Centre for Research in Primary and Community Care, University of Hertfordshire, on behalf of NICE.

UK Youth Parliament (2007) *Sex and Relationships Education: Are You Getting It? A Report by the UK Youth Parliament*. London: UKYP.

Warwick, I., Aggleton, P. and Rivers, K. (2005) 'Accrediting success: Evaluation of a pilot professional development scheme for teachers of sex and relationship education', *Sex Education*, 5(3): 235–252.

Wellings, K., Wadsworth, J., Johnson, A. M., Field, J., Whitaker, L. and Field, B. (1995) 'Provision of sex education and early sexual experience: The relationship examined', *British Medical Journal*, 311: 417–420.

WHO (World Health Organization) (2006) *Defining Sexual Health*. Report of a technical consultation on sexual health, 28–31 January 2002, Geneva. Available at www.who.int/reproductive-health/gender/sexual_health.html#3 (accessed 2 July 2007).

Wight, D., Raab, G., Henderson, M., Abraham, C., Buston, K., Hart, G. and Scott, S. (2002) 'The limits of teacher-delivered sex education: Interim behavioural outcomes from a randomised trial', *British Medical Journal*, 324: 1430–1433.

Chapter 9

Children and young people as partners in health and well-being

Jo Butcher

Children and young people's participation in matters affecting them is not a new concept, and, encouragingly, over the last ten years a range of policy, guidance, practical resources and research dedicated to understanding, promoting and improving children and young people's involvement at all levels has been developed. As a result, the concept of participation has grown beyond a narrow focus on children and young people simply being present at a meeting or an event, to reflect a wider commitment to children and young people sharing power and being active partners in decision-making in relation to policy, services and their own lives.

Despite the growth in awareness of the importance of children and young people's participation, time pressures and limited resources are constant challenges and represent potential barriers to effective participation (McNeish and Newman, 2002). Organisations and individuals need to be committed in the long term to carving out an enduring space for children and young people to be active decision-makers and influencers. Genuine involvement is a journey, not an end point, and requires organisational commitment to actively seeking and responding to children and young people's views (Kirby *et al.*, 2003). Expertise in involving children and young people is not absolutely necessary; however, careful thinking, planning and commitment as well as skills in participation are needed to do it well, to ensure it is a positive experience for children and young people and that their views, ideas and suggestions result in positive change now and in the future.

Through supporting meaningful participation now, adults can invigorate children and young people's faith in decision-making processes, mobilising them to shape and improve services and communities for themselves, their families and future generations. This will ensure that services for children and young people better meet their needs and that children use services that aim to improve their health and well-being.

This chapter begins by summarising progress to date in promoting participation of children and young people generally in England and highlights schools' roles and responsibilities in enabling students to participate, the benefits in doing so and common principles of effective participation, based on practice, guidance and evidence. It then explores in more detail how schools can create the right conditions for effective participation in health and the different methods they can use, drawing on practice and evidence. Unless stated otherwise, the chapter refers to legislation, policy and practice developments in England only.

Involving children and young people: summary of progress

In general, awareness of and commitment to children and young people's participation has increased considerably in recent times. Promoting participation is much more likely to be seen as the right and good thing to do. This shift has been influenced at least in part by recent policy and practice initiatives. Government has sought to integrate the concept of participation in its policies and strategies and within its structure. *Every Child Matters* states as a national outcome that every child should have the support they need to 'make a positive contribution' (Department for Education and Skills, 2004a). 'You're Welcome' criteria have been published to support the provision of child-centred health services.

At the heart of the National Healthy Schools Programme, a cross-government initiative launched in 1999 in England, is a commitment to student voice. Citizenship and Personal, Social, Health and Economic Education (PSHE) programmes of study in the school curriculum aim to encourage active participation of students in the democratic life of the school and the wider community, and nurture them to become compassionate, thoughtful and responsible citizens. National and local organisations such as children's charities and youth and community services have tirelessly advocated for children and young people's involvement (Carnegie UK Trust, 2008), and various local initiatives (announced by central government) such as the Children's Fund and Connexions strive to involve children and families in planning and delivering services.

There has been progress within the National Health Service (NHS) to involve young patients in the development and delivery of health services (Zachary, 2009). Children and young people make one of the greatest demands on NHS provision, but historically their views have not been included.

Despite this positive shift there are still some areas of participation practice that evidence suggests remain underdeveloped or neglected. More opportunities are needed for example for young people to engage in strategic decision-making where they contribute, through positive dialogue and partnerships with adults, new ideas and solutions to complex issues and problems. National Healthy Schools Programme research identifies a need for improvements in young people's involvement as decision-makers at national, regional, local and school levels (Warwick *et al.*, 2004).

National practice on engaging some of the most disadvantaged and marginalised children and young people in society is growing. Owing to their life experiences and negative perceptions and/or experiences of organisations aiming to work with them, they are less likely to experience participation opportunities. For example, younger children, disabled children, looked after children, young people in the youth justice system and young people from ethnic minority communities are still more likely to be excluded (Oldfield and Fowler, 2004; Francique, 2008). The Carnegie UK Trust has identified the need for more professionals skilled in engaging young people across public services. Workforce development builds capacity and helps embed participation within organisational cultures by ensuring that their own workforce can promote participation, rather than relying on external 'experts' (Carnegie UK Trust, 2008).

What do we mean by participation?

There are various definitions of children's participation, each reflecting the context in which it takes place (e.g. education, health or social care settings) and the level of influence or decision-making promoted. The Department for Children, Schools and Families (DCSF; formerly DfES) defines participation in the context of schools as when children and young people:

- become more active partners in their education, including planning and evaluation of their own learning;
- participate in creating, building and improving services to make them more responsive to their needs and those of the wider community;
- make a difference in their schools, neighbourhoods and communities;
- contribute to a cohesive community;
- learn from an early age to balance their rights as individuals with their responsibilities as citizens; and
- develop, through the way they are involved, the knowledge, understanding and skills they will need in adult life.

(Department for Education and
Skills, 2004b: 2)

Traditionally, the 'ladder of participation' (Arnstein, 1969; Hart, 1992) has been used to describe the different levels of involvement, each rung representing increased empowerment; for example, the bottom three rungs illustrate non-participation and the top three rungs reflect authentic participation. However, this can imply a hierarchy where organisations are failing if they have not reached the top of the ladder. Blake and Frances (2004) have subsequently proposed a new model called the 'journey of participation'. This starts where the organisation is at, echoes the voluntary nature of participation and promotes a flexible approach reflecting the confidence and enthusiasm levels of young people and staff. They state:

> Remember that insisting on everybody's participation goes against an ethos in which individuals are encouraged and given responsibility to make their own decisions. Children and young people need to be supported in participating when they are ready, able and in the right mood for it.
>
> (Blake and Frances, 2004: 12)

They describe the journey of participation as 'one of collaboration, mutuality, exploration, discovery, excitement and disappointments as well as successes' (Blake and Frances, 2004: 12).

Adults can create new participation opportunities and, whilst doing so, work towards empowering children and young people to maximise opportunities for themselves and speak out independently. However, research shows that children and young people want to work with and alongside adults (Franklin and Sloper, 2005).

Why is participation important?

There are several very important reasons why it is essential that children and young people have opportunities to participate. First, participation is a child's entitlement enshrined in law. It is a right preserved in Article 12 of the UN Convention on the Rights of the Child (UNCRC), which states that children have the right to express their views and have them taken into account in all matters that affect their lives. Second, morally it is the correct thing to do. Adults who respect children and young people will listen to what they say. Government guidance on the children's workforce promotes listening as a primary skill for children and youth professionals, and understanding and respect as preconditions of listening (Department for Education and Skills, 2005). Willow (2002) states: 'Continuing to exclude children from decision making is not a sign of respect for their youth or for their relative lack of life experience. Rather it disregards their basic human need to be valued and treated with importance' (p. 42).

Participation, when carried out well, benefits the children and young people involved, those seeking their views, and future beneficiaries of policies and services shaped by the results. There is a limited but growing evidence base on the benefits of involving children and young people. However, much participation to date is based on the benefits as perceived or interpreted by those doing the involving or the participants themselves, and it is problematic attributing outcomes to particular activities, with little research into costs and benefits (Davies et al., 2005a). Nevertheless, in general, evidence identifies definite and significant benefits (Blake and Frances, 2004; Davies et al., 2005a, 2005b).

For young participants, participation opportunities enable them to have fun, feel valued and respected, develop emotionally and socially, learn skills that improve their health, well-being and preparedness for life, improve services, policies and the environment, and help them take control of their own lives. For organisations, the benefits include a positive and inclusive atmosphere based on trust, respect and a sense of belonging, services that are well used and respected by children and young people and that use resources wisely, a growing culture of participation through ongoing dialogue with children, a more powerful voice with and for children on key issues affecting their lives, and new and creative ways to tackle problems informed by their ideas.

Communities that involve their young members can demonstrate love, care and pride for them and celebrate and promote their achievements. Consequently, children's increased feelings of self-worth in the places they live will contribute to whole communities becoming more welcoming, inclusive and cohesive, reflected, for example, in improved public spaces and intergenerational cooperation.

Why is participation important for schools?

First, schools have duties laid down in statute to promote the participation and well-being of their students. The Education and Skills Act 2008 strengthens legislation for schools on participation to include a duty for local authorities and governing bodies of maintained schools to actively consult students on matters affecting them. Schools are also expected to report on consultation with students as part of their self-evaluation process as well as demonstrate how they are meeting the five national outcomes within *Every Child Matters*.

The Education and Inspections Act 2006 (which came into effect in September 2007) places a duty on all schools and pupil referral units in England to promote the well-being of their students. Participation can be a powerful vehicle to help schools meet their responsibilities with regard to this duty as well as positively impact on school ethos and teaching and learning (Madge *et al.*, 2003; Davies *et al.*, 2005a, 2005b). More particularly, meaningful participation in schools can foster positive relationships among students, teachers, staff, parents and carers, and help students to develop key life skills, confidence and self-belief that enable them to pursue goals, live healthier and fulfilling lives, and become active and responsible citizens. It can help children and young people in finding solutions to issues affecting their lives or their community and improve learning, achievement and behaviour. It can also help schools improve their performance. Research indicates that schools which take participation seriously tend to have better GCSE results, fewer exclusions and better attendance (Hannam, 2003).

Participation is in itself health and well-being promoting. If done well, it can contribute to students feeling valued, confident, energised and more in control of their lives:

Contributing to change and seeing the impact of that change was clearly identified by children and young people as having a positive impact on their self-esteem, confidence and motivation.

'It is a real motivator because you feel like this is my school and I am doing something to make it better' [young person].

(Blake, 2005: 8–9)

The National Healthy Schools Programme in England is underpinned by the premise that students who are healthier and feel happier are more likely to commit to learning, which is good for educational attainment. Fuller (2009) explains that there is extensive research that correlates physical and mental health and attainment, but there is a dearth of research that unpicks these links. Student engagement also ensures that teaching and learning is responsive to their needs. It features in national policy and guidance for schools on key health education topics such as sex and relationships and drug and alcohol education.

Creating conditions for effective participation

Research has shown that participation activity is most likely to have a positive impact when organisations, including schools, sustain and embed participation activities within their structure:

Building participatory cultures is a complex and dynamic process. Change has to be negotiated between policy makers, senior managers, other staff and younger people and may be unpredictable. This is a creative process that involves eliciting and fostering enthusiasm, sharing ideas and learning through doing. Only by discussing, listening to each other, trying things out, and continuing to do so, will it be possible to decide each next step. It is a process that highlights that older and younger people have something to learn from and with each other, not least how to work well together.

(Kirby et al., 2003: 24)

Engaging children and young people as partners in health and well-being

Emerging evidence indicates that at the heart of successful health and well-being initiatives are two elements: a commitment to participation, and working through relationships that are defined by mutual respect, exploration, learning and support. There is a growing awareness of the links between attachment (defined as significant positive emotional connections by a child with important adults in their life) and positive well-being, which can be achieved through meaningful participative approaches. Exciting developments in research and practice demonstrate the value of positive relationships and attachment in achieving emotional and physical health and well-being for children and families and wider outcomes such as economic self-sufficiency, which can inform schools' approaches to promoting students' health and well-being (Barnes *et al.*, 2008).

Evidence from children and young people reinforces the significance that they place on their friendships and relationships with peers, family and professionals. Key findings from the National Healthy Schools Programme research into the key factors that work in promoting children's well-being in relation to particular health topics identifies the importance of taking children's views into account. The evaluation report states:

> . . . successful programmes build on children's and young people's own needs, concerns and interests with regard to a health issue; are responsive to issues such as age, gender, and vulnerability; are interactive (rather than didactic) in nature, and enable children and young people to acquire new knowledge, clarify their values, and to practise new skills.
>
> (Warwick *et al.*, 2009: 32)

A good knowledge base exists on children and young people's views on health, well-being and health services that schools can build on when planning health-participation activity. Children and young people have been consulted extensively on a range of health and well-being issues and health services. The National Children Bureau's Research and Evaluation Department summarised some of these consultations in a literature review in 2005. Consistent messages and themes identified in this report include:

- being healthy for children and young people isn't simply about being well or unwell, but is strongly influenced by how they feel and their relationships with friends, family and others;
- the environment in which children love, live, learn and play has a strong influence on how healthy they feel. They want their environments to be safe, welcoming, enjoyable and free from bullying, and offer appropriate activities for children and young people;
- the importance for children and young people of the confidential relationship when accessing health services;
- a desire that all practitioners are skilled and confident in talking with, listening and responding to children and young people, and that they show them respect;
- that children are seen as experts on their own health and well-being and capable of being partners in their own health care; and
- children want choice in relation to the information and support they receive on health and well-being.

(National Children's Bureau Research and
Evaluation Department, 2005)

Schools' role in enabling children's participation in health and well-being

Examples of participation work in schools are well documented on national and local websites and in research and guidance. Schools can use various approaches to involve children and young people in decision-making in relation to health and well-being at individual, family, school and community levels. Partnerships with parents and carers and a range of statutory, voluntary and private sector agencies can help schools to capitalise on opportunities for students to inform decision-making within their school and community. Businesses may be willing to donate equipment that promotes healthy behaviours such as lights for bikes and pedometers, although schools will want to balance these opportunities with their responsibilities to protect students from aggressive marketing and commercialism (Mayo and Nairn, 2009).

Children's Trusts have representation from commissioners and managers across children's services in a locality, including school governors, and are underpinned by the Children Act 2004 duty to cooperate and improve outcomes for all children. This mechanism can be used to develop consensus on children and young people's roles in shaping local services such as health services, and to create shared opportunities for their sustained involvement.

Participation methods and approaches

Children and young people being active decision-makers in relation to their own health and well-being behaviours

Effective ways to encourage health behaviour change among children have occupied the minds of policy-makers, researchers, academics and health professionals for many years, for example on smoking, drugs and alcohol, sexual health and obesity. The challenges of helping children and families apply their knowledge of health issues to make and sustain positive lifestyle changes have been documented in national policy (Department of Health, 2004).

An approach developed by the National Children's Bureau (NCB), commissioned by the Food Standards Agency, called *The Health Challenge*, provides an effective model for empowering children and young people to make and sustain lifestyle changes that promote their health and well-being based on exercising choice, self-exploration and learning. The programme, piloted in schools, uses a challenge approach where students choose one thing that they are going to change for four weeks to improve their health and well-being from any of the following areas: healthy eating, physical activity and feeling good inside. The initiative is student led: students have a say in how the programme is run in their school and in choosing their individual health challenge. Students are encouraged to buddy up with a friend and provided with practical tips on how to succeed in their challenge. In a recent evaluation, both primary and secondary school students reported success in sticking to their challenges. The research identified that having choice early on about the challenge contributed to students enjoying and committing to the programme. Collective action by students, parents, carers, teachers and school staff was also a significant motivator, supported by the whole school approach (Mainey *et al.*, 2009). The programme was rolled out nationally in 2009 under the new name *SmallSteps4Life*.

Supporting a whole school approach to health and well-being

The concept of a settings-based approach that harnesses the power of the entire setting for promoting health and well-being has its roots within the World Health Organization Health for All Strategy (World Health Organization, 1980) and the Ottawa Charter for Health Promotion (World Health Organization, 1986). Everyone living and working in the setting is committed to and has responsibility for making the environment as healthy as possible. 'Health is created and lived by people within the settings of their everyday life; where they learn, work, play and love' (World Health Organization, 1986).

The National Healthy Schools Programme is underpinned by a whole school approach to health and well-being that recognises that being healthy is not just about children and young people, but the whole school community. There are ten elements to this work:

- leadership, management and managing change;
- policy development;
- curriculum planning and resources, including work with outside agencies;
- learning and teaching;
- school culture and environment;
- giving children and young people a voice;
- support services for children and young people;
- staff professional development needs, health and welfare;
- partnerships with parents/carers and local communities; and
- assessing, recording and reporting children and young people's achievement.

(Healthy Schools, 2007: 5)

Students have valued the improvements in school ethos and quality of social relationships that had been achieved through the Healthy Schools' Whole School Approach (Warwick *et al.*, 2004).

The Health Challenge Programme evaluation, mentioned earlier, reported that 'embedding the Health Challenge Programme through class and whole school activities was valuable, and helped to support students doing individual challenges: "a groundswell" was created which appears to have maintained staff and student motivation and commitment to the programme' (Mainey *et al.*, 2009: 90).

Shaping the design and delivery of health services, within both the school and the community

Schools can promote students' involvement in local authority and primary care trust-led engagement processes, for example in connection with the Children and Young People's Plan owned by the Children's Trust. Many local authorities have set up young people's forums, youth parliaments, councils and children's rights groups mainly made up of representation from schools to tackle health and well-being issues such as bullying. Some have won awards as well as made films or held exhibitions of young people's artwork.

Initiating and leading health-related projects within the school that also have benefits for the community

Students may be asked to identify a need within the school and find solutions to problems. These include setting up initiatives to improve the environment such as reducing litter, promoting recycling and improving school dinners. Students can also help plan and deliver community improvement initiatives that contribute to positive health outcomes such as providing support to the elderly.

Informing teaching and learning content and delivery to promote healthy behaviours

This may focus on a particular curriculum area or be expanded to include health and well-being issues that are emerging within the school or local community, for example alcohol misuse. Activities can include students being asked their views on issues that encourage or hinder their learning and participating in evaluating lessons, so that the quality of teaching is improved.

Participating in training and development opportunities so young people feel equipped to participate in decision-making that improves health and well-being

Opportunities include training for children and young people that further develops their skills in communicating with their peers and adult decision-makers, increases their understanding of decision-making processes and how they can influence and understand any statutory or legal responsibilities connected to their role in the school, organisation or local authority and governance. Children can also lead or co-deliver training with professionals.

Involving children and young people in the design and implementation of school policies

These can include policies on health and well-being such as anti-bullying strategies and drug, alcohol, smoking, homework or behaviour policies. Students' engagement can help ensure that policies are realistic, benefit them and the wider school community, contribute to a positive atmosphere, support the aims and ethos of the school and are understood and implemented.

Involving children and young people in communications and media activities

Communications and media activities can be used to celebrate students' and the school's achievements and promote positive images of children and young people as active citizens. They can also develop students' media literacy skills.

Promoting access to and engagement in creative activities such as play, arts and leisure which promote health and well-being, relationship building, self-expression, enjoyment and participation has been particularly effective in engaging children and young people who ordinarily do not benefit from participation and support opportunities, for example children looked after by the local authority (National Children's Bureau, 2006).

Multi-media tools such as videos and audio recordings, text messaging, electronic voting and online discussion spaces and surveys can motivate creative expression among children and young people. Student newsletters may also enable them to communicate their views on school issues (Davies, 2008).

Supporting young people to become peer researchers, campaigners and fundraisers

Many children have won awards through the Diana Award and Anne Frank Awards, which recognise young people who contribute to their communities and improve the lives of others, for being champions in anti-bullying work. Young people on school councils undertake surveys with other students to find out about their health and well-being concerns. Some students may get involved in petitioning on issues such as school dinners.

In recent months, there has been an explosion of young ambassador programmes on climate change and sustainable living in England in response to children and young people's real concerns about the impacts of climate change. These new coalitions aim to involve children and young people in decision-making processes nationally, internationally and in their communities. There is also a strong global dimension recognising that connecting to children's stories in other parts of the world is important for mobilising collective action. Children may also become involved in fundraising for their school or community.

Students acting as peer mentors and supporters on health and well-being issues and related topics

Friendships are very important to children and young people (Layard and Dunn, 2009), and careful mentoring can harness children and young people's desires to be supportive of their peers. A variety of peer-support approaches exist, including peer mediation, peer advocacy, peer education and peer mentoring. Blake and Parsons (2004) describe peer mentoring as usually involving a supportive, one-to-one relationship between two peers for a defined period of time. A mentor may provide friendship and support for a peer during a difficult time, such as after a family bereavement. Peer mentoring and buddy schemes are becoming increasingly common as a way of involving children and young people in supporting others who may be worried about bullying or experiencing conflict in schools across the country.

Involving children and young people in school planning and governance

There are a variety of ways in which young people can be involved in planning and governance – for example, in staff recruitment, including headship appointments and school inspection. School councils and school committees linked to the school council can address specific issues such as environmental awareness, curriculum and health and safety. Research suggests that a number of elements contribute towards successful school councils, including a clear rationale as to why students are being involved, the availability of teacher input, the utilisation of strategies for engaging all students and provision of training and support (Whitty and Wisby, 2007).

Conclusion

There is a good evidence base and a range of levers to provide impetus for children and young people's involvement in schools. Schools have a vital role to play in ensuring that students experience participation as an integral part of school life, learning and their overall health and well-being. Increasing acceptance of the value of whole setting-based approaches, including whole school activities, in promoting health and well-being means that participation is more likely to be seen as a key aspect and product of whole school life. In order to be effective, participation needs to be implicit within the functions of the entire school and be evaluated as part of a school's effectiveness.

The wider context of children and young people's lives also influences aspirations and opportunities to participate. In general, more work is needed to communicate adults' love and care for children within wider society and to promote realistic and positive attitudes towards children and young people and images of them that acknowledge their importance within families and communities and the tangible differences they make. Children and young people need to feel connected, valued and optimistic about their place in society:

> We need a more positive attitude to children, where we welcome them into our society and want to help them . . . So it is possible to construct a modern society in which there are higher levels of child well-being than in Britain. The key is an ethic in which we care more for each other. As the psychological evidence shows, this yields a double benefit – other people treat us better and we feel better from helping them. It is a world like this, built on the law of love, that we should create with our children.
>
> (Layard and Dunn, 2009: 162–163)

A range of research, policy and guidance exists that can help to ensure that children's rights to participate are not undermined by poor principles and practice. Measuring the changes arising from participation and the resources required to bring about the change remains difficult, but the challenge of doing so should not be ignored. Resources such as *Measuring the Magic?* (Kirby with Bryson, 2002) and the *What's Changed Participation Outcomes Tool* (National Youth Agency, 2006) can help schools and other organisations examine and demonstrate the outcomes of children's involvement.

Through an ongoing commitment to student participation, schools can make a long-term commitment to children and young people's health and well-being. Schools will help to ensure that children and young people grow up happy and healthy and optimistic about life and their opportunities, are able to communicate and relate confidently at home, work or in their community, and ultimately become a force for positive change now and in the future.

References

Arnstein, S. (1969) 'A ladder of citizen participation in the USA', *Journal of the American Institute of Planners*, 35(4): 216–224.

Barnes, J., Ball, M., Meadows, P., McLeish, J., Belsky, J. and the FNP Implementation Research Team, Institute for the Study of Children, Families and Social Issues, Birkbeck, University of London (2008) *Nurse–Family Partnership Programme. First Year Pilot Site Implementation in England: Pregnancy and the Post-partum Period*. Research Information. London: DCSF.

Blake, S. (2005) *Don't be Afraid – Have Your Say! Children and Young People's Views on Participation at School*. London: National Children's Bureau.

Blake, S. and Frances, G. (2004) *Promoting Children and Young People's Participation through the National Healthy School Standard*. London: Department of Health.

Blake, S. and Parsons, M. (2004) *Spotlight Briefing. Peer Support: An Overview*. London: National Children's Bureau.

Carnegie UK Trust (2008) *Empowering Young People: The Final Report of the Carnegie Young People Initiative*. Dunfermline: Carnegie UK Trust.

Davies, L., Williams, C., Yamashita, H. with Ko Man-Hing (2005a) *Inspiring Schools. Impact and Outcomes: Taking Up the Challenge of Pupil Participation*. London: Carnegie UK Trust.

Davies, L., Williams, C., Yamashita, H. with Ko Man-Hing (2005b) *Inspiring Schools. Case Studies for Change: Taking Up the Challenge of Pupil Participation*. London: Carnegie UK Trust.

Davies, T. (2008) *How to Use Multi-media Tools to Engage Children and Young People in Decision Making*. London: National Children's Bureau and Participation Works.

Department for Education and Skills (2004a) *Every Child Matters: Change for Children*. London: The Stationery Office.

Department for Education and Skills (2004b) *Working Together: Giving Children and Young People a Say*. London: DfES.

Department for Education and Skills (2005) *Common Core of Skills and Knowledge for the Children's Workforce*. London: DfES.

Department of Health (2004) *Choosing Health: Making Healthy Choices Easier*. London: The Stationery Office.

Francique, M. (2008) 'Engaging young people from minority ethnic backgrounds', *Vibes and Voices*, 6 (Spring/Summer): 14–15.

Franklin, A. and Sloper, P. (2005) 'Listening and responding? Children's participation in health care within England', *International Journal of Children's Rights*, 13: 11–29.

Fuller, E. (2009) *The Relationship between National Healthy School Status and Selected School Outcomes*. London: National Centre for Social Research.

Hannam, D. (2003) 'Participation and responsible action for all students: The crucial ingredient for success', *Teaching Citizenship*, Issue 5, Spring: 24–33.

Hart, R. (1992) *Children's Participation: From Tokenism to Citizenship*. Florence: UNICEF International Child Development Centre.

Healthy Schools (2007) *Whole School Approach to the National Healthy Schools Programme*. London: DCSF and Department of Health.

Kirby, P. with Bryson, S. (2002) *Measuring the Magic? Evaluating and Researching Young People's Participation in Public Decision Making*. London: Carnegie Young People Initiative.

Kirby, P., Lanyon, C., Cronin, K. and Sinclair, R. (2003) *Building a Culture of Participation: Involving Children and Young People in Policy, Service Planning, Delivery and Evaluation. Handbook*. London: DfES.

Layard, R. and Dunn, J. (2009) *A Good Childhood: Searching for Values in a Competitive Age*. London: Penguin Books.

McNeish, D. and Newman, T. (2002) 'Involving children and young people in decision making', in D. McNeish, T. Newman and H. Roberts (eds) *What Works for Children? Effective Services for Children and Families*. Milton Keynes: Open University Press: 186–204.

Madge, N., Franklin, A. and Willmot, N. (2003) *Research Summary: National Healthy School Standard and Pupil Participation*. Unpublished. Available at http://www.wiredforhealth. gov.uk/PDF/NHSS_research_summary.PDF (accessed 20 April 2009).

Mainey, A., Gibb, J., Dillon, L. and Lewis, J. (2009) 'The Health Challenge Programme: Evaluation of a Pilot Intervention in Kent Schools'. Commissioned by the Food Standards Agency. Final Evaluation Report, August 2009. Unpublished. London: National Children's Bureau and Food Standards Agency.

Mayo, E. and Nairn, A. (2009) *Consumer Kids: How Big Business is Grooming Our Children for Profit*. London: Constable.

National Children's Bureau (2006) *Healthy Care Briefing: Arts in Partnerships to Promote Health*. London: National Children's Bureau.

National Children's Bureau Research and Evaluation Department (2005) 'Children and Young People's Views on Health and Health Services: A Review of the Evidence'. Unpublished. London: National Children's Bureau.

National Youth Agency (2006) *What's Changed Participation Outcomes Tool*. Leicester: National Youth Agency and Local Government Association.

Oldfield, C. and Fowler, C. (2004) *Mapping Children and Young People's Participation in England*. London: DfES.

Warwick, I., Aggleton, P., Chase, E., Zuurmond, M., Blenkinsop, S., Eggers, M., Schagen, I., Schagen, S. and Scott, E. (2004) *Evaluation of the Impact of the National Healthy School Standard*. London: Thomas Coram Research Unit and National Foundation for Educational Research.

Warwick, I., Mooney, A. and Oliver, C. (2009) *National Healthy Schools Programme: Developing the Evidence Base*. London: Thomas Coram Research Institute and Institute of Education, University of London.

Whitty, G. and Wisby, E. (2007) *Research Brief: Real Decision Making? School Councils in Action*. Institute of Education, University of London. London: DCSF.

Willow, C. (2002) *Participation in Practice: Children and Young People as Partners in Change*. London: Children's Society.

World Health Organization (1980) *European Regional Strategy for Health for All*. Copenhagen: WHO Regional Office for Europe.

World Health Organization (1986) *Ottawa Charter for Health Promotion*. Copenhagen: Health Promotion International.

Zachary, L. (2009) *PALS: Getting It Right for Children and Young People. Good Practice Case Studies*. London: National Children's Bureau.

Chapter 10

The contribution of parents

Claire James

This chapter looks at the contribution that parents can make to health and well-being in schools. Children and young people spend only a limited amount of their time at school, and families not only influence what children do when they are not at school, but also shape their attitudes to and understanding of a range of issues, including health and well-being. Much more can be achieved with regard to children and young people's health and well-being when schools and parents work together.

Three key issues are covered in this chapter: healthy eating and, in particular, the introduction of healthier school meals; improving young people's sex and relationships education; and promoting children's emotional well-being and mental health through family support. Although there are potentially a number of other topics on which to focus, these three areas have attracted particular attention with respect to parental engagement with schools. The chapter then focuses on some general principles of how best to work with and involve parents and concludes with suggestions as to how schools might better involve parents in health-related programmes and activities.

Schools, parents, health and well-being

Healthy eating and school meals

In 2005, amid mounting concern about childhood obesity, the TV chef Jamie Oliver became the public face of a campaign to improve school meals which received heavy coverage in the media. In response, the Government pledged to invest £220 million over three years to make school food healthier, with additional funds to set up the School Food Trust to give independent support and advice to schools.

However, in many schools not enough was done to involve pupils and parents in these changes. In Rotherham, South Yorkshire, for example, two mothers became the focus of media attention in 2006 when their local school changed its mealtime policies. The school no longer allowed pupils outside the school at lunchtime, so the mothers took orders for fish and chips, burgers, jacket potatoes and sandwiches and delivered them to pupils through the school railings. The mothers told journalists that they did this because many children did not like the new 'healthy' menu and their lunch break had been reduced from 45 minutes to half an hour, which did not leave children enough time to queue for and eat their food (BBC, 2006; Perrie, 2006).

More generally, a recent Ofsted review of the national situation found that in 19 of 27 schools inspected, the take-up of school meals had fallen by between 9 per cent and 25 per cent since new interim standards for food in schools came into force in September 2006 (Ofsted, 2007). More children were bringing packed lunches, which were sometimes much less healthy than the new school meals. This trend was attributed to a number of factors, including the cost of school meals for low-income families, a lack of choice, a lack of consultation with pupils over the content of menus, pupils' unfamiliarity with some of the food being provided by the school, and poor marketing of the new menus.

However, although between 2006–07 and 2007–08 the overall decline in take-up seems to have halted, there is clear variation across and within local authorities (Nicholas et al., 2008). For those local authority school caterers who were experiencing a fall in demand, the most common explanation given was that the new 'healthy' menus resulted in more pupils bringing packed lunches. Where demand was steady or had increased, the most common reasons caterers gave were a whole school food policy, marketing of school meals to pupils, and marketing to parents.

The School Food Trust, which seeks to promote healthy food in schools, has developed a number of case studies, several of which feature good practice in involving parents.[1] In some schools, school food policy was shaped by a steering group that included parents. Wider consultation with parents was also perceived to be important, as was ongoing consultation with pupils. In one school in the north of England, for example, initial attempts to ban soft drinks and unhealthy foods from packed lunches were resented by pupils and not supported by parents. A new policy, agreed by the pupil council, was promoted to parents by the children themselves, with pupil helpers checking packed lunches. The new rules were more acceptable to pupils and to parents, who ensured that packed lunches almost always complied with the new rules.

Another way in which parents were engaged in some of the case study schools was to run tasting sessions of the new menus at parents' evenings. In some of the primary schools, parents had been invited to have lunch in the dining room with pupils. School-based courses in cookery and healthy eating have also sometimes proved popular. These have ranged from one-off sessions to a ten-week accredited course run for parents in schools in Newcastle. To ensure that childcare is available, this latter has usually been held at nurseries attached to schools or children's centres which have their own cooking facilities. Other schools have held sessions in which children learn about healthy eating alongside their parents. Hampshire's 'Cook and Eat' project, for example, is mainly an after-school club activity designed for parents and pupils, but some schools run it just for parents or just for pupils.

In some instances, parents may even be ahead of schools in calling for changes towards healthy eating. In the London Borough of Merton, for example, a group of parents began a campaign in 2005 for better meals in primary schools. Working with headteachers in some of the schools, the parent-led campaign lobbied the council, and achieved healthier food in all the borough's primary schools. A new catering contract is now in place and the council also employs a full-time nutritionist (Topping, 2008).

Parents and sexual health in schools

While healthy eating can occasionally trigger tensions with parents, the topic of sex and relationships education (SRE) is perhaps more controversial (see Chapter 8, this volume). This need not be the case, but SRE can be an issue which raises fundamental questions about the rights of parents and those of young people and children.

Henricson and Bainham (2005) have highlighted some of these. For example, Protocol 1 in Article 2 of the European Convention on Human Rights states that 'In the exercise of any functions which it assumes in relation to education and to teaching, the State shall respect the right of parents to ensure such education and teaching is in conformity with their own religious and philosophical conditions' (Council of Europe, 1952). Meanwhile, the UN Convention on the Rights of the Child states: 'State Parties shall respect the right of the child to freedom of thought, conscience and religion' (United Nations General Assembly, 1989).

Schools, therefore, need to consider not only their legal obligations, but also the underlying principles and values with which they operate. The school has a responsibility to ensure that the information it provides is scientifically and legally accurate. It also has a responsibility to protect young people from discrimination on the grounds of ethnicity, religion, gender or sexual orientation.

The interface between SRE and religious belief may be particularly sensitive. It has been argued that children are entitled to an 'open future', with the education system 'offering children a cultural, moral and spiritual framework for development, and equipping them with a capacity to criticise that framework and a knowledge of alternatives' (Henricson and Bainham, 2005: 72). In a similar vein, Halstead and Reiss (2003) have argued that monocultural sex education which presents only one religious perspective does not respect the future autonomy of the child. However, they also state that sex education cannot truly be 'value-free'. In trying to make it so, values are still present but will be implicit and unquestioned, which does not help children identify and develop their own values or challenge those presented in the media.

Given these principles, the Sex Education Forum has explored how parents in multi-faith communities can be consulted on SRE (Blake and Katrak, 2002). They argue that, while consensus should not necessarily be an expected outcome of consultation, open discussion can reduce mutual misunderstandings. They note that such consultation needs to be skilfully facilitated.

One example of such consultation has been with Turkish Muslim parents on sex and relationships education in a girls' school in a multi-racial area of London. The headteacher attended consultation sessions, which were arranged at times to suit parents. The consultation reassured parents that sex education would help children avoid abusive and exploitative situations. The sessions also challenged staff perceptions that parents would not be interested in SRE, or that open discussion would lead to girls being withdrawn from SRE (Blake and Katrak, 2002).

Issues that have generally been found to be important to Muslim parents include sex education being delivered in single-sex groups, not using visual aids that are too explicit and avoiding the provision of sex education during Ramadan. Underlying this was their concern that SRE should be presented in a context which explains different faith perspectives on sex before marriage (Blake and Katrak, 2002).

However, a degree of caution is needed when engaging parents in discussion about SRE to ensure that the voices of the children and young people who are directly affected by these decisions are not overlooked (Halstead and Reiss, 2003). This includes the voices of disabled pupils as well as lesbian and gay pupils. With regard to the latter, the school should highlight to pupils and parents that people have a right to express their sexuality in any way which is within the law and that homophobic bullying will not be tolerated.

Regarding the division of responsibility between parents and schools for SRE, some parents would like to play a greater role in informing their children about sex-related issues, but feel they lack the confidence to do this. Over half of parents, for example, have been reported to find it embarrassing to talk about sex with their child – yet many also say that being able to talk about sex, sexual health and relationships with their teenager would make them feel like a better parent (Department for Children, Schools and Families, 2008).

If schools can help parents feel more confident about talking to their children about sex and relationships, this may be a potentially effective way of helping young people to learn about relationships and sexual health. A national survey, for example, found that 44 per cent of all 11 to 14-year-olds said they would like to talk about sex with parents, because they did not trust the information they received from friends. One-third felt that talking about sex and sexual health would help them feel closer to their parents (Department for Children, Schools and Families, 2008).

One way to support parents in such discussion may be for schools to provide information to parents on talking about relationships and sex in day-to-day conversations with their children. As part of the 'Time to Talk' campaign, government advice to parents suggested that they could, for example, use the storylines in television programmes to start conversations with their children (Department for Children, Schools and Families, 2008).

Another approach is that taken by the 'Speakeasy' course for parents run by the Family Planning Association. This course greatly increased parents' confidence in talking to their children about sex through increased factual knowledge as well as providing guidance on specific strategies to approach difficult topics and reduce the embarrassment associated with discussion of sex. Parents reported that the course was relaxed and informal and helped them to 'get together' with other parents (Coleman *et al.*, 2007). Two to three years after the course, parents reported that they still found what they had learned in the course to be useful in responding to their children's questions.

However, involving fathers, in particular, can prove difficult. Very few men attended the 'Speakeasy' course, and those who did were often there as foster parents or because they undertook voluntary work with young people (Coleman *et al.*, 2007). Mothers appear more likely to discuss sex and relationships with young people, and boys are particularly likely to miss out on advice from parents. While 66 per cent of boys receive sex information and 68 per cent advice on relationships from their mothers, only 6 per cent and 11 per cent respectively get advice on these subjects from their fathers (Department for Children, Schools and Families, 2008).

Young people whose parents had completed the 'Speakeasy' course reported that they could talk to their parents more easily about sex, and some young people felt that the way they themselves now thought about sex was different from that of many of their peers at school (Ramm and Coleman, 2008).

Mental health and well-being: family support

Family circumstances and relationships are a major influence on children and young people's emotional health and well-being. Alongside direct support for children and young people such as through the provision of counselling services, schools can help more indirectly by providing support to parents.

Some schools have successfully run structured parenting courses to help parents who are having difficulty managing their children's behaviour. Other schools believe that these would not be popular. Some have used fun activities such as family cooking to engage parents, enabling discussion of parenting issues as part of this. Others have used drop-in groups for informal support, either universally or targeted at particular groups of parents (Apps *et al.*, 2007).

One successful way of supporting parents is through Parent Support Advisers (PSAs), which have been piloted in schools in 12 local authorities. Parents who had sought help from PSAs recognised that many problems related to their children's behavioural, emotional and social development arose from events at home. These included problematic parental relationships, child–step-parent relationships, depression and mental health problems, drug and alcohol misuse, housing problems, and domestic violence (Lindsay *et al.*, 2008).

PSA assistance ranged from informal support, through individual and group support such as parenting classes, to intensive support for parents in substantial need. Parents valued the confidentiality of their service and the balance between professionalism and being 'like a friend'. PSAs were seen as engaging and empowering parents, improving parents' relationships with their children and improving their children's behavioural, emotional and social development (Lindsay *et al.*, 2008).

Providing family support in this way may seem to be beyond schools' traditional remit, but is part of an increasing understanding that children and young people's well-being cannot be separated from their family circumstances. Supporting parents is an integral part of the extended schools agenda, which aims to improve children's outcomes through schools providing a wider range of services (Department for Children, Schools and Families, 2007).

However, schools can experience difficulties in finding appropriate services to which they can refer parents. Key staff need to be aware of, and may need to work closely with, local agencies and local child and adolescent mental health services. With regard to support to families, links between schools and social services mainly take the form of signposting and referral of families (Apps *et al.*, 2007). However, there can be difficulties where schools operate with information-sharing policies but where parents' confidentiality must be maintained and trust built. Guidelines regarding confidentiality need to be understood by all those involved.

In a review of full service extended schools, some schools had a range of professionals working on the school site for at least part of the week. These could provide support to both pupils and their families more quickly than would be the case if a referral to an outside agency were required, and were able to offer continuing, rather than time-limited, support (Cummings *et al.*, 2007).

Parental engagement in schools: some general principles

Policy and practice

Government policy on parental involvement appears to take three different views of parents: as consumers, as problems or as partners (Reynolds, 2006). Over the last two decades, parents have increasingly been viewed as purchasers or service consumers, with government policy highlighting parents' rights to access information about schools. There has also been more emphasis on parental 'choice' in the school admissions process.

However, parents have also been viewed as a problem, especially where children's misbehaviour is linked to poor parenting. For example, schools have been encouraged to use formal 'parenting contracts' with parents regarding their children's poor behaviour or truancy. If parents fail to meet their legal duty to ensure their child attends school regularly, they can be fined or, in some circumstances, sent to prison. Home–school agreements signed by parents have also been viewed by some as an attempt to 'police' the actions of parents (Reynolds, 2006).

More positively, parents can also be viewed as partners in educating children. There is considerable evidence that parents' involvement in their children's learning at home, starting in the first year of life, has a significant impact on children's educational achievement (Desforges with Abouchaar, 2003; Department for Children, Schools and Families, 2008). There has been a particular focus on how best to reduce the difference in educational outcomes between children from different socio-economic groups. A number of programmes have concentrated on early years provision, but others are aimed at parents of older children, for example through providing family learning projects in schools. Some programmes have sought to involve fathers in particular, since there is evidence that fathers' interest and involvement in their children's learning is associated with better educational outcomes (Goldman, 2005).

The degree of parental involvement in schools can be measured in at least two different ways. The first relates to the effort put in by parents, such as helping with their children's homework and volunteering in the school. The second identifies the extent to which parents' voices are heard within the school – both in regard to their own children and in wider school decision-making. The benefits of the former to a school may be obvious; the latter perhaps less so. However, the latter (which includes the quality of home–school communication) may have a significant impact on whether parents are prepared to put effort into the former.

In thinking about the concept of 'parental voice' in schools, a 'ladder' of participation and engagement may be useful. The ladder moves from the lowest level, which is simply informing parents of decisions; through consultation, which gives parents limited opportunities to influence certain decisions; and finally to partnership, where decisions are made and agendas are set together. One advantage of this model is that it requires an explicit decision as to what is the appropriate level of engagement for any issue; what parents can expect to change as a result; and what the limits to their involvement will be.

A guide for professionals using this type of model in working with parents is provided by the Council for Disabled Children and Contact a Family (2004). The National Healthy Schools Programme also attempts to divide parental/carer engagement and participation into different types, distinguishing at each level what is essential practice, best practice and exemplary practice (DH/DCSF, 2008). At the level of consultation, for example, essential practice is said to include 'feedback requested on a regular basis, e.g. termly questionnaires', while exemplary practice would include 'whole school surveys with focus groups that include hard to reach parents/carers, new parents/carers, [and] parents/carers that have had a difficult relationship with the school' (DH/DCSF, 2008: 38).

Specific barriers to involvement

Not all parents feel comfortable in a school environment. Some may recall negative experiences from their own schooldays (Apps *et al.*, 2007). There may also be logistical problems to involving parents. Many parents, for example, find it difficult to come into school because of work and other demands on their life, and may also experience problems regarding childcare and transport to and from the school (Reynolds, 2006).

Some groups of parents are more likely not to be involved in schools. These include fathers (and particularly non-resident fathers), parents whose first language is not English, and families with complex problems or multiple needs (Apps *et al.*, 2007). Teachers may assume that those who are not visibly involved are not interested in their children's education (Page, 2009). This is one reason why parental engagement should be designed to ensure that some groups of parents are not systematically excluded.

The transition from primary to secondary school is a significant change for both children and parents. Parents tend to be much less involved in their children's secondary education than they were during primary school. Factors contributing to this are that secondary schools tend to be larger and more formal than primary, that subjects are more advanced (so parents feel less capable of helping children with homework), and that children themselves may seek increasing independence from their parents (Page, 2009).

Teachers, too, may wish to set clear limits to parental involvement, because they are not sure what demands parents will place on them. Some teachers may fear the extra workload involvement with parents may bring. Moreover, parents can be perceived as a potential threat to teachers' authority and autonomy. Some teachers may feel that they do not have the training and skills to work with parents (Reynolds, 2006). One survey of teachers, for example, found that 70 per cent did not think that training and professional development prepared teachers to work with parents successfully (Hallgarten, 2000).

Teachers may also either believe that parents are not interested in their child's education or, alternatively, feel that some parents are a little too interested and will try to manipulate the system for the benefit of their children. In the same survey cited above, 74 per cent of respondents disagreed that parents should have a greater say in how schools are run (Hallgarten, 2000). In a well-publicised comment, David Hart, general secretary of the National Association of Head Teachers, told the union's annual conference in 2005 that giving more power to parents who lack responsibility was like 'putting an alcoholic in charge of a bar' (Garner, 2005).

Good practice in engaging parents

There are a number of ways in which parents can be supported to become more fully involved with schools. Four elements of good practice are highlighted here. These are: communicating with parents to provide them with relevant and timely information about the work of the school; building a culture within schools of listening to parents and responding to their agendas (so reaching higher levels of the 'ladder of participation' described above); having in place a non-teaching specialist link worker who can build up good relationships with parents and support families; and putting in place programmes and activities to engage those parents considered 'hard to reach' (Page, 2009).

Useful ways of communicating with parents include letters, telephone calls, e-mails, newsletters, websites and face-to-face meetings. E-mail is seen by many parents as efficient (Page, 2009), while a study on parental involvement in multi-ethnic schools found that personal phone calls were appreciated (Department for Education and Skills, undated). One message from parents is that the 'letter in the schoolbag' can be a very unreliable way of communicating with them (Page, 2009).

Some of the most basic information and communication requirements are a welcoming and informative reception area with reception staff trained to be courteous and helpful to parents; a clear system for answering telephone, e-mail or written enquiries from parents and responding promptly; information provided to parents in good time, for example about term dates; and a clear complaints policy, which responds to complaints positively (Page, 2009).

Transition information sessions for all parents can lay the foundations for a good parent–school relationship from the beginning of a child's time at the school. These inform parents on what to expect from the new school and how to access local services, and help them understand about child development and learning. They also enable parents to meet each other as well as school staff (Page, 2009).

Building a culture of listening to parents means moving beyond a notion of 'parental involvement' as simply informing parents and enlisting their help. It requires developing a culture within schools of listening to parents, children and staff, using what has been learned to develop new ways of working. This more open culture can only arise with strong leadership from headteachers and senior staff, which can help ensure all teachers know the importance of working with parents – and feel able to do so.

Parents should know how they can offer suggestions as well as complaints. A clear response to parental concerns can increase parental engagement with the school (Harris and Goodall, 2007). This can take the form of highlighting parents' concerns and noting what action has been taken as a result of these – using, for example, the format of 'You said, we did'.

In order to elicit the concerns of a particular group of parents, one London school has created a forum for parents of African Caribbean/Black African students. Parents set the agenda and discuss issues such as cultural differences and racism openly to address issues behind the low attainment of pupils from these backgrounds and to try to resolve conflict. The school staff present at the meetings feed back to a teaching staff meeting. The group has since taken on other projects such as a mentoring scheme (Carpentier and Lall, 2005).

With regard to working with and supporting parents, a non-teaching link worker who is the first point of contact for parents can facilitate the school's relations with parents and increase parents' involvement in their children's education (Page, 2009). The role of the link worker (or home–school liaison officer) includes establishing contact and building ongoing relationships. For some families, home visits can be an important element of this work (Department for Education and Skills, undated).

Other activities undertaken by the link worker may include helping parents to support their children's learning in school and at home; organising specific activities and parents' groups; helping parents to have a voice in the work of the school; dealing with attendance issues; identifying and responding to the needs of individual families, in partnership with other agencies and services; or mediating between teachers and parents to share information and clear up misunderstandings.

These three elements of good practice – providing relevant information, adopting a listening approach and employing a link worker – apply when engaging with all parents, but are particularly important when addressing the fourth element of good practice: reaching those who may be 'harder to reach'. These can include fathers, ethnic minority parents, parents with low literacy or any parents who do not feel comfortable in a school environment.

As far as possible, schools should aim to make their work as inclusive as possible, to avoid attempts at parental involvement unintentionally reinforcing existing educational inequalities around class, gender and ethnicity. This may require 'consultation about consultation', for example finding out which parents might find it difficult to attend a meeting at school, why this is and what could be done to help, or whether additional consultation methods might be needed.

Projects or events focused exclusively on, for example, fathers or parents from a particular ethnic background can make a dramatic difference in building confidence to engage with the school (Carpentier and Lall, 2005; Goldman, 2005). A long-term commitment to working with some groups may be necessary to establish trust. As one author has noted, 'Parents are not alike – they differ in their commitments, skills and confidence in dealing with teachers – but all parents overwhelmingly appreciate being consulted, valued and welcomed by their child's school' (Page, 2009: 68).

One final principle to keep in mind is that a positive relationship often comes from celebrating success. This includes informing parents about the good things their children do as well as the bad, and helping parents to build their own confidence and skills in supporting their children's learning.

Conclusion

No matter what the issue, the role of parents should not be ignored in any attempt to improve the health of children and young people. Working with parents on health should be seen to be an integral part of the school's overall approach. Consultation with parents can help them to feel listened to, valued and welcomed, which, in turn, can promote cooperation. The examples provided in this chapter illustrate good practice in engaging parents in health and well-being in schools. Lessons may also be drawn from what has worked more generally in involving parents in school life and their children's education.

Overall, for example, it is important to work with parents as partners, building a culture of listening to parents about their children's health and well-being, and responding to what parents say. In this way, parents are more likely to engage with school programmes and activities. However, slightly different strategies may be needed depending on a school's history of parental involvement and its starting point. For example, in primary schools, parents may already be more involved in school programmes and activities than in secondary school and further education settings.

Particular effort may need to be made to engage with parents who traditionally have been 'harder to reach', be they fathers, ethnic minority parents or those who do not feel comfortable in a school environment. Having in place a non-teaching link worker who can act as the first point of contact for parents may be of particular benefit in these circumstances. The work that family link workers undertake with families to help them cope with difficulties they are facing may have a significant impact on their children's health and well-being. At the other end of the scale, link workers can also be involved in the development and implementation of healthy school policies by engaging parents in relevant events and activities. These could be tailored to the needs of particular parents, a sports event for fathers, for example, or a multicultural food fair.

More structured consultation may be appropriate when school policies on, say, healthy eating or SRE are being drawn up or revised. The 'ladder' model of participation may be useful in distinguishing between the provision of information, consultation and more in-depth participation. Consultation and participation should be seen as an ongoing process, reviewing which parents were reached, what they said, what changed as a result and how the process could be improved.

Including parents as partners in promoting health and well-being will not necessarily be straightforward, since there are at least three important sets of perspectives to keep in mind – the teachers', the parents' and those of children and young people themselves. Although the rights and needs of children and young people will necessarily be the school's primary concern, these cannot be seen in isolation from the broader family context. An open and respectful approach will minimise conflict, and understanding parents' perspectives is likely to increase any programme's chance of success.

Note

1 See www.schoolfoodtrust.org.uk (accessed 24 March 2009).

References

Apps, J., Ashby, V. and Bauman, M. (2007) *Family Support in Extended Schools: Planning, Commissioning and Delivery*. London: Family and Parenting Institute.

BBC (2006) 'Parents feed pupils through gates', *BBC News* [Online], 15 September. Available at http://news.bbc.co.uk/1/hi/england/south_yorkshire/5349392.stm (accessed 9 February 2009).

Blake, S. and Katrak, Z. (2002) *Faith, Values and Sex & Relationships Education*. London: National Children's Bureau.

Carpentier, V. and Lall, M. (2005) *Review of Successful Parental Involvement Practices for 'Hard to Reach' Parents*. London: Institute of Education, University of London.

Coleman, L., Cater, S., Ramm, J. and Sherriff, N. (2007) *Evaluation of fpa Speakeasy Course for Parents: 2002 to 2007*. Brighton: Trust for the Study of Adolescence.

Council for Disabled Children and Contact a Family (2004) *Parent Participation: Improving Services for Disabled Children*. London: Council for Disabled Children and Contact a Family.

Council of Europe (1952) *Protocol 1 to the European Convention for the Protection of Human Rights and Fundamental Freedoms*. Strasbourg: Council of Europe.

Cummings, C., Dyson, A., Muijs, D., Papps, I., Pearson, D., Raffo, C., Tiplady, L. and Todd, L. (2007) *Evaluation of the Full Service Extended Schools Initiative: Final Report*. London: Department for Children, Schools and Families.

Department for Children, Schools and Families (2007) *Extended Schools: Building on Experience*. London: Department for Children, Schools and Families.

Department for Children, Schools and Families (2008) *Everyday Conversations, Every Day*. London: Department for Children, Schools and Families.

Department for Education and Skills (undated) 'Parental involvement in multi-ethnic schools', *The Standards Site* [Online]. Available at www.standards.dfes.gov.uk/parentalinvolvement/pics/pics_multiethnic_menu (accessed 9 February 2009).

Desforges, C. with Abouchaar, A. (2003) *The Impact of Parental Involvement, Parental Support and Family Education on Pupil Achievements and Adjustment: A Literature Review*. London: Department for Education and Skills.

DH/DCSF (2008) *Engaging Parents and Carers: Guidance for Schools*. London: National Healthy Schools Programme.

Garner, R. (2005) 'Many children "do not know how to hold a knife and fork" ', *The Independent* [Online]. Available at www.independent.co.uk/news/education/education-news/many-children-do-not-know-how-to-hold-a-knife-and-fork-491498.html (accessed 9 February 2009).

Goldman, R. (2005) *Fathers' Involvement in Their Children's Education*. London: Family and Parenting Institute.

Hallgarten, J. (2000) *Parents Exist, OK!? Issues and Visions for Parent–School Relationships*. London: Institute for Public Policy Research.

Halstead, M. and Reiss, M. (2003) *Values in Sex Education: From Principles to Practice*. London: Routledge.

Harris, A. and Goodall, J. (2007) *Engaging Parents in Raising Achievement: Do Parents Know They Matter?* London: Department for Children, Schools and Families.

Henricson, C. and Bainham, A. (2005) *The Child and Family Policy Divide*. York: Joseph Rowntree Foundation.

Lindsay, G., Cullen, M., Band, S., Cullen, S., Davis, L. and Davis, H. (2008) *Parent Support Advisor Pilot Evaluation*. London: Department for Children, Schools and Families.

Nicholas, J., Wood, L., Morgan, C., Lever, E., Russell, S. and Nelson, M. (2008) *Third Annual Survey of Take-Up of School Meals in England*. Sheffield: School Food Trust.

Ofsted (2007) *Food in Schools: Encouraging Healthier Eating*. London: Ofsted.

Page, A. (2009) *School–Parent Partnerships: Where Next? Emerging Strategies to Promote Innovation in Schools*. London: Family and Parenting Institute.

Perrie, R. (2006) 'Sinner ladies sell kids junk food', *The Sun* [Online], 16 September. Available at www.thesun.co.uk/sol/homepage/news/article63611.ece (accessed 9 February 2009).

Ramm, J. and Coleman, L. (2008) *Evaluation of the Effects of the Birmingham Speakeasy Course*. Brighton: Trust for the Study of Adolescence.

Reynolds, J. (2006) *Parents' Involvement in Their Children's Learning and Schools: How Should Their Responsibilities Relate to the Role of the State?* London: Family and Parenting Institute.

Topping, A. (2008) 'Appetite for a fight', *The Guardian* [Online], 16 September. Available at www.guardian.co.uk/society/2008/may/21/children.health (accessed 3 April 2008).

United Nations General Assembly (1989) *United Nations Convention on the Rights of the Child*. UN General Assembly Resolution 44/25. New York: United Nations.

Chapter 11

The role of the school nurse

Viv Crouch and Helen Chalmers

In recent years, 'there has been a paradigm shift in school nurse practice from a medical model to a social model of working' (DeBell and Tomkins, 2006: 18). This chapter is set against this background of change and considers how registered nurses, who work primarily in schools, can contribute to the health and well-being of children and young people in England. In it, the term 'school nurse' is used to denote those qualified nurses whose work with children and young people takes place in and around schools.[1] Nurses working in schools may have other titles such as school health nurse or school health adviser. They respond to differing challenges and opportunities and as such their work may vary from area to area and even from school to school.

Nurses have a long history of working in primary and secondary schools and with children of all ages. Since its inception in 1892, when school nurses were in uniform and worked under the direction of medical staff, the role of the school nurse has changed considerably. It was after the Boer War (1899–1902), however, that the need for a school-based nursing service was highlighted, at a time when the potential health impacts on children as a result of insanitary living conditions and malnutrition were becoming better understood (Nash *et al.*, 1985). Early school nurses were therefore employed to fulfil a public health agenda that focused on checking for health problems (health screening) and on preventing childhood infectious diseases, such as diphtheria and measles, through immunisation programmes.

For many years, a task-oriented approach dominated the way in which school nurses went about their work. For example, all children, irrespective of need, would be weighed and have their height measured as an apparently simple way of identifying some of the more obvious health and nutritional problems. The inadequacies and non-individualised nature of these activities resulted in some disillusionment among school nurses about the value of what they were doing. At the same time, some health and local authorities were unconvinced about the value of the school nursing service, seeing the responsibilities as more properly those of parents or of primary health care systems. Taken together, these negative views explained, in large part, the fall in school nurse numbers in the early 1990s. Indeed, during this time some authorities considered discontinuing the service altogether (Turner, 1998).

Attitudes towards the service began to change during the mid-1990s when there was concern about a national outbreak of measles. The outbreak began in London and then spread to areas in both the north and the south of England (Hanratty *et al.*, 2000). Carrying out immunisations in schools was thought to be the most cost-effective way of curbing the spread of the infection. Suddenly, school nursing became a valued service again as school nurses successfully managed the immunisation campaign and delivered the programme in schools (Queen's Nursing Institute, 1994).

Since the 1990s the school nursing service has regained its reputation as an important player in delivering the national public health agenda. Indeed, the role of the school nurse is now wider than ever before. However, despite this and the many challenges threatening children and young people's health, there remains a serious disparity between the number of school nurses, the number of schools in which they practise and the number of children with whom they come into contact. The latest NHS figures indicate that there were 1,062 whole time equivalent school nurses in post in September 2008 for an estimated population of 7.3 million school-aged children (NHS and Social Services Workforce Statistics, 2008). Government plans include an expansion in school nurse numbers so that by 2010 there will be a school nurse team led by a qualified nurse for every cluster of schools (DH, 2004). Within this developing service, there are opportunities for school nurses to engage in both established and new practice initiatives (DH, 2006a) and in partnership working to achieve a whole school approach to health.

Partnership working

For children and young people to obtain maximum benefit from health initiatives in schools, effective partnership working is essential. There have been times when health and education staff have not worked well together. Some school staff have perceived addressing health issues at school as an intrusion into the more academic aspects of the school day and as an interruption to the important business of education. However, despite these misgivings, there is growing recognition that education and health need to work 'hand in hand' if they are to impact on the current and future well-being of children and young people (DH, 2001).

Considerable progress in the relationship between health and school staff has been made in many areas through school nurses and teaching staff working together and thereby developing greater understanding of each other's roles. A variety of government initiatives and goals have also helped develop a culture of working together. The five outcomes of *Every Child Matters* (DfES, 2004a) (be healthy; stay safe; enjoy and achieve; make a positive contribution;

achieve economic well-being) are examples of health and education outcomes for children predicated on successful partnership working.

All schools now have to show how they are meeting the five outcomes of the *Every Child Matters* agenda. This has led to greater school nurse involvement in the planning of curricula, in extra-curricular activities in schools and with other initiatives such as *Choosing Health* (DH, 2004). *Choosing Health* encourages schools to focus on specific health issues, such as bullying, and to make plans accordingly. A more recent strategy for children and young people's health, *Healthy Lives, Brighter Futures* (DH and DCSF, 2009), aims to improve the health of school-aged children by supporting the duty of schools to promote well-being (Croghan, 2009).

The new Children's Trusts, set up after the death of Victoria Climbié in 2000 and in response to the report that followed her death (Secretary of State for Health and Secretary of State for the Home Office, 2003), aim to bring key local agencies together in a cooperative manner. Al Aynsley-Green, as the then director of the Children's Taskforce, expected Children's Trusts to break down barriers between different professions. He anticipated that concern to ensure children acquired key competencies would over-ride concerns about professional boundaries (Carlisle, 2003). More recently the *Children's Plan* (DH, 2007) has recognised the importance of strengthening Children's Trust arrangements further, so that the needs of children and young people are the central focus of integrated services, with increasingly effective links between health services and schools.

In 2006, additional recognition of the importance of partnership working came when the Department of Health (DH) issued guidance for school governors and teaching staff about the skills and services available to them from school nurse teams. The guidance highlighted the general benefits for children, young people and schools as a whole from the increased involvement of school nurses (DH, 2006b).

Drivers for change

Widespread concern about the health of children and young people has led to a number of national policies and programmes, most of which recognise schools as key environments in which positive change can be effected. School nurses are ideally placed to contribute to health-promoting activities, to support public health and safeguarding initiatives, and to provide health services on school sites.

For example, aims incorporated within the national Teenage Pregnancy Strategy have had a direct impact on school nurse practice and on funding. The Social Exclusion Unit (SEU) set out an ambitious target of halving the rate of teenage pregnancies by 2010 (SEU, 1999). In some schools, this resulted in a more open attitude which encouraged and empowered nurses to offer sexual health services on school sites. Services such as emergency contraception and, in some schools, a more comprehensive sexual health service were established (Chase *et al.*, 2005). School nurses have an important role in communicating with governing bodies and school staff about the importance of such initiatives, especially as sexual health promotion in schools may be regarded by some as controversial.

Policy papers such as *Youth Matters* (DfES, 2006) and *Aiming High* (HMT and DCSF, 2007) emphasise the importance of partnership working and of shared responsibility if children are to be safeguarded and their health promoted. A significant driver for the development of partnership working in school nurse practice was the National Healthy School Standard (DfEE, 1999). To begin with, some schemes associated with the Standard did not include an obvious health component in the way the government had envisaged (DfES, 2004b), leading to concern that they did not have a clear enough health agenda. In 2005, the criteria were formalised into a national programme which was launched jointly by the DH and the DfEE (now the Department for Children, Schools and Families (DCSF)) as the National Healthy Schools Programme (NHSP) (DH and DCSF, 2005).

School nurses' role and ways of working

In many schools, nurses now have a much wider role than ever before. Broadly speaking, their work falls into three main categories. There is contact with individual pupils and their families or carers, activities with groups of children and young people, and partnership work with school staff. As well as offering help and advice, the school nurse is also a resource to those with whom she comes into contact. With a background in health and social care and with specialist clinical expertise, she is likely to be well equipped to provide information about other services and how to access them.

For some children and young people, and for some topics, an individualised approach through one-to-one contact and drop-in sessions is invaluable. Indeed, such an approach may be the only one deemed acceptable, particularly when issues such as bullying, sexual health or obesity are involved. For some children and young people, the school nurse may be a sole point of professional contact about such issues, and meeting one to one provides opportunities for talking through problems in private. A school nurse may also be seen as less of an authority figure than some teaching staff, and someone who understands and respects confidentiality. This may make it easier for some pupils to talk to her.

Drop-in sessions are a particular, less formal and less structured way for young people to make contact with a school nurse. Whereas one-to-one sessions often involve having an appointment time, drop-in sessions allow young people to be self-referrers and to see a nurse at a time of their choosing. For such meetings to be accessible, the nurse usually needs to be available at known times each week. The more discreet and private the venue, the better, so that those seeking help can do so unobserved and in an environment where they will not be overheard. Nevertheless, locating an appropriate room for drop-in sessions remains a challenge in many schools.

Some school nurses also run drop-in sessions for parents, particularly of primary school children, in an effort to learn of any parental concerns at an early stage. Parents may have concerns, for instance, about their child's behaviour or about physical or emotional development. By providing opportunities to talk privately about a child's progress, drop-in sessions can lead to early intervention to help the child.

Seeing children on an individual basis also offers opportunities for school nurses to fulfil their obligations with regard to safeguarding. Whilst children can only be safeguarded properly when all relevant agencies work together, the school nurse is in a unique position to monitor and work with vulnerable children on a one-to-one basis. Sometimes, vulnerable pupils in secondary schools will take advantage of confidential drop-in sessions to talk with the nurse. This provides an opportunity for the nurse to build relationships and to offer support. As part of the safeguarding role, school nurses may contribute at case conferences and at Local Safeguarding Children Boards (LSCBs). In some instances, nurses may find safeguarding issues so time-consuming that it is difficult to fulfil their public health role in the way that they would like.

Group work involves rather different activities. It might involve the school nurse organising lunchtime activities to assist with smoking cessation, or might involve organising clubs for those children who need and want to lose weight. In addition there may be more timetabled group work within and outside the classroom as part of a school's Personal, Social and Health Education (PSHE) programme. Often there will be opportunities for a school nurse to speak in assemblies about health issues and to be involved with parents' evenings on PSHE topics.

For many school nurses, PSHE is an important focus for their work. Sex and relationships education (SRE), as a part of PSHE, is now a mandatory curriculum subject (DCSF, 2008). In some schools, SRE continues to be taught by teachers who may not have specialist knowledge but have space in their timetable. The Office for Standards in Education (Ofsted) (2002) has commented about this lack of specialist teachers in at least two reports. The government has responded by allocating money and resources for the training of both community nurses (including school nurses) and teachers to help them develop better teaching skills for the delivery of PSHE and in particular for SRE.[2]

Work by school nurses may include delivering health-promotion topics alongside teachers in the classroom and helping with curriculum planning. In SRE, in particular, nurses have a key role to play in teaching about sensitive topics such as puberty and sexual health, in both primary and secondary schools.

Classroom teaching provides both opportunities and challenges. Team teaching between a school nurse and a member of the teaching staff can help to develop the skills of both teachers and nurses and thus benefit pupils directly. In addition, some children find it easier to engage with certain issues in a less personalised way than is possible through one-to-one sessions. For a group to participate in the same teaching session also provides opportunities for them to carry on discussing issues outside the classroom.

Another role for the school nurse lies in developing ways of involving young people in promoting health. An initiative (the peer sign-posting scheme) that is widely used in parts of south-west England involves young people (Year 10 volunteers) as 'peer sign-posters'. The scheme works by the sign-poster directing other young people to professional services that can help them, including the school nurse. Volunteers take part in a four-week training session which includes 'mystery' shopping at various services for young people so the sign-poster can become familiar with what is available. They also learn how the C card scheme[3] works and are encouraged to develop assertiveness skills. Opportunities are provided to discuss a variety of teenage health issues. Participating schools provide notice boards with a picture of the peer sign-poster alongside the nurse from the school. The sign-poster's remit is to facilitate others getting help. The scheme also includes a one-day peer sign-posting conference for teachers, school nurses and other agencies working with young people. All secondary schools in a local authority are invited to participate, and lunch in a local sports club offers the opportunity for professionals and peer sign-posters to meet informally. A training session for everyone involved, including teachers and nurses, takes place in the afternoon so that everyone is helped to understand the boundaries and possibilities of the scheme.

Specific health concerns

Key health priorities in which school nurses play an important part include sexual health, emotional health and well-being, maintaining a healthy weight, healthy eating and drinking, physical exercise, smoking cessation and anti-bullying initiatives. In this section we will briefly consider a number of practice initiatives relevant to these health concerns.

Sexual health

For many school nurses, sexual health is a priority public health concern. The UK has high rates of teenage pregnancies, and the incidence of young people acquiring sexually transmitted infections, including chlamydia, is increasing (Harvey, 2008). Sexual health initiatives for young people may be very complex or relatively straightforward. For instance, nurses may be encouraged to promote chlamydia awareness and screening programmes in schools to help young people understand the nature and effect of the infection and the ease with which it can be detected and treated. In a straightforward way, the nurse can make accessible information available and can reassure young people that newer screening tests do not involve intimate or uncomfortable examinations.

On the other hand, involvement with sexual health issues can be challenging. A young person may have complex concerns to address, such as low self-esteem and a history of sexual abuse. For some young people, such concerns may be complicated by drug or alcohol misuse. There are also challenges when initiatives in school attract negative feedback. There may be disquiet among some parents, or the local media may not be supportive. Because of this, school nurses need the support of school head teachers, governors and primary care trusts if they are to develop effective young people-friendly initiatives around sexual health. Successful negotiation with governing bodies and head teachers opens the way for a range of sexual health promotion services, such as the issuing of emergency contraception and providing access to comprehensive sexual health services.

Another sexual health initiative concerns those nurses who work to Patient Group Directions (PGDs). These Directions allow nurses who are specifically trained to issue prescribed drugs according to a strict protocol. The introduction of PGDs has made it possible for girls who need emergency contraception to obtain it from the school nurse. Given the sensitive nature of offering emergency contraception, some school nurses have developed new ways of being in contact with young people. For some young people, text messaging is proving a favoured way of communication. Where a school does not allow emergency contraception to be issued on the school site, nurses have to look to other nearby venues such as local children's centres or health centres.

Alcohol misuse

The misuse of alcohol by children and young people is an important health issue. Although the majority of young people do not drink to excess, the numbers who are drinking in quantities that threaten their health are increasing (see Chapter 6, this volume). Whilst the proportion of 11 to 15-year-olds in England who reported having drunk alcohol decreased from 62 per cent to 54 per cent between 1988 and 2007, the amount consumed by those who do drink increased from 6.4 units per week in 1994 to 12.7 units in 2007 (Fuller, 2008). There has also been a sharp increase in alcohol-related hospital admissions for both boys and girls in the 15–18 year age group (Seabrook and McNeill, 2008). The government has an overall approach in place to try to minimise the risks of alcohol use. It includes the National Alcohol Harm Reduction Strategy, which was implemented in March 2004.[4] National Institute for Health and Clinical Excellence (NICE) guidelines (2007) suggest school nurses are key players and should become actively involved in tackling the problem of alcohol misuse by children and young people.

Many school nurses see young people with problems related to alcohol consumption in drop-in sessions. For some pupils, a multi-agency approach may be appropriate and nurses are in a good position to work effectively with workers from other agencies. This may be achieved by sign-posting to other services (for example, Young People's Drugs and Alcohol Services) or by joint working with other practitioners, such as the Local Authority Drugs and Alcohol Specialist. There can be benefits in joint working as young people are offered expertise from more than one professional. Such arrangements require a young person's consent, especially as some young people may perceive a threat to confidentiality if practitioners other than the school nurse come into school to see them.

Some schools offer pupils a drop-in service every lunchtime. One such service, for example, occupies an unused bungalow in school grounds. Although not designed exclusively to offer advice about drinking, drop-in sessions have proved useful for young people with alcohol-related problems. Students can access a variety of health and non-health personnel, including the school nurse. One specific example (Teenage Information Centre, Teenage Advice Centre – Tic-Tac) was highlighted as an example of good practice in SRE (Ofsted, 2002). Initiatives of this nature succeed best in a supportive school environment where the value of young people with health concerns being able to access expert help on the school site is recognised.

Emotional health and well-being

It has been estimated that 10–20 per cent of children and young people have mental health problems (DH, 2006a). In a secondary school of a thousand pupils, it is estimated that fifty will experience depression to some degree, a hundred will suffer from serious distress and between ten and twenty will have an eating disorder (Wilson, 2006). Emotional problems can occur at all ages and can therefore be experienced by children at primary and secondary schools. This is an important health and educational concern because there are strong links between untreated childhood mental health and emotional problems and educational failure, alcohol and substance misuse and offending behaviour (DH, 2006a).

The school nurse has opportunities to help children and young people in a number of ways. She may aim to foster a positive sense of well-being for all children and young people and to encourage the development of coping strategies when difficulties occur. Some school nurses deliver programmes based on a cognitive behavioural therapy (CBT) model to whole classes of primary-aged pupils. One such programme, called 'Friends', is recommended as good practice by the World Health Organization (WHO, 2004). It aims to reduce anxiety by helping children pay attention to thoughts that make them feel anxious and enabling them to develop strategies to change unhelpful thoughts to helpful ones. The programme is delivered to classes of 8 and 9-year-olds. The benefit of universal delivery to whole classes is that it is non-stigmatising so children with specific anxiety and/or anger problems are not singled out. Another benefit is the increased chance of detection of difficulties at an early stage when interventions are more likely to be successful (Bartlett et al., 2002).

Other approaches seek to help children and young people who are known to be particularly vulnerable to emotional problems, often because of social and/or family circumstances. When a school nurse has good relationships with children and young people in school, she may be in a position to help with emotional problems such as those associated with major changes in a child's life. Parental divorce or family bereavement, for example, may create circumstances in which children are particularly susceptible to anxiety and loss of self-esteem. Some school nurses offer a six-week bereavement course based on guidance from 'Winston's Wish',[5] a UK childhood bereavement charity. The course, designed to be run by school nurses, has been beneficial for both younger and older children (Stokes, 1992).

There will also be some children for whom more expert help is needed. The nurse has a key role in recognising when other professional help is indicated and in making a timely and appropriate referral (DH, 2006a).

Healthy eating

Childhood obesity is now recognised as a major health concern, and school nurses view the encouragement of healthy eating as an important part of their role. The Health Survey for England (HSE) in 2002 revealed that obesity in children is on the increase and physical activity on the decline (DH, 2004). Between 1995 and 2006 the percentage of boys aged 2 to 10 years who were overweight or obese in England increased from 22 to 29 per cent. For girls in the same age group the increase was from 23 to 26 per cent (Greenaway, 2008).

In addition to including healthy eating sessions in the curriculum, the government's strategy in England for the management of childhood obesity requires the weighing and measuring of children at specific ages in primary school as part of the National Child Measurement Programme (NCMP) (DH, 2009). Such measurements are usually undertaken in school by members of the school nurse team. The data gathered are 'to inform local planning and delivery of services for children' and 'to allow analysis of trends in growth patterns and obesity'.[6]

The need to be weighed and measured can cause difficulties and unhappiness for some young people, especially those who are already concerned or embarrassed about their weight. With a marked increase in the number of children and young people with an eating disorder, there are challenges for the school nurse in facilitating the need to weigh and measure children in school. One way of managing the NCMP to minimise embarrassment and distress is for a member of the school nurse team to talk with a class beforehand, explain what is planned and answer any queries. Children can be reassured that their own measurements will not be made known to other people (except their parents, who receive a personal letter of notification), and that there will be privacy for them when they are being weighed and measured. For children in the final year of primary school (Year 6), there may be value in talking about different growth rates as well, especially as they are reaching puberty.

School nurses are well placed to be involved with other healthy eating activities and programmes in schools. They may be able to advise about establishing tuck shops that stock healthy food and about ways to encourage healthy lunches. Specific projects can be managed by the school nurse working alongside parents and children. One project is organising a 'food bus' to park in school for several days. Working together, a nurse, parents and children plan strategies to encourage parents and children to come and explore different food options and attend cooking demonstrations (South West Public Health Observatory, 2008).

Physical activity

An increase in children and young people's participation in physical activity and exercise is one way of helping them manage their weight within healthy limits and develop a healthy lifestyle. The school nurse can be involved with a plethora of activities that encourage and promote increased physical activity. Many schools have community sports facilities on site with a range of activities that young people can take part in.

One primary care trust (Bath and North East Somerset (BANES)) has developed an after-school club coordinated by a school nurse and involving both parents and children. The club is called 'Physkids' (Physkids and Mend, 2007) and offers various activities ranging from those that focus on physical exercise to more creative endeavours. The 'Cook It' programme (BANES PCT, 2008) runs free 'fun' cooking sessions for both children and families attending 'Physkids'.

One school has created a new faculty[7] called 'Self, Health and Exercise'. Year 7 pupils (aged 11) develop a personal health portfolio which includes their aims for physical exercise and PSHE. Achievements and challenges documented in the portfolio are reviewed each year. The aim is to raise the profile of healthy living for both pupils and staff and to extend extra-curricular activities that are thought to contribute to health. As part of the scheme, pupils agree to participate in exercise of some sort, to assess their own fitness levels and to examine their lifestyles (Read and Sargent, 2004). One result of this initiative has been that PSHE within the school has increased from fifteen sessions a year to one hour each week. The school nurse was involved from the beginning both with planning for the new faculty and with responding to the aims identified in the pupils' portfolios.

Confidentiality

Confidentiality is of central importance for anyone, including children and young people, accessing health or social care services. Its purpose is to set a limit on personal information that can be disclosed without consent. When issues of a personal nature are disclosed to a health professional, there is an expectation that the information will be treated as confidential and that the individual's privacy will be protected. It is the fulfilment of this expectation that leads to relationships of trust. For those working with children and young people in schools, confidentiality is similarly important if relationships of trust are to develop. However, the entitlement of young people to confidentiality has not always been straightforward and education staff may sometimes have different views to health professionals. Confidentiality is complicated for some by concerns about safeguarding issues and for others by concerns that parents have a right to be told about their children's health problems.

Guidance on these matters was issued jointly by the Royal College of General Practitioners and Brook in 2000 (Donovan *et al.*, 2000). It recognised that young people, including those under 16, are entitled to confidential health services and that health professionals have a duty not to disclose any information about individuals without their consent, whatever their age or maturity, except in exceptional circumstances. However, despite guidance and professional codes of practice for health staff that reinforce the importance of confidentiality, it continues to be an area of concern for young people, parents, carers and professionals. For example, one of the main reported barriers for young people accessing contraceptive and sexual health advice is the fear that confidentiality will not be maintained (DfES, 2004b).

Of particular relevance for school nurses is the degree to which understandings about confidentiality can be agreed with school staff. Some staff regard a commitment to confidentiality as being at odds with their *in loco parentis* responsibility for children and young people while they are in school. They believe that there is a need to know about personal issues in order to fulfil their responsibilities to act on parents' behalf. However, increasing recognition of the importance of confidentiality in relation to health concerns means that most secondary schools now offer pupils the opportunity to see a health professional on a one-to-one basis and in confidence (DfEE, 2000).

School nurses are bound by *The Code: Standards of Conduct, Performance and Ethics for Nurses and Midwives* (Nursing and Midwifery Council, 2007), which states that 'you must respect people's right to confidentiality', in addition to explaining the circumstances (risk of self-harm) under which this element of the Code can be breached. School nurses have a key role in helping school staff understand confidentiality and in assisting with related policy development in schools. Schools are expected to have clear policies on confidentiality to help teachers, nurses, pupils and parents understand the boundaries of confidentiality (DfEE, 1999). So, for instance, a policy may recognise the need for young people to be able to see a nurse in confidence, whilst at the same time clarifying the particular circumstances under which information may need to be communicated to another person(s). Workable policies generally develop when there is inclusive consultation with, and input from, pupils, parents and governors as well as school nurses and teaching staff. Time spent achieving an agreed and understood policy is worthwhile as it can reduce disagreement and dispute when difficult situations arise.

Breaches of confidentiality can have wide-ranging, sustained and detrimental effects on the reputation and take-up of the school nurse service. At an individual level, a child or young person may feel let down. More generally, if a nurse is perceived to breach confidentiality, her credibility will be undermined and the services she offers may be shunned. Young people may opt to do without advice and help, especially around sexual health and personal issues. For example, a girl who believes the nurse cannot be trusted may not seek contraceptive advice if she fears her parents will be informed.

Future challenges

Involving young people more fully in the development of initiatives to improve health and well-being is perhaps the key challenge for future work in schools. Greater engagement of young people provides opportunities for developments that reflect young people's concerns. In some areas, young people contribute to the interviewing process for new school nurse appointments. Initiatives such as this hold the potential for a better-understood and better-tailored service as both pupils and nurses learn from each other about which health issues are of most concern and about how they might be most effectively addressed. More remains to be done in this area.

The opportunities afforded by new technology also hold the potential to change the school nurse role in the future. To date, the use of text messaging and e-mailing has developed considerably as a means of easy and accessible communication for children and young people, despite the risks to confidentiality that can ensue. Careful evaluation of future technological changes will be needed to see what benefit can be gained for the promotion of health and well-being for children and young people.

School nurses play a crucial role in helping to tackle some of the ever-increasing public health concerns. Unacceptable inequalities in health persist and, like poor educational achievement, compound poverty by reducing young people's life chances (DH, 2001). Many children and young people live in less than ideal circumstances and their experiences often impact on their life in school as well. For some children, hardship and unhappiness at home will interfere with their ability to make the most of the educational opportunities afforded them. For some, school will be a refuge and a safe place.

The recent joint strategy from the DH and the DCSF, *Healthy Lives, Brighter Futures*, reiterates the importance of effective partnership working and places school nurses at the centre of future initiatives in school:

School Health Teams provide a key link between education and health services, providing guidance and support on a range of health-related issues. Though their composition will vary across different primary care trusts (PCTs), school health services will usually have at their core a group of school nurses working with or supported by a range of other practitioners and support staff.

(DH and DCSF, 2009: 38)

Learning from the experiences of school nursing teams in other countries is also likely to stimulate key developments in the future, as local experience and good practice are shared across international boundaries.

Notes

1 The majority of school nurses are female and therefore 'she' will be used in preference to 'he'.
2 The National PSHE Continuing Professional Development (CPD) Programme is the main body offering training and accreditation for this area of work.
3 C card schemes allow young people access to free condoms from various local outlets.
4 www.cabinetoffice.gov.uk/strategy/work_areas/alcohol_misuse.aspx (accessed 26 May 2009).
5 www.winstonswish.org.uk (accessed 26 May 2009).
6 www.dh.gov.uk/en/Publichealth/Healthimprovement/Healthyliving/DH_073787 (accessed 26 May 2009).
7 Where two or three departments in school work together.

References

BANES PCT (2008) *Cook It*. Available at http://healthyweight4children.org/resource/view.aspx?RID=59739 (accessed 26 May 2009).

Bartlett, P., Webster, H. and Turner, C. (2002) *Friends for Children*. Bowen Hills: Australian Academic Press.

Carlisle, D. (2003) 'Building the framework', *Community Practitioner*, 76(6): 202–203.

Chase, E., Goodrich, R., Simon, A., Holtermann, S. and Aggleton, P. (2005) 'Evaluating school-based health services to inform future practice: Lessons from Teen Talk at Kidbrooke School in Greenwich', *Health Education*, 106(1): 42–59.

Croghan, E. (2009) 'The child health strategy: Implications for school nursing', *British Journal of School Nursing*, 4(2): 86–87.

DCSF (Department for Children, Schools and Families) (2008) *Government Response to the Report by the Sex and Relationships Education (SRE) Review Steering Group*. Nottingham: DCSF.

DeBell, D. and Tomkins, A. (2006) *Discovering the Future of School Nursing: The Evidence Base*. London: Routledge.

DfEE (Department for Education and Employment) (1999) *National Healthy School Standard Guidance*. London: DfEE.

DfEE (2000) *Sex and Relationship Education Guidance*. London: DfEE.

DfES (Department for Education and Skills) (2004a) *Every Child Matters: Change for Children*. London: DfES.

DfES (2004b) *Independent Advisory Group on Teenage Pregnancy Annual Report 2003/2004*. London: DfES.

DfES (2006) *Youth Matters: Next Steps*. London: DfES.

DH (Department of Health) (2001) *School Nurse: Practice Development Resource Pack*. London: DH.

DH (2004) *Choosing Health: Making Healthy Choices Easier*. London: DH.

DH (2006a) *School Nurse: Practice Development Resource Pack*. London: DH.

DH (2006b) *Looking for a School Nurse*. London: DH.

DH (2007) *The Children's Plan: Building Brighter Futures*. London: DH.

DH (2009) *National Childhood Measurement Programme*. London: DH.

DH and DCSF (2005) *National Healthy Schools Programme*. Nottingham: DfES.

DH and DCSF (2009) *Healthy Lives, Brighter Futures: The Strategy for Children and Young People's Health*. London: DH and DCSF.

Donovan, C., Hadley, A., Jones, M., Martin, J., Mawer, C., McPherson, A. and Romano-Critchley, G. (2000) *Confidentiality and Young People: Improving Teenagers' Uptake of Sexual and Other Health Services*. London: Woodworks.

Fuller, E. (ed.) (2008) *Drug Use, Smoking and Drinking among Young People in England in 2007*. London: National Centre for Social Research, National Foundation for Educational Research.

Greenaway, J. (2008) 'Children's obesity: Bringing children's rights discourse to public health policy', *Community Practitioner*, 81(5): 17–21.

Hanratty, B., Holt, T., Duffell, E., Patterson, W., Ramsey, M., White, J. M., Jin, L. and Litton, P. (2000) 'UK measles outbreak in non-immune anthroposophic communities: The implications for the elimination of measles from Europe', *Epidemiology and Infection*, 125: 377–383.

Harvey, R. (2008) 'Sex education at school'. *British Journal of School Nursing*, 3(2): 62–64.

Healthy Weight for Children Hub (Cook It) Available at www.healthyweight4children.org.uk (accessed 26 May 2009).

HMT and DCSF (2007) *Aiming High: A Ten Year Strategy for Positive Activities*. London: HMT.

Nash, W., Thruston, M. and Baly, M. (1985) *Health at School: Caring for the Whole Child*. London: Heinemann Nursing.

National Institute for Health and Clinical Excellence (2007) *School-Based Interventions on Alcohol*. London: NICE.

NHS and Social Services Workforce Statistics (2008) Available at www.dh.gov.uk/en/Publication sandstatistics/Statistics/StatisticalWorkAreas/Statisticalworkforce/DH_582 (accessed 26 May 2009).

Nursing and Midwifery Council (2007) *The Code: Standards of Conduct, Performance and Ethics for Nurses and Midwives*. London: NMC.

Ofsted (2002) *Sex and Relationships: A Report from the Office of Her Majesty's Chief Inspector of Schools*. London: Ofsted.

Physkids and Mend (2007) For targeted overweight/inactive families. Available at www.barhnes.gov.uk/committee_papers/PBHW/PBHW080917/09zAppx1HealthInequal ities.pdf (accessed 26 May 2009).

Queen's Nursing Institute (1994) *Operation Safeguard: The Measles and Rubella Campaign 1994*. London: Queen's Nursing Institute.

Read, M. and Sargent, J. (2004) 'The SHE faculty', *Teaching Expertise*, 3: 37–39. Devizes: Smale Consulting.

Seabrook, R. and McNeill, A. (2008) 'Drinking by children and adolescents: A role for school nurses', *British Journal of School Nursing*, 3(1): 45–47.

Secretary of State for Health and Secretary of State for the Home Office (2003) *The Victoria Climbié Inquiry: Report of an Inquiry by Lord Laming*. London: The Stationery Office.

SEU – Social Exclusion Unit (1999) *Report on Teenage Pregnancy.* London: The Stationery Office.

South West Public Health Observatory (2008) *Healthy Weight for Children.* Available at www.healthyweight4children.org.uk (accessed 26 May 2009).

Stokes, J. (1992) *Winston's Wish Bereavement Programme for Children.* Gloucester: Gloucester Royal Infirmary.

Turner, T. (1998) *Healthy Futures: The Diversity of School Nursing.* London: CPHVA.

WHO – World Health Organization (2004) *Prevention of Mental Health Disorders: Effective Interventions and Policy Options.* Geneva: WHO.

Wilson, P. (2006) 'Promoting Good Mental Health and Psychological Wellbeing in Your School', keynote speech, Adolescent Development and Mental Health, SfE conference, Bristol.

Chapter 12

Evaluating health and well-being in schools

Issues and principles

Catherine Dennison, Ian Warwick and Peter Aggleton

A huge amount of energy and enthusiasm has been invested in work through schools to improve the health and well-being of children and young people. Throughout the UK and in many other countries, significant effort has been expended in planning, securing funding, building partnerships and delivering services, programmes and activities to achieve this goal. Too often, however, evaluation is an afterthought or is even omitted completely. Without evaluation, however, many opportunities can be lost. It will be hard to understand what has been achieved, to share learning with others and to make the case for continuation or expansion of the activity.

This chapter therefore encourages readers to think of evaluation as a priority from the earliest stages of planning their work. It identifies some of the ways in which, by understanding what evaluation can and cannot achieve, it can become a useful and less onerous task. Our aim is not to review the literature on evaluation and healthy schools (for a valuable overview, see St Leger *et al.*, 2007), but to draw out some key principles of best practice that can be used to frame local – and often small-scale – evaluations of healthy schools. Recent national and local examples of evaluations of the National Healthy Schools Programme in England are used to illustrate the issues discussed.

Why is evaluation essential?

There are many different ways of evaluating health-related programmes and projects – be these national-level initiatives or local activities. Broadly speaking, evaluation can take two main forms. Summative evaluation focuses on identifying the effects of an initiative – not only whether intended goals have been achieved, but also whether unintended consequences have come about. Formative evaluation, on the other hand, sets out to assist in the development of a project (Robson, 2002). Good-quality evaluation should provide a mechanism for understanding two key issues: *how* health-related activities have an impact and *what* that impact is. Evaluation also provides an opportunity to draw together the views of different stakeholders to reflect upon the activity

(Patton, 1997). This may lead to the identification of elements that facilitate and elements that act as barriers to having impact.

In principle, information about both 'has it worked?' and 'how has it worked?' should feed back into practice. Together, these different sources of information can be used to reshape an activity or stop the activity altogether if it is shown to be having no or negative impact. Evaluation findings, when positive, can play a role in illustrating the worth of the project, showcasing it to young people, parents, potential partners and funders, and the wider community. They may also be used to demonstrate the need for continued or expanded resources to be dedicated to a programme or activity, such as the contribution of a school nurse drop-in or the benefits of a breakfast club. Crucially, evaluation provides an opportunity to share what has been learned with other schools and to contribute to building the evidence base. In a context where 'evidence-based interventions' are increasingly advocated for, but where there has been relatively little evaluation of school-based health and well-being programmes and interventions, there is real value to extending our knowledge of what has worked and why.

Designs and approaches

The expected function that evaluation findings will serve should, in principle, determine the design and scale of the evaluation (Patton, 2008). In general terms, evaluation approaches can be placed along a continuum from those modelled most closely on the natural and medical sciences to those that have been developed from within the fields of qualitative sociology, anthropology and education. On the whole, natural scientists and those within medicine favour the use of comparative studies of one kind or another (Hansen and Rieper, 2009). Most usually, these take the form of experiments in which a group of people (most usually called 'subjects' because they are subjected to a manipulation or intervention) receive a special treatment, whose effects are measured. This is the same logic underlying drug trials in which the effects of a new treatment are identified by comparing the response of a group which receives the treatment with that of a comparable group which does not.

Borrowing from this 'medical model' of establishing effectiveness, a very vocal group of public health practitioners hold strongly that it is only when the impacts of an intervention are directly compared to that of another, or no, intervention, and ideally where people are randomly allocated to one or other group, that an evaluation can truly tell us about effectiveness. Randomised controlled trials (RCTs), are often held up as the 'gold standard' for evaluation, enabling one to be clear about cause and effect. They are usually tightly controlled, expensive and lengthy to conduct. How appropriate they are for implementation in schools and colleges, or for evaluating initiatives where multiple factors (rather than one easily controlled-for factor) influence outcomes and different elements interact with each other, is questionable (Davies et al., 2008).

Designs which allow some degree of comparison between groups are often more practical. Frequently, baseline and follow-up designs are used in which participants are tested before and after they have been part of an intervention, and improvement between the two time periods is taken as indication of a positive impact. Although attribution to the intervention can never be certain, an observed change after the intervention does suggest a possible linkage. Such a design may be more feasible in a school setting and where it is to be implemented by a practitioner. A slightly more rigorous design can use a naturally occurring comparison group consisting of individuals who are broadly similar to those who have received the intervention.

In some instances, comparative designs may not be open, or be desirable, to the evaluator. Here, instead, they may want or need to rely on gathering or perceptions of impact from children and young people themselves, parents or school staff. Such reports can be obtained either quantitatively, perhaps through ranking or the use of rating scales, or qualitatively, in the form of opinions and descriptions. More qualitative methods such as semi-structured and open-ended interviews, focus groups and case studies all have real value in exploring if and also how an initiative works. In what are sometimes called mixed methods studies, qualitative methods (where the focus is on gathering accounts of what has happened) may also be used in combination with more quantitative approaches (where the focus is on gathering numbers).

Whilst some insist there exists a 'hierarchy of evidence' when it comes to evaluation (with RCTs at the top) (Parsons and Stears, 2002; Hansen and Rieper, 2009), others take a more pluralistic view. For example, where we can be reasonably sure of both cause and effect, and where the investment of significant resources and decisions as to policy direction rely on the findings, then a stricter, more experimental design might be appropriate. However, where work is in its infancy, when causal pathways are less clear, and when budget, time, skills and/or need are more modest, a more descriptive approach may be all that is possible, and may be just what is needed. At the end of the day, it is better to do a simple evaluation well than to attempt a complex evaluation badly.

In order to illustrate the range of approaches that can be taken to evaluation, the next section looks at examples of how the National Healthy Schools Programme in England has been evaluated at local and national levels.

Evaluating healthy schools

As part of a wider study conducted during 2007 to provide an overview of existing evidence related to the National Healthy Schools Programme in England, there was an opportunity to identify and learn from evaluations of how the programme is implemented at the local level (Warwick et al., 2009). As well as drawing together and summarising findings from local evaluations, it was also possible to gain an insight into the characteristics of these often small-scale evaluations – the sorts of issues and topics asked about, the sources of information used, as well as the methods of data collection applied. Although there are many views about what might constitute an ideal evaluation of healthy school activities, knowing about what is actually happening in practice is an indispensable step in building on existing strengths.

Local evaluations

In response to a request to all local healthy school programmes in England for evaluations and reviews of their programmes, 15 evaluations or reviews were returned. These 15 reports focused chiefly on work undertaken during 2006–2007, although two were conducted during 2003–2005.

Most local evaluations did not have a clearly specified evaluation design. Nonetheless, in two local evaluations, comparisons were made between schools more involved in a local programme with schools less or not involved. Both of these local evaluations used existing data to try to identify the impact of being a healthy school. In the first, information was collected from schools across the local authority area. Around 24 schools had achieved healthy school status with 92 others not yet achieving status. Information regarding pupil achievement was analysed and findings suggested that those schools which had achieved healthy school status had a greater percentage of pupils achieving a higher level in English, Mathematics and Science. Although an encouraging finding, it was not possible to state with any certainty that healthy schools involvement had contributed to this – those schools that were operating more successfully overall may have been better placed to achieve healthy school status.

The second local evaluation with a comparative element sought to compare one group of schools which had achieved healthy school status with another group of schools which were working towards it. This evaluation used existing inspection information from Ofsted (the organisation which inspects and regulates schools in England). This information provided a rating of the overall effectiveness of schools as well as each school's success in supporting pupils' personal development and well-being. The ratings (outstanding, good, satisfactory or inadequate) of 161 schools which had achieved healthy school status were compared with those of 51 schools that were reported to be 'working towards' status. A greater proportion of schools with healthy school status were rated as good or outstanding (with regard to overall effectiveness and support for personal development and well-being) than of those working towards status. Again, this was an encouraging finding – especially as Ofsted reports commented favourably on healthy schools-related activities. However, it was not possible to identify the specific contribution of these activities to the ratings in isolation from other school improvement measures.

More commonly, local evaluations do not have a comparative design yet seek to gather information about, among other things, perceptions of change or of impact, as well as processes involved in the development and implementation of schools' involvement in local healthy schools programmes. Among these evaluations, a range of methods of gathering information were used. Six evaluations, for example, used postal surveys to invite respondents to comment on the process of being involved in their local healthy school programme and to ask about what had worked well and what might be improved. Often, one or two questions were included in these surveys about what changes or benefits had arisen as a result of developing and implementing healthy school activities.

A further six evaluations used a wider range of methods – including face-to-face individual interviews, small group interviews and questionnaires – as well as drawing on existing information such as that contained in Ofsted reports. Those evaluations that used a number of methods of data collection tended to invite responses from a broader range of respondents to a wider set of questions than those that relied on one method. More often than not, there was an interest in collecting information about whether participation in healthy schools had an impact on the school as well as seeking to identify what had contributed to these changes. In five of these evaluations, the views of children and young people were sought – particularly through the use of small group interviews.

In one evaluation of this kind, for example, a number of methods of data collection were used across primary, secondary and special schools to identify perceptions of involvement in the local healthy school programme, the impact of this involvement and the processes of working towards becoming a healthy school. Methods included interviews with pupils and parents, a self-completion questionnaire for key school staff, observations of changes to the physical environment of schools (such as changes to playgrounds), and use of existing information to identify changes (such as that related to pupil attendance, curriculum development and Ofsted reports of healthy school activities). Drawing these different sources of evidence together, findings suggested that positive changes were perceived to have come about as a result of involvement in the healthy school programme. These included changes to some health-related practices among pupils, particularly in primary schools – such as healthier food and drink being consumed, greater levels of physical activity and an increase in initiatives to promote pupil participation in the school. However, while schools were said to be making progress in 'embedding' healthy school activities into the life of the school, there remained significant difficulties in engaging parents and carers in the development and implementation of these activities.

Again, the specific contribution of being engaged in a local healthy school programme cannot be separated out from the influences of other initiatives focused on school improvement. Notwithstanding this, collecting information about perceived impact (or outcomes) from a range of people (including children and young people themselves), using a number of methods of enquiry, appears useful in generating a degree of insight into both the strengths of a healthy school approach, what is yet to be achieved and what factors might have contributed to particular outcomes.

Although it may be useful to draw on a number of different methods to collect information from a range of respondents, deciding on what information to collect about which topics or issues can remain challenging. With regard to evaluations of local healthy school programmes in England, few attempts appear to have been made to collect information about changes to children and young people's health status, such as levels of obesity and engagement with substance misuse. In part, this may be due to the challenges of collecting such information, it being much more feasible to collect information about more immediate changes that might result from participating in a healthy school programme (such as improvements to Personal, Social, Health and Economic (PSHE) education, increases in the number of pupils walking to school, increases in pupil participation). While such activities might be expected to contribute to improvements in health and well-being, broader social and environmental factors will also have influence. Evaluation, therefore, needs to reflect the range of activities and levels at which the programme operates and be realistic about the changes that would result.

Across the local evaluations, changes that were perceived to occur as a result of participation in the healthy schools programme could be characterised under three broad headings: changes to the school environment; changes in knowledge and practices (among pupils and staff); and wider benefits. There were, for example, changes to the school environment – including a strengthened PSHE education curriculum; improvements to play facilities; healthier food offered (including water being more readily available, and breakfast clubs introduced); and improved processes for pupil participation. There were also reported to be changes among pupils, such as improved concentration in classes, improved attendance, increased understanding of sex and relationship issues, and a greater number of children involved in physical activity and in choosing healthier food. Among staff, a better understanding of health-related issues and more effective teaching of PSHE education were seen to result. Examples of wider benefits to the school of being involved in a local healthy school programme included having a useful tool for school improvement more generally and supporting processes of school self-evaluation for use in external school inspections.

Although these are just a few examples from local evaluations, there is a range of sources of information from which information can potentially be collected for evaluation purposes. The audit tool for the National Healthy Schools Programme in England[1] enables a school to review the extent to which it meets 41 criteria that centre on four topics: PSHE education, healthy eating, physical activity and emotional health and well-being. The self-evaluation form used by Ofsted as the basis for school inspections in England[2] contains many direct and indirect references to improving health and well-being among pupils (for example, whether learners are adopting healthy lifestyles and whether they feel safe). Both these documents can be used to identify the sorts of information it might be useful to gather to compare what the situation was like at the beginning and end of a piece of work.

One other area to collect information about – and one which was often missing from local evaluations – relates to the broader school context. Some schools, perhaps those that have been successfully involved in other school improvement activities, might more readily develop and implement healthy schools activities than those schools which struggle to improve. Moreover, the type of school (primary, secondary or special) and the diversity among pupils (such as the proportion of those who have English as an additional language, who come from minority ethnic groups or who are eligible for free school meals) are likely to influence what and how health issues can best be addressed. Collecting information about these factors, among a number of others, will provide greater insight into why activities put in place in one school may have a similar, greater or lesser impact when placed in a different school context.

National evaluations

Since its instigation, the National Healthy Schools Programme in England has been subjected to external evaluation. Early studies were more formative pieces of work, reflecting the need for research to shape the programme in its infancy (Aggleton *et al.*, 2000). More recently, the focus has shifted to using evaluation to establish programme impact, as well as to provide feedback to inform ongoing programme development. The National Foundation for Education Research and Thomas Coram Research Unit at the Institute of Education, University of London partnered to undertake an evaluation which gathered a wide range of perspectives through interviews with school staff, governors, children and young people, parents and local and national programme staff. The consensus among staff, governors and parents was that the programme had enabled them to develop and implement a wide range of health-related activities that had contributed to important changes within their school (Warwick *et al.*, 2005). Alongside this, the research team undertook a statistical comparison of schools participating and not participating in the programme using a range of existing national health and well-being datasets, the aim being to get early insight as to whether the programme could be linked to positive outcomes (Schagen *et al.*, 2005).

With this limitation in mind, an innovative evaluation design is currently being implemented. The National Centre for Social Research (NatCen) has been commissioned to assess the impact of the programme, in a context where there is no possibility for a controlled design. Although participation in the programme is voluntary, the number of schools engaged with it has increased very rapidly over the last few years, so that participation is now almost universal (Barnard *et al.*, 2009). Instead, the research team has sought to capitalise on naturally occurring differences between schools in the speed and extent to which they implement the programme. Schools in the early stages of participating have been invited to join the evaluation by asking small groups of their students to complete questionnaires to capture health-related attitudes, beliefs and behaviours that relate directly to the themes of the National Healthy Schools Programme. Two years later, the same year groups are being revisited to assess how far these may have changed and whether the degree of change can be linked to engagement with the programme over that time. In addition, in-depth interviews in a sample of schools are exploring how the programme is perceived to be impacting in schools, and this information will inform interpretation of the more quantitative impact data.

Principles of good practice

A number of principles can be identified from the evaluation experiences described above. In this concluding section, we highlight a few of these.

Choosing an appropriate design or approach should be the starting point for an evaluation. Much depends on what we want to find out. Well-designed comparative and experimental studies are good at determining cause and effect, but may not always be practical to implement. Insights into possible causes and influences can be obtained from before and after studies, especially if a comparison or control group is included. However, understanding more about how a particular change is brought about calls for more in-depth enquiry. Semi-structured interviews, focus group discussions and case studies can be useful in painting a rounded picture of the work of a new initiative or programme (Yin, 2003).

Using a number of methods of collecting information from a range of people involved in developing and putting in place health and well-being activities – as some of the local evaluations described above were able to do – can be useful in building an understanding of both the strengths and the weaknesses of a project. Methods used included individual and group interviews, questionnaires, as well as observation. There may, however, be value in testing out other methods, such as participant observation or even visual methods such as maps, diagrams and drawings (Laws *et al.*, 2003).

Identifying the topics or issues to collect information about is also key in the early stages of planning an evaluation. Information can be collected about the context of the work, about the processes involved, or the resources needed to make things happen (Pawson and Tilley, 1997; Timmins and Miller, 2007). Any outcomes measured should relate directly to the objectives of a programme. From these, 'indicators of success' can be identified – which should be realistic with regard to what can be achieved within the timeframe, resources and activities put in place.

Considering whether to conduct an evaluation 'in house' or to commission an external individual or body can be an important early decision. Which is decided upon will depend on a number of factors, including the scale of the project and resources available. All practitioners should put in place a certain level of self-evaluation, but opportunities to gain support and advice, with limited costs attached, from those with expertise in evaluating health and well-being initiatives, should always be made the most of.

Building partnerships among those involved in the evaluation is central to success (St Leger, 2006). School staff, parents and students should be consulted on evaluation plans, and alerted to findings. The potential to involve them as co-researchers or in some other participatory way in the evaluation could be considered (Laws *et al.*, 2003). Their perspectives will make evaluation more relevant. In turn, this may make them more willing to participate in the research. Partnership with those who will use the evaluation findings can assist by ensuring what emerges from the evaluation is relevant and useful (Patton, 1999).

Finally, effective dissemination is key to evaluation success. Without it, there will be missed opportunities for others to gain from the learning. Those who participated in the evaluation, whether staff or students, should receive appropriate feedback to show recognition of their contribution. Good dissemination involves more than providing information. It can be tied into wider professional development opportunities for teachers, health professionals and others involved in healthy schools work. When organised effectively, it should not only enable managers and practitioners to learn about what has been tried out elsewhere, but also help them to think about how this learning might be applied within their own school context (Cordingley *et al.*, 2003).

Ultimately, it is the knowledge base established through health-promoting schools work that will lay the foundations for new and more effective ways of promoting health and well-being in and through schools. Good-quality evaluation, be it conducted by outside experts, by teachers and health professionals, or by partnerships established between different groups of healthy school stakeholders, is central to realising these goals.

Notes

1 Available at www.healthyschools.gov.uk (accessed July 2009).
2 Available at www.ofsted.gov.uk (accessed July 2009).

References

Aggleton, P., Rivers, K., Mulvihill, C., Chase, E., Downie, A., Sinkler, P., Tyrer, P. and Warwick, I. (2000) 'Lessons learned: Working towards the National Healthy School Standard', *Health Education*, 100(3): 102–110.

Barnard, M., Becker, E., Creegan, C., Day, N., Devitt, K., Fuller, E., Lee, L., Neil, H., Purdon, S. and Ranns, H. (2009) *Evaluation of the National Healthy Schools Programme: Interim Report.* London: NatCen.

Cordingley, P., Bell, M., Rundell, B. and Evans, D. (2003) 'The impact of collaborative CPD on classroom teaching and learning', in *Research Evidence in Education Library*. London: EPPI-Centre, Social Science Research Unit, Institute of Education, University of London. Available at http://eppi.ioe.ac.uk/cms/Default.aspx?tabid=132 (accessed July 2009).

Davies, R. S., Williams, D. D. and Yanchar, S. (2008) 'The use of randomisation in educational research and evaluation: A critical analysis of underlying assumptions', *Evaluation & Research in Education*, 21(4): 303–317.

Hansen, H. F. and Rieper, O. (2009) 'The evidence movement: The development and consequences of methodologies in review practices', *Evaluation*, 15(2): 141–163.

Laws, S. with Harper, C. and Marcus, R. (2003) *Research for Development: A Practical Guide.* London: Sage.

Parsons, C. and Stears, D. (2002) 'Evaluating health-promoting schools: Steps to success', *Health Education*, 102(1): 7–15.

Patton, M. Q. (1997) *Utilization-Focused Evaluation*, 3rd edn. London: Sage.

Patton, M.Q. (2008) *Utilization-Focused Evaluation*, 4th edn. Newbury, CA: Sage.

Pawson, R. and Tilley, N. (1997) *Realistic Evaluation.* London: Sage.

Robson, C. (2002) *Real World Research*, 2nd edn. Oxford: Blackwell.

Schagen, S., Blenkinsop, S., Schagen, I., Scott, E., Eggers, M., Warwick, I., Chase, E. and Aggleton, P. (2005) 'Evaluating the impact of the National Healthy School Standard: Using national datasets', *Health Education Research*, 20(6): 688–696.

St Leger L. (2006) 'Improving the quality of school health evaluations', *Health Education*, 106(4): 261–264.

St Leger, L., Kolbe, L., Lee, A., Douglas, S., McCall, D. and Young, I. M. (2007) 'School health promotion: Achievements, challenges and priorities', in D. V. McQueen and C. M. Jones (eds) *Global Perspectives on Health Promotion Effectiveness.* New York: Springer.

Timmins, P. and Miller, C. (2007) 'Making evaluations realistic: The challenge of complexity', *Support for Learning*, 22(1): 9–16.

Warwick, I., Aggleton, P., Chase, E., Schagen, S., Blenkinsop, S., Schagen, I., Scott, E. and Eggers, M. (2005) 'Evaluating healthy schools: Perceptions of impact among school-based respondents', *Health Education Research*, 20(6): 697–708.

Warwick, I., Mooney, A. and Oliver, C. (2009) *National Healthy Schools Programme: Developing the Evidence Base.* London: Thomas Coram Research Unit, Institute of Education, University of London. Available at www.healthyschools.gov.uk (accessed July 2009).

Yin, R. K. (2003) *Case Study Research: Design and Methods*, 3rd edn. London: Sage.

Index

abortion 113
abuse 11, 14
active lifestyles 18 *see also* physical activity
Advisory Council on the Misuse of Drugs 75, 87
Advisory Group on Drug and Alcohol Education 75
Aiming High 150
alcohol use 3, 4, 15, 16–17, 19, 69–80, 89; awareness and implementation of national guidance by schools 79; and *Blueprint* initiative 77; government response to problematic 74–5, 153; and *Healthy School and Drugs Project* (HSDP) 77–8; hospital admissions caused by 17, 72, 153; information resources 80; multi-component intervention 76, 77, 79; negative impact of excessive 69, 71–2; and *Positive Futures* initiative 70, 77; prevalence of 69–71, 153; protective factors 73–4; reasons 71; risk factors 72–3; role of families in prevention of 74, 78–9; and *School Health and Alcohol Harm Reduction Project* 78; and school nurses 153–4; school-based programmes 75–8, 89; and whole school approach 76
Anne Frank Awards 129
anti-bullying initiatives 3, 34
anti-social behaviour 26
anxiety 26
APAUSE project 105
assets-focused frameworks: and obesity 60, 63
asthma 12
attachment 124–5
attendance, school 45, 46, 52; and behaviour and attendance partnerships 52; and persistent absence 46, 47, 48

attention deficit hyperactivity disorder 37
Australia: mental health promotion in schools 27–28; and *School Health and Alcohol Harm Reduction Project* 78
autism 12

Back on Track (White Paper) 51
Bangladeshi community 14, 58
Bath and North East Somerset (BANES) 156
behaviour and attendance partnerships 52
behavioural disorders 12
bereavement courses 155
binge drinking 69
Black and Black African/Caribbean community 14, 15, 46, 58, 142–3 *see also* BME Communities
Blueprint initiative 77, 88, 91
BME (black and minority ethnic) communities 10, 12, 14
body image: and self-esteem 19
Body Mass Index (BMI) 18, 57
British Crime Survey 11
Brooks, Fiona 3, 8–20, 63
buddy schemes 33, 126–7, 130
bullying 10, 113, 128, 149; anti-bullying initiatives 3, 34

C card scheme 152
cannabis 17, 84–5
carers, young 9–10
Carnegie UK Trust 121
Children Act (2004) 126
Children and Young People Child Protection Registers 11
Children and Young People's Plan 128
Children's Fund 120
Children's Plan 43–4, 45, 51, 75, 149

Children's Taskforce 149
Children's Trusts 126, 128, 149
chlamydia 16, 152
Choosing Health 149
Citizenship curriculum 108
Climbié, Victoria 149
Cognitive Behavioural Therapy (CBT) model 37, 154
communications and media activities 129
community-improvement initiatives 128
comparative studies 163–4, 165, 169
condoms 15, 105
confidentiality 156–8
Connexions 120
contraception 15, 110, 111, 153
contraceptive pill 15
Council for Disabled Children 140
crime: young people as victims of 11
Curriculum for Excellence 29

data collection: and evaluation 166–7, 169
decision-making: engagement of by young people 46, 61, 119, 120
Department for Children, Schools and Families (DCSF) 27, 94, 121
depression 26, 154
Developing Emotional Awareness and Learning (DEAL) project 29
diet 3, 18, 66; benefits of healthy 60; fruit and vegetable consumption 18; guidelines for healthy 60; and obesity 56, 60–1; and parental involvement 5, 134–6; and school nurses 155–6; ways to improve 64–5
disadvantaged children: and participation 121
disaffection: reducing 3, 42–53; *see also* school engagement
disengagement 3–4; factors underlying 3–4, 47; *see also* school engagement
drinking *see* alcohol use
drop-in sessions 150–1, 154
drug education 4, 84–94; affective approaches 86, 87; aim of 88; challenges faced 88–9; effectiveness of school 86–8, 94; knowledge-based approaches 86, 87; meeting needs of those who are at risk 92; peer approaches 90; and PSHE 75, 90, 94; reasons for schools as setting for 85; and school ethos 93; and skills-based approaches 86; and special needs children 93; teachers and external contributors

90–1; universal approach and challenges 91–2; working with wider community 93–4; and zero tolerance policies 92
drug use 4, 17; and alcohol use 72; prevalence 84–5
dysgu 42, 44

eating disorders 19, 26, 154, 155
Education Act (1996) 106
Education and Inspections Act (2006) 123
Education and Skills Act (2008) 123
emotional well-being 13–4, 31, 45, 54; levels of satisfaction 13; promotion of through family support 5, 134; and school nurses 154–5; *see also* mental health; mental health promotion
engagement *see* school engagement
English Alcohol Needs Assessment Research Project 69
ethnic minority community 121, 144 *see also* BME communities
European Convention on Human Rights 136
European Network of Healthy Promoting Schools 64
European School Survey Project on Alcohol and Other Drugs (ESPAD) 8, 69
evaluation 6, 162–70; building partnerships among those involved in 170; data collection methods 166–7, 169; designs and approaches 163; and effective dissemination 170; local 165–8; national 168–9; of National Healthy Schools Programme 164–9; principles of good practice 169–70; reasons for importance 162–3; sources of information 167–8; summative and formative 162
Every Child Matters 2, 43–4, 45, 50, 74–75, 120, 123, 148–9
exclusion 46, 51; and alcohol use 70; and drug use 92; factors underlying 47
Exeter Schools Health Study 8
Extended Schools Programme 1, 45, 50, 139
external contributors: and drug education 91; and SRE 113

faith schools 107
families: promotion of emotional well-being 5, 134; role of in alcohol use prevention 74, 78–9; *see also* parents
Family Fund Trust 12
family link workers 142, 143, 144

Family Planning Association 138
fathers 138, 140, 141, 143, 144
Food Standards Agency 126
'Friends' programme 154
friendship groups 10
friendships 125, 130
fruit and vegetable consumption 18
fundraising 129

gay relationships 109, 110, 137
gender: and alcohol use 17, 19; and
    emotional disorders 13; and health 8; and
    physical activity participation 18, 19, 62
General Household Survey (GHS) 12
general practitioners (GPs): consultation
    rates with 11
gonorrhoea 16
government: and children and young
    people's participation 120; and obesity
    155; and parental involvement 139–41;
    response to problematic alcohol use
    74–5, 153
Growing through Adolescence (GTA) 64

Health Behaviour in School-aged Children 81
Health Challenge Programme 126–8
Health Development Agency (HDA) 104
Health Promoting Schools initiative
    (Scotland) 2, 94
Health Survey for England (HSE) (2002) 62,
    155
healthy eating see diet; school meals
Healthy Lives, Brighter Futures 149, 158–9
Healthy School and Drugs Project (HSDP)
    77–8
Healthy Schools Programme see National
    Healthy School Programme
HIV 16
home-school agreements 140
hospital admissions 11; alcohol related 17,
    72, 153; and asthma 12
household structures 9
HSBC Study 12, 13
hyperkinetic (hyperactivity) disorders 13, 37

illnesses, longstanding 12
Incredible Years 29
internalising disorders 37

'journey of participation' model 121–2

Kirby, Douglas 103–104, 124
knowledge-based approaches: and drug
    education 86, 87

'ladder of participation' 121, 140, 144
Learning Behaviour: Lessons Learned (Steer
    Report) 44, 45
Learning and Skills Act (2000) 106
Learning Support Units (LSUs) 52
Life Skills Training 86
link worker see family link workers
Linking the Interests of Families and Teachers 79
Local Authority Drugs and Alcohol
    Specialist 154
Local Safeguarding Children Boards (LSCBs)
    151
lone parenthood 9
'looked after children' 14, 16, 37, 48, 62,
    92, 129
LSUs (Learning Support Units) 52

Macdonald Review 45
masturbation 111, 115
measles outbreak 148
Measuring the Magic? 131
mental health 13–14
mental health promotion (in schools) 3,
    24–38; evidence of effectiveness 31;
    global overview 26–30; holistic approach
    32–3; implementation of 32–8; links
    between mental health and learning 26,
    31–2; and parental involvement 34,
    138–9; positive mental health approach
    25; and SEAL 29–30, 35, 37; and skills
    development 29, 34–5, 37; and staff
    development 36; supporting those with
    special needs 36–8; supportive contexts
    and environments 33–4; targeted
    approaches 30; 'three-wave' model 27;
    whole school approaches 28–9, 31, 32;
    see also emotional well-being
mentoring 33; peer 130
mortality 10–11

National Alcohol Harms Reduction Strategy
    153
National Centre for Social Research
    (NatCen) 168–9
National Challenge Programme 53
National Child Measurement Programme
    (NCMB) 57, 58, 155

National Children's Bureau (NCB) 125, 126
National Foundation for Education Research 168
National Health Service 120
National Healthy School Standard 150
National Healthy Schools Programme (NHSP) 1, 2, 44, 50, 60, 94, 120, 124, 125, 127, 140, 150; evaluation of 164–9
National Institute for Health and Clinical Excellence *see* NICE
National Programme for Specialist Leaders of Behaviour and Attendance 53
National Strategies 42, 48
National Strategy for Sexual Health and HIV 100
National Survey of Sexual Attitudes and Lifestyles (NATSAL) 105
Netherlands 13; and *Healthy School and Drugs Project* (HSDP) 77–8; and SRE 115
newsletters, student 129
NICE (National Institute for Health and Clinical Excellence) 59, 64, 76, 104, 153
Norway, and SRE 114
nurses, school 5, 147–59; and alcohol use prevention 153–4; change in attitudes towards 148; and confidentiality 156–8; contributions to health-promoting activities 149–50; and drop-in sessions 150–1, 154; emotional health and well being promotion 154–5; future challenges 158–9; group work 151; and healthy eating 155–6; history of 147; impact of Teenage Pregnancy Strategy on 149–50; and measles immunisation campaign 148; numbers of 148; partnership working 148–9, 150, 158–9; and Patient Group Directions (PDGs) 153; and physical activity 156; and PSHE 151; relationship with school staff 148–9; role of and ways of working 150–2; safeguarding role 151; and sexual health 152–3; and SRE 151
nutrition *see* diet

obesity 4, 18, 56–66, 155; and assets-focused frameworks 60, 63; challenges in tackling 58–9; definition 56, 57; government strategy 155; and Growing through Adolescence (GTA) 64; health consequences of 58; importance of healthy diet 56, 60–1; and parental Body Mass Index 18; prevalence and rates of 18, 56, 57, 155; social determinants of 18, 57; socio-cultural frameworks 59, 63, 64–5; ways to tackle 63–5; whole school approach 64–5, 66
Ofsted (Office for Standards in Education) 107, 151, 165; drug education survey 89; inspections by 45–6; report (2005) 91; self-evaluation form used by 167–8; 'TellUs3' survey 70; well-being indicators 53
oppositional defiant disorders 37
outside contributors *see* external contributors

Parent Support Advisers (PSAs) 138–9
Parent to Parent peer education scheme (Sheffield) 113
parental involvement (in schools) 4, 5, 134–43; barriers to 141; good practice in increasing 142–3; healthy eating and school meals 134–6; and mental health promotion in schools 34, 138–9; policy and practice 139–41; secondary school compared with primary 141, 144; and SRE 106, 113, 136–8
parenting contracts 140
parenting courses 138
Parentline Plus 113
parents; and alcohol use 72–3; communicating with by schools 142; listening to 142, 144; and non-reaching link worker 142, 143, 144; responding to concerns of 142–3; and school nurses drop-in sessions 151; supporting of by schools in dealing with mental health 138–9; and Transition Information Sessions 142
participation, children and young people's 4, 119–31; barriers to 119; benefits 122–3; creating conditions for effective 124–30; definitions 121–2; engaging as partners in health and well-being 124–5; and *The Health Challenge* 126–7; methods and approaches 126–30; reasons for importance of 122–3; reasons for importance for schools 123–4; summary of progress 120–1
PATHS 27, 28, 29
Patient Group Directions (PDGs) 153
PE lessons 62–3
peer approaches: and drug education 90

peer learning 33
peer mentoring 130
peer relationships 125
peer sign-posting scheme 152
Penn Prevention Programme 37
persistent absence 46, 47, 48
Personal, Social and Health Education *see* PSHE
personalisation 44
physical activity 3, 4, 6, 18; benefits of 62, 63; factors facilitating increased 62–3; plans to increase provision through schools 62; prevention of obesity and 56, 62–3; recommended guidelines for 62; school nurses' involvement with 156
'Physkids' club 156
Place 2 Be 28
Plan for Action on Alcohol Problems (Scotland) 72
play-based therapies 37
Positive Futures initiative 70, 77
postal surveys, and evaluation 166
poverty 9
pregnancy 14, 15, 16, 100, 112
PRUs *see* Pupil Referral Units
PSAs (Public Service Agreements) 45
PSHE (Personal, Social and Health Education) 44–5, 88, 156; and alcohol education 75, 76; and drug education 75, 90, 94; encouragement of student's active participation 120; informing parents about 93; Macdonald Review of 45; and school nurses 151; as statutory part of the curriculum 94, 99, 107
PSHE education certification programme 107
psychiatric disorders 14
Public Service Agreements (PSAs) 45
Pupil Referral Units (PRUs) 51, 52, 123
Pyramid Clubs 28

randomised control trials (RCTs) 163
reception staff 142
religion: and SRE 136–7
RIPPLE programme 105
Royal College of General Practitioners 157

Safe, Sensible, Social 75
Samaritans 29
school councils 130
School of Emotional Literacy 29
school engagement 42–53; and alternative provision 51–2; and attendance 45, 46, 47, 52; behaviour and attendance partnerships 52; building on children and young people's strengths 43–7; contribution to health and well-being 42; focus on partnerships 45; identifying those who are at risk of disaffection 47–8; as learners mindset 42–3; and SEAL 50–1
school ethos 48–9; impact on effectiveness of drug education 93
School Food Trust 134, 135
School Health and Alcohol Harm Reduction Project 78
school meals 48, 61; and parental involvement 134–6
school nurses *see* nurses, school
school planning: involving young people in 130
school policies: involving young people in 129
school staff 77, 127; and confidentiality 157; and development 36, 51; engagement of 43; meeting with parents 142–3; relationship with school nurses 148–9
Scotland: and alcohol use 75; drug education 88, 89, 90; Health Promoting Schools initiative 2, 94; and mental health promotion 29; *Plan for Action on Alcohol Problems* 72; *Youth Commission on Alcohol and Young People* 75
SEAL (Social and Emotional Aspects of Learning) 29–30, 35, 37, 45, 50–1
Seattle Social Development Program 79
Second Step 28, 29
Section 28 101
sedentary behaviours 18, 19
self-esteem: and body image 19
self-harm 26
self-rated health 12
Senior Leadership Team 48
Sex Education Forum 99, 137
Sex and Relationships Education *see* SRE
sexual health 3, 4–5, 14–16, 90–115; and alcohol use 71; and contraception use 15, 110, 111, 153; definition 99–100; prevalence of early sexual experiences 15; public health strategy 15; and school nurses 152–3; 'sex positive' approach 100–1; STIs and HIV 14, 15, 16, 100, 109, 152; teenage pregnancy 14, 15, 16, 100, 112; and Teenage Pregnancy Strategy 149–50; *see also* SRE

sexual health services 111
sexually transmitted infections *see* STIs
SHARE programme 105
skills development: and mental health
    promotion in schools 29, 34–5, 37
skills-based approaches: and drug education
    86
SmallSteps4Life (was The Health Challenge)
    127
smoking 17, 84, 89
Social Exclusion Unit (SEU) 149
'socialisation gap' 9
socio-cultural frameworks: and obesity 59,
    63, 64–5
socio-economic status: impact on health 9
solvents 17
Speakeasy 113, 138
special needs children: and drug education
    93, 107
SRE (Sex and Relationships Education) 4,
    99–115; biological, physical and practical
    issues 109–10; compromises made over
    years 102–3; curriculum issues 108–12;
    dealing with differences 112; emotional
    well-being and relationships element 109;
    evidence of effectiveness 103–106; need
    for change in general culture regarding
    114–15; objections to greater provision of
    99, 101–2; and parental involvement 106,
    113, 136–8; policy position 106–8, and
    religion 136–7; and school nurses 151;
    skills and competencies element 110–11;
    as a statutory part of curriculum 99;
    teachers and outside contributors 113;
    unevenness in provision of 107; values,
    rights and responsibilities element 108–9;
    young people's view of 106, 108
staff *see* school staff
Steer Report *see Learning Behaviours: Lessons
    Learned*
STIs (Sexually Transmitted Infections) 14,
    15, 16, 100, 109, 152
Stradling, Robert 4, 84–94
Strengthening Families Programme (US) 78–9
substance use 10, 17; negative impact of 84;
    prevalence 84–5; treating of tobacco,
    alcohol and drugs separately or together
    issue 89; *see also* alcohol use; drug use;
    smoking
suicide 13–14, 26
Sweden: SRE 114
syphilis 16

talktofrank website 80
targeted action 43
Targeted Mental Health in Schools (TaHMS)
    project 29, 30
teachers: and parental involvement 141,
    142; *see also* school staff
teenage pregnancy *see* pregnancy
Teenage Pregnancy Strategy 149–50
Teenage Pregnancy Unit: Independent
    Advisory Group 99
text messaging 129, 153, 158
'three-wave' model 27
Tic-Tac 154
'Time to Talk' campaign 138
Transition Information Sessions 142
truancy 46
21st Century School 43, 44, 45, 46, 53

UN Convention on the Rights of the Child
    (UNCRC) 103, 122, 136
UNICEF 26
United States: mental health promotion in
    schools 27; role of families in protection
    against alcohol-related problems 78–9

Welsh Substance Misuse Strategy 75
What's Changed Participation Outcomes Tool 131
White, D. 87
whole school approach 3, 4, 127–8, 130;
    and alcohol harm prevention 76; and
    mental health 28–9, 31, 32; tackling
    obesity 64–5, 66
Winston's Wish 155
World Health Organization (WHO) 60,
    100, 104, 154; Health for All Strategy
    127; Ottawa Charter for Health
    Promotion 127
wrap-around services 45, 50

young ambassador programmes 129
Young People's Drugs and Alcohol Services
    154
Youth Alcohol Action Plan 75
Youth Commission on Alcohol and Young People
    (Scotland) 75
Youth Matters 150
Youth Matters Review 75

zero tolerance policies: and drug use 92
zero-exclusions policy 46
Zippy's Friends 29